ALSO BY ALAN PELL CRAWFORD

Thunder on the Right

UNWISE PASSIONS

A TRUE STORY *of a*
REMARKABLE WOMAN—
and the
FIRST GREAT SCANDAL
of EIGHTEENTH-CENTURY AMERICA

Alan Pell Crawford

Simon & Schuster

New York   London   Toronto   Sydney   Singapore

SIMON & SCHUSTER
Rockefeller Center
1230 Avenue of the Americas
New York, NY 10020

SIMON & SCHUSTER and colophon are registered trademarks
of Simon & Schuster, Inc.

Book design by Ellen R. Sasahara
Map copyright © 2000 Jeanyee Wong

Manufactured in the United States of America

10   9   8   7   6   5   4   3

Library of Congress Cataloging-in-Publication Data

Crawford, Alan Pell.
    Unwise passions : a true story of a remarkable woman—and
the first great scandal of eighteenth-century America / Alan Pell
Crawford.
        p. cm.
    Includes bibliographical references (p.).
    1. Morris, Anne Cary Randolph, 1774–1837. 2. Morris,
Gouverneur, 1752–1816. 3. Randolph family. 4. United States—
History—1783–1865. I. Title.
CT275 .M6397 C73 2000
973.4'092'2—dc21
[B]
                                                                00-061872

ISBN 0-684-83474-X

to Sally

I regret that I am now to die in the belief, that the . . . sacrifice of themselves by the generation of 1776, to acquire self-government and happiness to their country, is to be thrown away by the unwise and unworthy passions of their sons and that my only consolation is to be, that I live not to weep over it.

THOMAS JEFFERSON, 1820

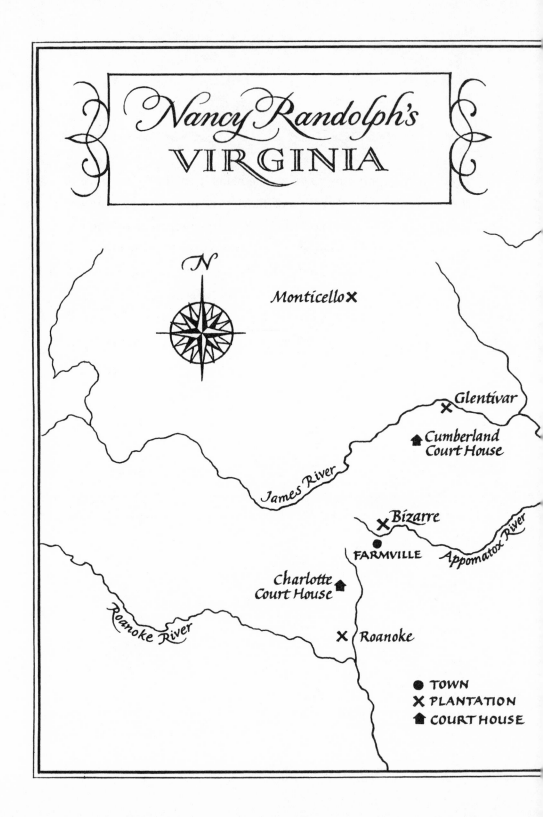

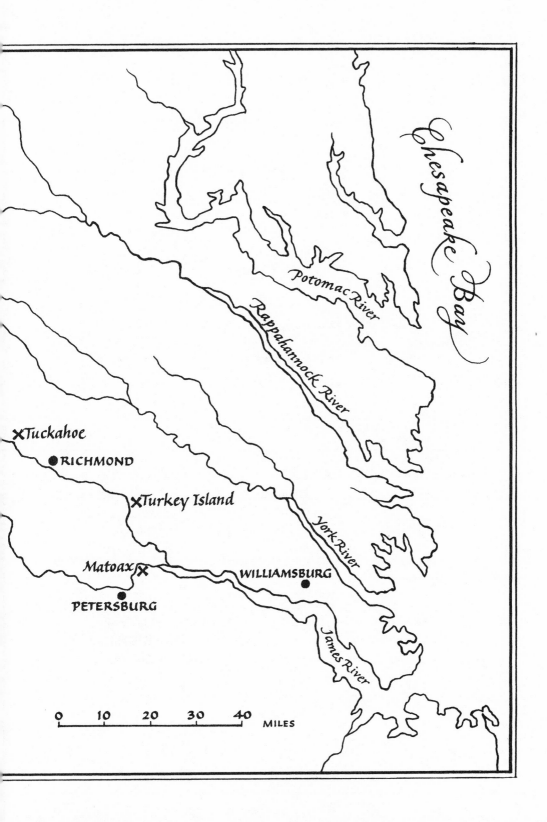

Chesapeake Bay

Potomac River

Rappahannock River

X Tuckahoe

● RICHMOND

X Turkey Island

York River

Matoax X

WILLIAMSBURG ●

● PETERSBURG

James River

0   10   20   30   40   MILES

Isham Randolph of
Dungeness
(1685–1742)
m. Jane Rogers

Nine children, including

Thomas Isham Randolph
m. Jane Cary of Ampthill

Susannah Randolph
m. Carter Harrison

Jane Randolph
m. Peter Jefferson
(1707–1757)

Mary Randolph —— m. ——
(1771–1835)

Randolph Harrison of
Glentivar
(1769–1830)

Thomas Jefferson
(1743–1826)
m. Martha Wayles
Skelton

Mary (Maria) Jefferson
(1778-1804)
m. John Wayles Eppes
(1773-1823)
(cousins)

Martha (Patsy) Jefferson
m. Thomas Mann Randolph, Jr.
of Tuckahoe
(1768-1828)
(cousins)

The Randolphs of Virginia
1651 to 1857

William Randolph of Turkey Island (1651–1711) m. Mary Isham

Nine children, including

Thomas Randolph
of Tuckahoe
(1683–1729)
m. Judith Fleming

Richard Randolph of Curles
(1690–1748)
m. Jane Bolling

Elizabeth Randolph
m. Richard Bland

Theodorick Bland
of Cawsons
m. Frances Bolling

William Randolph
of Tuckahoe
(1713–1746)
m. Maria Page

Mary Randolph
m. Archibald Cary of
Ampthill
(1721-1787)

Frances Bland
m.
John Randolph
of Matoax
(1742–1775)

Colonel Thomas Mann
Randolph, Sr.,
of Tuckahoe
(1741-1793)
m. Anne Cary
of Ampthill
(cousins)

Theodorick
Randolph
(1771–1792)

John Randolph
of Roanoke
(1773–1833)

Thirteen children, including

— m. — Thomas Mann
Randolph, Jr.
(1768–1828)

Anne Cary (Nancy)
Randolph
(1774–1837)
m. Gouverneur
Morris
(1752–1816)

Judith Randolph — m. – Richard Randolph
of Tuckahoe   of Bizarre
(d. 1816)   (1770–1796)
(cousins)

Gouverneur Morris II
m. Patsy Jefferson Cary
(cousins)

St. George Randolph
(1792–1857)

Tudor Randolph
(1796–1815)

PROLOGUE

On Wednesday, August 26, 1818, on a patch of ground in the Bronx where cars by the thousands now clamor onto the Triborough Bridge, a woman walked out of an old stone mansion that has long since vanished. She had once been beautiful but was now in her mid-forties in an era when many women considered themselves fortunate to live that long.

Strangers had hauled a wagon into the woman's orchard and were helping themselves to the apples. She approached them and ordered them to leave. The next day, the woman received a letter repeating rumors that had pursued her for twenty-five years, since she had left her home on a Virginia plantation and come to this now-dilapidated mansion in New York. The letter accused her of "poisoning a man and trying to seduce his sons."

Such accusations were nothing new to Nancy Randolph. In the days before she discarded that name and took another, her father's tobacco plantation had been one of the finest in Virginia, where such illustrious men as George Washington and the Marquis de Lafayette had come to call. Thomas Jefferson, who had been one of her father's closest friends, grew up there.

But in 1792, the gracious life Nancy had known seemed to

disappear overnight, consumed by a scandal that she was still unable to put behind her. Even in New York, she discovered that boys "of 12 and 14 are warned against me!"

Most of what the gossips said about her was without foundation. They said she had killed her brother-in-law after having borne his baby. They said she had killed the baby, too, then carried on an illicit love affair with a Negro slave. She had been banished from the plantation, and once she had gone, people claimed she became a prostitute.

During the desperate years that followed, in which Nancy made her way north, there were times when she would look back "with wonder to what my condition was, in the morning of life."

At a time when the world of the great Virginia planters was disintegrating beneath their feet, she, far better than most, had managed to meet the unrelenting challenges of a new, more democratic age. What happened to the South after the War Between the States—the crushing poverty and enormous social and political upheaval that brought it on—was already being visited on the Virginia grandees three decades before the first guns fired on Fort Sumter. Their expansive way of life was rapidly coming to an end by the time Nancy Randolph left Virginia. The tobacco economy was collapsing, and the great fortunes that depended on it were rapidly dwindling. Anti-slavery sentiment was building, and even the churches the Virginia gentry attended were falling into disrepair. The confidence of an entire class was crumbling, and many of the young men and young women with whom Nancy had grown up would never recover from the blow.

But she had struggled, endured and overcome even more horrendous circumstances than they had faced, some of which, she would no doubt be forced to admit, were of her own making. But the recognition of her own responsibility would not defeat her. When first threatened with exile from her plantation home, she had declared: "I shall rally again."

Part One

CHAPTER ONE

PATRICK HENRY

Such an unspeakable crime!

The accusation was this: A blameless babe had been torn
from its screaming mother's womb, either strangled or stabbed
(the method of its murder had not been determined), its bleeding body hustled down the cold stairs into the still, starlit night
and flung like the contents of a chamber pot onto the nearest
trash pile.

The defendants were so obviously guilty that people would wonder why the great Patrick Henry would represent such wretches. How could Henry take these monsters' money without bloodying his own hands and good name?

And Henry may well have wondered if the esteem in which he was held by his countrymen—esteem for which he had struggled so hard for so many years—could withstand the sheer tawdriness of it all. Would he not be irretrievably dragged, along with his dishonored clients, through the muck and mire?

The girl accused of this awful deed was just eighteen—a coldhearted young female, if the charges were true. Her family, which included the man she had been with that cold, clear September night, swore that nothing had happened. They claimed that there had been no baby born, so there had been no baby killed. They said ignorant slaves had concocted the tale, which had started in the quarters, then spread with maddening ferocity until it was whispered at every racetrack and dancing academy in Virginia.

Before the year was out, the girl had become the Jezebel of the Old Dominion, and the young man who was the alleged father had become its laughingstock. Idlers in taverns made ribald jokes at his expense; in stables and tailor shops, sons of the great planters remembered how they had danced with the little slut but swore they would never make that mistake again.

Her name was Nancy Randolph. The fetching daughter of one of the greatest of the great planters, Nancy had surely been one of the most marriageable and evidently desirable girls on the plantations, but no more. Even if she were to be exonerated of the charges, no man would ever look at her the same way again. She was ruined.

The young man's name was Richard Randolph. Richard of Bizarre, they called him, after the plantation he owned. He had married Nancy's sister Judith. Nancy had shown up at Bizarre, and they had taken her in. There, the gossips said, Nancy had managed to seduce her own sister's husband and was soon pregnant. Suddenly there was hell to pay. Richard got thrown in Cumberland County jail, on charges of murdering Nancy's baby. In mid-April, shortly after he was locked up, a messenger galloped up to Patrick Henry's plantation with a note from Richard begging the old trial lawyer to take the case and offering him 250 guineas to do so.

Richard was no doubt outraged that anyone would dare lay a hand on him, yet terrified he would hang. Henry knew the type. Richard was a Randolph, a member of as an illustrious a clan of Virginia bluebloods as had ever looked down their aquiline noses at the likes of an upcountry tavern keeper like Patrick Henry.

For almost a century, the Randolphs had made their own rules and carried on with what ordinary folks deemed astonishing license. For as long as Henry could remember, the overbred young men of the gentry families had run amok in the slave quarters and had their way with the young ladies of their own set, and no one had dared question it. But now that one of these haughty princelings had been called to answer for his conduct, he needed Henry to save him. Henry declined Richard's offer, but a few days later, the messenger returned with another note. Henry put on his eyeglasses, read it, and looked up at his wife.

Not much older than Henry's eldest daughter, Dorothea was a Dandridge, the daughter of Martha Washington's first cousin and, as such, irrefutable evidence that Patrick Henry— no matter what the Randolphs might say—was no inconsequential backwoods demagogue.

"Dolly, Mr. Randolph seems very anxious that I should appear for him, and five hundred guineas is a large sum," he said. "Don't you think I could make the trip in the carriage?"

Within days, Henry's one-horse gig was rattling out of the wilderness and down the trail alongside the tobacco fields, where patches of muddy bottomland extended as far as he could see. It would be this way, more or less, all the way to Cumberland Court House. Where the seedlings had begun to break through monotonous rows of mud hillocks, barefoot slaves, ankle-deep in mire, had covered the young plants with bundles of green brush; until warmer weather arrived, a frost could kill them. Once the threat of frost passed, swarms of deadly tobacco flies would descend, and then the only thing to do was send the Negroes out to flood the fields, in hope that the flies would be washed away. If the plants survived until midsummer, worming would begin. This meant trudging along, plant by plant, row by row, usually in steamy and malarial conditions, picking off the worms by hand and mashing the odious lumps underfoot.

Forty years before, when he was not yet twenty, Henry had learned all he cared to know about tobacco by working a small farm called Pine Slash in Hanover County, north of Richmond. The property was part of his first wife, Sallie Shelton's, dowry.

There, with six slaves whom he had also received through marriage, Henry did the plowing and planting and worming himself. Today, as master of a 3,500-acre plantation, he owned close to a hundred Negroes who did the dirty work for him.

Henry had discovered something along the way that an astonishing number of the proprietors of the great estates and inheritors of proud old Virginia names did not yet realize or would not face: their great golden age was drawing to a close. It was virtually impossible to make a profit in tobacco. Its price was collapsing; exports had been falling for thirty-five years and would probably continue to do so until all the great planters went broke.

Just thirty years before, when Henry was coming up in the world, people feared the great planters. They had to doff their hats whenever they met these so-called aristocrats prancing down the road on their fine imported saddle horses, but that was changing. Now most of the big planters lived off credit extended on the value of next year's crop, and year after year, their precious soil was wearing out, which meant smaller and less desirable yields. And although the grandees still adorned themselves in the finest fabrics and still furnished their mansions with Hepplewhite tea tables and Scottish carpets, nobody took them quite so seriously. Merchants no longer feared approaching them on the streets of Petersburg or Richmond in the harsh and unforgiving light of midday to demand payment for goods their servants had carted off weeks before.

The great estates—cracked windowpanes, falling-down fences and all—had begun to reflect the precarious foundation of the planters' putative wealth. Even their churches seemed all but abandoned as folks flocked to new ones in the woods, where they cringed in fear of God and sought His healing hand with a fervor unheard of in the bloodless murmurings of the Randolphs' English church. Nowadays, more and more men like Henry, who had not studied at the Inns of Court but had read their Bibles, were practicing law, entering politics, and questioning the way things had been done in Virginia for the past hundred years.

Convinced that dependence on tobacco would bankrupt a man, Henry grew wheat and other grains at his plantation where the soil was so rich that folks said he could feed everybody in the county. He had become one of the largest landholders in Virginia, owning huge tracts in North Carolina, Kentucky, and Georgia, and he had grown richer than some of the grandees who scorned him. But he knew you could never be rich enough, especially when you were the father of sixteen children and had scores of Africans to feed and clothe, so he still practiced law when his health would allow it, the price was right and the case offered him the opportunity to advance himself. The prospect of extricating the Randolphs from the mess they had gotten themselves into surely gratified the still ambitious old man. For most of Henry's life, the Randolphs had been the most important family in Virginia, and because Virginia had been the largest and richest of the colonies, many people considered the Randolphs the most important family in America.

Energetic and industrious men, the Randolphs had come to the sandy shores of the Chesapeake and built their baronial manor houses in primeval wilderness. They had cleared vast stretches of fertile acreage, chased off the Indians and put African slaves to work in the fields. In what seemed an instant, they had established a civilization on a single cash crop three thousand miles from supplies of the manufactured goods on which they relied. The great manor houses had not gone up until the 1700s, scarcely a century before. Rome might not have been built in a day, but Virginia was, and for a great many years Randolphs ran it, as Henry had discovered when he was still a young man.

Shortly after Henry's first failure at farming, he showed up in Williamsburg still wearing the linsey-woolsey of the backwoodsman, seeking a license to practice law. He was directed to Tazewell Hall, an estate on the edge of town, to be examined by its master, one John Randolph, the king's attorney and son of a colonist of the same name who, a generation earlier, had pleaded the cause of Virginia tobacco planters before the British Crown.

For what seemed like hours, John of Tazewell Hall bombarded the tavern keeper with questions on every aspect of the common law, the more abstruse the better. When the interrogation was complete (or Randolph tired of the game), he waggled his head back and forth, chuckled, and swore he would never trust appearances again. He dipped his quill pen into ink, signed the parchment that would serve as Henry's law license and affixed his seal.

By the time Henry was thirty-five, he was a member of the House of Burgesses, an orator whose power was recognized throughout the colonies and a lawyer with a brisk practice. He was also master of Scotchtown, a plantation as impressive as any in Virginia, but he still refused to live like a grandee. Henry covered his floors with animal skins, in the manner of an honest farmer.

Henry did not like to think about Scotchtown, however. His family—Sallie Shelton had borne him six children by the time they moved to the plantation—had lived there from 1771 until 1778. Henry did not spend as much time at home as Sallie would have liked, but those were busy years, and things are never perfect in any family.

In 1772, after giving birth to her sixth child, Sallie became deeply melancholic and, finally, violent. For the next three years, Henry confined her to a room in the basement. In time she was strapped down to prevent her from harming others and herself, and she was attended day and night by a slave woman. When Sallie died in 1775, at the age of thirty-seven, Henry stashed away everything that reminded him of his loss, put Scotchtown up for sale and found a new wife. She was the daughter of Nathaniel Dandridge, one of the leading men of Hanover County. In 1777, when Henry married her, Dorothea was twenty-two, the same age as his own son John.

Less than a month after the marriage, John, who was a captain in the American army, was walking across the field of battle after the victory at Saratoga. Recognizing the faces of his friends among the dead, the boy snapped his sword into pieces, flung it to the ground and, as Henry was told, went "raving mad." In September of 1778, General Washington wrote to Henry enclosing a letter, still unopened, that Henry had written to his son. The boy's "ill state of Health," the general wrote, "obliged him to quit the service about three months past. I therefore return you the letter."

Whether Henry knew it or not, the young man's miseries appear to have started well before he saw his comrades littering the ground at Saratoga. When his father began to court Dorothea, what might have happened did happen. John fell in love with the young woman, and it no doubt unhinged him when his own father married her.

Henry would need to bear in mind how vexing family affections could be as he prepared to defend Nancy Randolph and her alleged paramour. Perhaps people were being unfair to this young woman. Henry had made his share of compromises as he rose in the world, but there was still something in him of the idealistic stripling who read the law when trade was slow at his father-in-law's tavern. He had been moved by injustice then, and no matter how far he had come in the world and how rich he had grown, he could be moved by injustice still.

Perhaps this girl—for she was not much more than a child when the scandal erupted—was the victim of an unscrupulous brother-in-law. Perhaps she really was innocent. Who, at this point, could say?

Henry would know more when he reached Cumberland Court House. John Marshall had also agreed to appear for the defense, and they would interrogate witnesses, compare notes and ready their case. There were a great many questions to answer. What had led to this horrendous mess? What really had happened that night? Who was this girl?

CHAPTER TWO

‒‒‒‒‒~~~~~‒‒‒‒‒

She was born Anne Cary Randolph on Tuesday,
September 16, 1774, at Tuckahoe Plantation, on a wooded bluff
overlooking the James River, an hour's carriage ride west of
Richmond. One of thirteen children, Anne, or Nancy as she was
known, was the daughter of Colonel Thomas Mann Randolph,
Tuckahoe's genial and indulgent master, and his wife, the former Anne Cary, for whom she was named. The Sunday after she
was born, she was baptized by the Reverend William Douglas
at Saint James Church. When services were over, she was taken
back to Tuckahoe, where she spent what was by all indications
an idyllic childhood.

Tuckahoe was built by her great-grandfather around 1710,
some twenty years before Richmond was established, and was
the scene of boisterous barbecues, fish fries and fancy-dress
balls. The clapboard mansion was known throughout the
colonies for its fine walnut paneling and its fragrant boxwood
gardens. Done up in velvet and gold, the Colonel's bedroom
was the stuff of local legend; the stables housed some of the
fastest horses in the South.

For years the gentry would gather at Tuckahoe to drink
barrels of Madeira and feast on beef, pork and mutton raised on

TUCKAHOE

the farm and on game shot in its fields and forests. With an entire wing for the accommodation of visitors, the mansion was
designed, one visitor said, "solely to answer the purposes of
hospitality." When there were not enough visitors for dancing,
guests read plays by candlelight. William Byrd of Westover recalled passing a rainy evening at Tuckahoe acting out John
Gay's *Beggar's Opera*.

Nancy grew up with a strong sense of her place in society.
She was a descendent of Sir Thomas Randolph, the first earl of

Moray and a nephew of Robert the Bruce. In 1314, Sir Thomas had led a plucky band of Scottish patriots through the early morning mists and noiselessly scaled the steep stone cliffs of Edinburgh Castle. They flung their siege ladders over the battlements, overwhelmed the English guards, and reclaimed the castle for Scotland. Fourteen years later, when the Treaty of Northumberland recognized Scottish independence and Bruce's right to the throne, Sir Thomas was made guardian of David II and regent of the kingdom. Two centuries later, another Sir Thomas Randolph served as Chancellor of the Exchequer to Queen Elizabeth. A generation after that, yet another Sir Thomas was a renowned poet and friend of Ben Jonson. At the time of the English civil wars, the Randolphs became Cavaliers. The son of one such loyalist was a Warwickshire country squire named William Randolph, who sailed to the Chesapeake during the Restoration and established the family in Virginia. He built a plantation house on a peninsula of the James River and was known thereafter as William of Turkey Island.

William took a wife and sired seven sons, who in turn took wives, fathered children and established their own plantations. Around these plantations settlements grew, and then towns, with churches, courthouses, apothecaries and taverns. In their powdered wigs, white silk stockings and satin doublets, the Randolphs sat on the vestries of their complacent Anglican churches and served as gentlemen jurors in the county courts. They advised the king's colonial agents, legislated in the House of Burgesses, and took their turns as governors of the Commonwealth.

In time, the Randolphs became so numerous and intermarried with such regularity that it became impossible for all but the most devoted family historian to keep them straight, a veritable "tangle of fish-hooks so ensnarled together that it was impossible to pick up one without pulling three or four others after it." Amused by the tendency of Randolphs to marry their own cousins, less well born Virginians would say, "Only a Randolph is good enough for a Randolph." When Randolphs did condescend to marry outside the family, they did so smartly. One Jane Randolph married an enterprising Piedmont backwoodsman named Peter Jefferson and gave birth to a boy they named Thomas.

The third in a succession of William Randolphs, Nancy's paternal grandfather was a friend of Peter Jefferson. When William lay dying, he called his friend to his bedside, imploring him to look after the plantation in his absence, since he would leave the plantation to his only son, Thomas Mann Randolph, then but five years old. For seven years the Jeffersons lived at Tuckahoe, where Jefferson forged a lifelong friendship with young master Thomas of Tuckahoe, who grew up, took a wife and had six boys and seven girls. The fourth daughter was Nancy.

The Jeffersons were frequent visitors to Tuckahoe, where Nancy and her cousin Patsy Jefferson, the elder daughter of Thomas Jefferson, became friends. In 1790, Patsy would marry Nancy's brother Tom, binding the families ever tighter. Thomas Jefferson took a somewhat less than exalted view of the family's storied past. "They trace their pedigree far back to England and Scotland," he wrote of his maternal connections, "to which let everyone ascribe the faith and merit he chooses."

COL. THOMAS MANN RANDOLPH

By the time Nancy came along, many Virginians had already begun to sneer at such pretensions to noble birth. By the 1790s, the Randolphs were no longer so formidable as they had been three decades earlier, when Patrick Henry had journeyed to Williamsburg to be interrogated by John Randolph of Tazewell Hall. Even John of Tazewell Hall came to a bad end that many Virginians felt was richly deserved. Six months after Lexington and Concord, he declared his loyalty to the Crown and sailed for England. Cut off from his rich kinsmen in the colonies, he lived on a petty pension from the government and died—dishonored in Virginia and never wholly accepted in England.

Most Randolphs, however, were ardent patriots, bound together by their stake in the society they had established and their mounting anger at the British banking houses to which they owed money. By the time Nancy was learning to read, her father was one of the largest landholders in Henrico County and an officer of the local militia. Colonel Randolph considered himself a liberal in politics, contributed to the relief of Richmond's poor and took pride in what he saw as his democratic principles. Once, when he had extended Tuckahoe's legendary hospitality to a British officer, three local farmers ambled into the house to discuss their use of the Colonel's mill. They took chairs near the fire, pulled off their muddy boots and spat on the floor. After they left, the officer remarked on the great liberties the farmers had taken, and the Colonel tried to apologize for their antics. "No doubt," Nancy's father said, "each of those men conceived himself in every respect my equal."

Nancy's mother no doubt would have been appalled. A formidable woman with an imposing pedigree of her own, Mrs. Randolph was a daughter of Colonel Archibald Cary of Ampthill plantation, a forbidding brick fortress on the James whose proprietor seemed to enjoy intimidating his neighbors. A member of the Virginia House of Burgesses, Colonel Cary was an industrious, bullying man who established his own mill, ropery, iron furnace and foundry. As a gentleman justice of the Chesterfield County Court, he was known for persecuting Bap-

tists and other preachers of the dissenting sects. As a plantation master, he was ruthless with slaves, including those who
belonged to other planters. Cary's imperious outbursts were
matched by those of his wife, whose "rash humour" was attributed to her Indian ancestry. Mary Randolph Cary was descended from the marriage of John Rolfe to Pocahontas and,
like most Randolphs with Indian blood, took pride in the connection.

The family into which Nancy Randolph was born, by all appearances, possessed such wealth that it would endure for generations. Nancy's father indulged his children and liked to
reserve a barrel of tobacco every year for each of his daughters,
just so they could buy new clothes. He provided dancing classes
and music lessons and put the girls as well as the boys under
the instruction of tutors. They were afforded every opportunity
to refine their social skills at the most fashionable balls in the
southern colonies. He introduced them to famous visitors, including Washington, Lafayette and others who would loom
large in the war for independence. Colonel Randolph viewed
the war much as the other great planters did. They believed it
would solidify the tremendous gains the old Virginia families
had made in their years in the New World. Once the shackles
were cast off, the future of the great planter families would be
secure.

The world as Nancy had come to know it was a pleasant
blur of vague, agreeable possibilities, a seemingly endless arrival of crates of new dresses, dolls, books and musical instru-
ments. As it was for her older sisters, life would be a succession

of fish fries, barbecues, balls and horse races, crowned by marriage to a young gentleman from one of the nearby plantations.

Nancy was six years old in December 1780, when the first ominous signs of change—the sails of fearsome British gunboats—were spotted in the icy waters of the James River.

CHAPTER THREE

On that wintry day when the British came,
Nancy's first cousin John Randolph, Jr., born at Cawsons plantation near Petersburg on June 2, 1773, was seven years old. Jack and his brothers Richard, who was ten, and Theodorick, who was nine, imagined war to be glorious. They had no comprehension of the horrendous consequences the war would have for what Henry Adams would call the "small cheerful world" into which they had been born. This world, which had "produced the greatest list of great names ever known this side of the ocean, was about to suffer a wreck the more fatal and hopeless because no skill could avert it." The "dissolution was so quiet and subtle," Adams wrote, "that no one could protect himself or secure his children." The country had plunged into a war that

> in a single moment cut that connection with England on which the old Virginian society depended for its tastes, fashions, theories, and above all for its aristocratic status in politics and law. The Declaration of Independence proclaimed that America was no longer to be English, but American; that is to say, democratic and

popular in all its parts,—a fact equivalent to a sentence of death upon old Virginian society, and foreboding dissolution to the Randolphs, with all the rest, until they should learn to master the new conditions of American life. For passing through such a maelstrom a century was not too short an allowance of time, yet this small Randolph boy, not a strong creature at best, was born just as this downward plunge began, and every moment made the outlook drearier and more awful.

But for all Jack and his brothers knew, their future would be glorious. They lived at Matoax, the plantation of their late father, John Randolph, Sr. John Randolph of Matoax was a son of Richard of Curles Neck and grandson of William of Turkey Island. Richard of Curles Neck owned 10,000 acres in Cumberland and Prince Edward Counties, but like many great planters, his land and slaves were mortgaged to London brokerage firms. Most of this land, and these debts, were passed on to Jack's father. In 1769, John Randolph of Matoax married Frances Bland, the daughter of Theodorick Bland of Cawsons, a slaveholding member of the Virginia House of Burgesses, and in 1775 he died at the age of thirty-four.

Tall, clever and well connected, Frances Bland Randolph would not remain a widow for long. In 1777, at Bruton Parish Church in Williamsburg, she was observed at prayer by St. George Tucker, a young lawyer who, upon seeing the "tawny" beauty, promptly renounced a vow, taken at the age of eighteen, to "never marry a widow." The son of a British naval officer with shipping interests in the colonies, Tucker had come to Vir-

FRANCES BLAND RANDOLPH TUCKER

ginia at the age of twenty to study law. Eager to serve his
adopted country and make money, he returned to Bermuda in
the early days of the Revolution, bought a boat and ran arms
and ammunition past the British blockade. Tucker made a small
fortune with his derring-do, but he was no mere adventurer.
Tucker read Grotius, Montesquieu, Locke and Paine, studied
the movements of the planets, conducted experiments with
electricity and wrote verse inspired by Dryden and Pope. He
designed a steam engine and talked of a device, a precursor of

the telegraph, that would employ flashes of light to transmit messages over long distances. He was, in short, a man of the Enlightenment with all the virtues of the type. "Comfortable in this world and sanguine about the next," he was a well-rounded gentleman, liberal in his judgment, kindly, learned, tolerant of others, devoted to duty and—as his blockade-running enterprises demonstrated—capable of bold and decisive action, a quality the war would require.

The Randolph boys considered the arrival of British ships to be the prelude to greatness, when their stepfather— "a fine officer," Jack announced—would put the redcoats to rout, driving them away forever and ushering in a new and still more golden age. For days, the ships lay at anchor off Hampton Roads. Then, led by the fearsome forty-four-gun H.M.S. *Charon*, they sailed forward and, with what the Virginia gentry considered a savage disregard for common decency, plundered the countryside, putting the torch to tobacco barns and looting wine cellars.

As Christmas of 1780 came and went, the townspeople of Petersburg packed their belongings. Shopkeepers boarded up their stores. Periwig makers and dancing masters picked up their fowling pieces and drilled on the green. Wagons piled high with tea tables, silver, bridles and ball gowns disappeared down muddy streets, headed west. Trade was restricted, hogsheads of tobacco rotted in warehouses and prices of basic commodities soared. Disorder and deprivation were everywhere, but Jack and his brothers seem to have been too excited to feel the lack. They would flee with their mother as soon as they received word from St. George Tucker, who had joined the Virginia militia and was now hunkered down in a muddy camp near Williamsburg. If the British approached Matoax, he would order them to leave.

On December 29, 1780, Frances gave birth for the sixth time in eleven years. Less than a week later, on January 3, 1781, Tucker sent word that the British were heading toward Petersburg. There was no time to lose.

CHAPTER FOUR

They started out while the sun was still a ghostly glimmer through the barren trees to the east in an unwieldy, halting caravan of carriages and wagons. As the Randolphs crept past hard, flat tobacco fields and dark pine forests, eight hundred British soldiers landed just twenty-five miles east of Richmond. Governor Jefferson sent his family to stay with their Randolph cousins, including Nancy, her sister Judith and her brother Tom, at Tuckahoe.

By the time the redcoats entered Richmond, Jack's family had reached Bizarre. One of three plantations John Randolph, Sr., had left to his sons, Bizarre spread out along both banks of the slow-moving Appomattox in a sparsely populated part of Southside Virginia sixty miles west of Richmond. A handsome frame structure, the house stood on the north side of the river in Cumberland County, high on a bluff. For years, the house and outbuildings were the only outpost of civilization in a bound-less forest. In late summer the river was so shallow that wagons could cross it within sight of the house.

Just across Sandy Ford, where the wagons crossed, the Randolph boys could make out a peculiar sloping elevation of the ground. A hundred years earlier, this mound had been home to Indians of unknown tribe, who had hunted, fished, tended gardens, put up wood huts, fashioned clay-fired pottery, and then inexplicably disappeared. Many centuries earlier, after the bison had moved on, scattered bands of other natives had camped along the Appomattox. They had moved up- and down-river with the seasons, inhabiting in warmer weather the land that, given in a grant by the British Crown, would become Bizarre. When cooler weather came, they would move back east to the Tidewater lowlands. No one knows why they left, but when the first English explorers arrived by 1669 or there-abouts, the land was once again rich with deer.

Shortly after the English began to settle along the Appo-mattox, a wooden bridge was built to span the river at Sandy Ford. Wagons full of flour from the five-story mill at Muddy Creek rumbled across it, toward new settlements to the south. From Matoax, John Randolph, Sr., continued to direct opera-tions at Bizarre, Buffalo and Roanoke plantations, where his own sons might someday raise their families and watch as vil-lages—even cities—grew up around them. Jack's father had done much to make that dream attainable for Richard, who would inherit Bizarre. A path had been cut from the water's edge to the house, and docks were built for loading tobacco onto flat-bottomed bateaux. John Randolph of Matoax cleared land from the scrub forests around the mansion and, as that land wore out, cleared still more land, until tobacco fields, raw and barren when his sons sought refuge there, surrounded the lonely house. By the mid-1700s, other plantations were being hacked out of the wilderness around the Randolphs' holdings, and more English, Scots and German immigrants arrived. The nearest village was Cumberland Court House, twenty miles away. There was a general store at Cumberland Court House, a smattering of houses and a tavern.

The Randolph boys, their mother and her two little ones would spend the duration of the war at Bizarre. As Frances regained her strength and began to spruce up their "smokey Cabbin," and the young Randolphs wrote letters encouraging their stepfather to "make the militia fight," Tucker marched to North Carolina and engaged the British. News that he had been stabbed with a bayonet at Guilford Court House turned Frances "into an old Pumpkin faced, dropsical, Mope," but Tucker fretted less about his wound than he did about the moral development of his stepsons. It worried him that Jack, Richard and Theodorick were spending too much time without a tutor.

Even Jack, the most promising scholar of the three, needed discipline. A precocious child, Jack had a fierce temper, which his mother's indulgence did little to moderate. Frances allowed him to sleep in her bed from the time of his father's death until she remarried, and Jack was perhaps too devoted to her. When thwarted in his desires, he would sometimes swoon as if losing consciousness; unusually sensitive, he was like a child "without a skin."

In the days leading up to his mother's most recent confinement, Jack had entertained her with readings from Smollett's *Expedition of Humphrey Clinker.* When he was not reading to his mother, he read to himself, consuming books "more eagerly than gingerbread." By the time he was seven, he had already worked his way through Voltaire's *Charles XII, Gulliver's Travels, Don Quixote* and *Robinson Crusoe.* With Richard's help, he was learning Latin.

Richard admitted neglecting his own studies of Latin grammar as he dreamed of military glory. "I wish I was big enough to turn out, if I was I would not stay at home long," Richard wrote to his stepfather. Although he had not studied as diligently as Tucker would have hoped, the boy assured his stepfather that he would "have my syntax at my finger ends when you return."

Latin was important, not for its own sake but for the light that Tacitus, Cicero and other writers, orators and statesmen could throw on virtue. Tucker wanted his stepsons to be gentlemen who acted from duty, knew restraint and possessed a lofty sense of honor. When the war was over, Tucker intended to send them to grammar school and then to college. Tucker agreed with John Randolph, Sr. In his will, the boys' father decreed that his sons be educated "in the best manner without regard to expenses as far as their fortunes may allow, even to the last shilling." He also wanted them to learn a trade or profession, freeing them from financial dependence on tobacco.

Tutors were in short supply during the war, however, and without such discipline as tutors instilled, "our little monkeys," Tucker told his wife, might grow up to be ungovernable apes. His stepsons' taste for the *Arabian Nights, Orlando Furioso*, and *Gil Blas* offered scant assurance that they would grow to dutiful manhood. Virginia plantations were full of half-educated wastrels, lording it over their unlettered neighbors and running in and out of the slave quarters at all hours of the night.

These fops, Tucker believed, had no sense of decency or decorum. Unless Frances could find a stern tutor, and she never could, the boys might become "quite spoilt."

And spoilt boys too often become irresponsible men, incapable of defending themselves or their way of life. Such men too readily fall prey to their passions and can be as easily overwhelmed by a pretty young girl as by an indignant mob or invading army. No infant country should be left, Tucker felt, in such unsteady hands.

CHAPTER FIVE

~~~~~~~~~~~~

After Yorktown, the great planters attempted to recapture the grandeur that had characterized the plantations before the British came, and on the surface of things, life there did indeed resume its prewar complacence. Jack Randolph and his two older brothers were sent off to school, where, confirming his stepfather's worst fears, Richard almost immediately ran out of money. Within hours of his arrival in Williamsburg, he bought a fiddle for ten dollars ("two dollars less than I can get it anywhere else," he told his parents), a pair of shoes, ice skates and a haircut. Deciding it is "hard trusting a boy to his own head," St. George Tucker recruited friends to keep an eye on Richard and serve as "a Check on the imprudences of youth," which proved "perfectly futile."

While Nancy Randolph's boy cousins were at school, the balls and barbecues at Tuckahoe started up again. As Nancy approached her adolescence, she watched with anticipation—and, no doubt, some envy—as her older sisters danced with the young men from neighboring plantations. After long afternoons in the schoolhouse near the mansion, Nancy could speak and read French, which she found enchanting. An enthusiastic reader, she began to work her way through *Tom Jones, Moll*

Flanders and other popular novels. She enjoyed poetry and considered the odes of William Collins "sublime."

Nancy's brother Tom, who had been sent to the University of Edinburgh three years after the war, thought Nancy was growing up much as young ladies should. He wanted his sisters to be smart and accomplished but only insofar as these attributes would render them attractive to men. Having developed strong opinions about the proper education of females, Tom asked John Leslie, a young instructor at Edinburgh, to return with him to Tuckahoe and tutor his younger siblings. Leslie was proficient in the departments of learning that "particularly belong to females," Tom told his father. The faculties women should cultivate are those of "imagination and taste." The "elegant and agreeable occupations of Poetry and the fine arts surely become the delicate sex more than tedious or abstruse enquiries" into philosophy. Nancy and her elder sister Judith should also be trained in music, which "alone raises them above the generality of ladies." Mastery of music would help them "shine in Company, & will insure their pleasing" of men. It is the admiration of men, above all, that "is to be sincerely wished for."

With this last sentiment, Colonel Randolph had no doubt come to agree most ardently. Despite the Colonel's efforts to make it appear otherwise, life at Tuckahoe was not as it had been before the war. Debts were steadily piling up, the land was wearing out and the Randolphs of Tuckahoe could no longer afford to live as grandly as they once had. He could no longer afford to set aside hogsheads of tobacco to pay for his daughters' clothing, and he would not be able to offer attractive dowries, except for land and slaves, the value of which was falling precipitously.

Colonel Randolph could consider himself fortunate that men seemed to consider his daughter Judith, who had turned fifteen in the spring of 1787, eminently marriageable. One day that summer, a young swain rode up the lane at Tuckahoe, decked out in his best nankeen breeches, white waistcoat and white stockings. Determined to "storm the citadel" that "contained [Judith's] virtues and accomplishments," he arrived just as her beauty was "in its meridian splendor." When Judith rose to greet him, "a small border of red occasioned by the blush of ingenuous modesty, tinged her lovely face, which opposed to the snowy whiteness of her skin formed an enchanting spectacle." The sight of Judith was "not much inferior to that which is exhibited in the eastern sky just at the moment when aurora is about to dispense the beams of her effulgence to the whole animate world." During dinner, the young man's hands trembled, his heart "palpitated and [his] eyes too well evinced [his] internal commotion." When the party adjourned to the parlor, Judith played as if "inspired by some deity of music, and . . . seemed to do it with a modesty which appeared to indicate an opinion of her own deficiency." In "plain words," Judith "is beautiful, sensible, affable, polite, good-tempered, agreeable, and to crown the whole, truly calculated both by her virtues and accomplishments to render any man happy."

Eager to provoke such powerful responses in men, Nancy seems to have given considerable thought to her strategies for attracting them. She was "captivated" by a vase that was decorated with a "modest violet" surrounded by leaves and en-

NANCY RANDOLPH

graved with the words, in French, "I must be sought." From that day forward, Nancy decided, "I must be sought" would be her motto. In the years to come, she assumed, it would serve her well.

CHAPTER SIX

Sent to the College of New Jersey in 1787,
Richard Randolph did better than his parents might have
expected. In September he won first prize in the school ora-
tory competition and, brother Jack reported, was "regular, studious, and above low company of any sort." He remained a
spendthrift, however, though a kindhearted one. On his journey north the previous July, he had given seven shillings, sixpence to a "poor woman on the road" and had his manservant
give two shillings, sixpence to a "poor, crippled, distrest" black
man they passed. But Richard also got his hair cut twice on his
three-day trip and added to his wardrobe a pair of boots
and boot buckles, silk stockings, gloves, a walking stick and a
stickpin.

Once established in Princeton, Richard began to spend his
weekends in Philadelphia, where he met Anne Bingham, whose
parties were the height of elegance. The daughter of Thomas
Willing, a prosperous merchant who became mayor of Philadelphia and served in the Continental Congress, Anne was just
eighteen when she married William Bingham, said to be the
richest man in America. The Binghams lived for a time in Eu-

rope, where Anne caused a sensation at Versailles. She had been presented with great success at the Court of St. James's, and engravings of her face were sold in the shops of London. When the Binghams returned to Philadelphia in 1786, they built the finest house and established the most fashionable salon in America. Anne liked Richard, and before long he was her "master of ceremonies," a kind of consort and cohost who initiated dancing at her parties. It was a role other gallant men, including Gouverneur Morris of New York, had performed for her in years past.

The parties at the Binghams' mansion were unlike anything Richard had ever experienced, and they appealed to his craving for urbanity, elegance and ease. The social circles through which he now moved impressed, and sometimes appalled, men who had known the royal courts of Europe. The Viscount de Chateaubriand was astonished by Philadelphia's "elegance of dress, the luxury of carriages, the frivolity of conversations, the disproportion of fortunes, the immorality of banks and gambling houses, the noises of dance halls and theaters." The Duc de la Rochefoucauld Liancourt, Grand Master of the King's Wardrobe, was amazed by the "profusion of luxury" in women's dresses. Jean Pierre Brissot de Warville was astonished by the enormous expense that went into the women's grooming and hairdos, which he considered "too affected to be pleasing." Philadelphians spent huge sums on their houses for no better purpose, he surmised, than to lure "a few European fops and empty-headed parasites."

The poet Peter Markoe felt much the same, expressing his disapproval of the Binghams, to whose

> *Mansion wits and fops repair,*
> *To game, to feast, to saunter, and to stare,—*
> *Thine eyes amid the crowd, who fawn and bend,*
> *View many a parasite, but not one friend . . .*

Most Virginia planters also tended to view Philadelphia society with disgust. They considered the entire city a hotbed of monarchists and merchants who relied on southern crops but professed to scorn the institution of slavery that supplied them. If Richard shared that view, he did not let it stop him from enjoying the bounty. At Mansion House, he could help himself to mustards, wines and blancmange from France, and oranges and lemons from the Binghams' gardens. In the parlors, drawing rooms and boudoirs, he could also sample the charms of Philadelphia's most beautiful women.

Richard's dazzling social whirl came to an abrupt halt in late 1787, when the Randolph boys learned that their mother was sick and they were needed at home. In November, when Frances was eight months pregnant with her eighth child, a slave from Bizarre showed up at Matoax. Tucker was not at home, so the slave told Mrs. Tucker of brutal conditions at Bizarre, upon which "anarchy" had descended. The overseer's "repeated cruelty" required immediate action, so, refusing to "leave the miserable creatures a prey to the worst of mankind," she repeated the arduous journey she had made six years before, restored order at Bizarre and returned to Matoax feeling "much disordered."

When Tucker came home in mid-December, Frances gave birth for the eighth time. Three weeks later, surrounded by her husband and her seven surviving children, including her newborn daughter, Frances Bland Randolph Tucker died at the age of thirty-six.

Her death seems to have hit Jack the hardest, and when he and Richard resumed their schooling at Columbia College in New York six months later, he turned to his older brother for companionship and comfort, sharing an enthusiasm for literature and a passion for politics. They followed the debates over the federal Constitution and, in April 1789, went to Federal Hall to watch George Washington take the oath of office.

Earlier in the day, the two young men stood in the street as the carriage bearing Vice President John Adams paraded by. Richard leaned forward to get a better look, and the vice president's coachman, seeing him approach the escutcheon of what Jack called "the vice-regal carriage," not only gave Richard a look of utter disdain but kicked at him to keep him away. Such contemptuous treatment was not to be borne, and Jack would never forget it.

The patient boy who had once tutored Jack in Latin had become, in his adoring eyes, "the most manly youth" he had ever known and the noblest. Although Richard stood to inherit slaves from his late father's estate, he claimed to want "not a single negro for any other purpose than his immediate liberation." The idea that "so insignificant an animal as I am, is invested with this monstrous, this horrid power" appalled him. Despite his taste for fine things, Richard claimed that a life of honest poverty would be preferable to dependence on a system in which men are "sacrificed at the shrine of unjust and lawless power."

For all his high-mindedness, Richard lacked direction. He does not seem to have considered how he would support himself without slaves, and his attitude toward money struck his stepfather as wildly impractical. St. George Tucker had built a thriving law practice, and he hoped Richard would do the same. But by the time he was attending Anne Bingham's parties, Richard had ceased to show any interest in the career for which he was being educated. As a Randolph, he seemed to feel that he was not required to concern himself with money and certainly not to go grubbing after a profession. He did not have to *be* anything, as such things are generally understood. He need not exert himself in pursuit of a position in society because he already had one by virtue of birth.

But Richard was also aware—because his mother had constantly told him so—that even if he tried, he could never meet the standard set by his father, his stepfather, and the men of their generation. These men had settled a wilderness, thrown off the shackles of an oppressive and tyrannous mother country and founded an Empire of Liberty. They carried themselves with a manliness and confidence that was grounded not in the acquisition of fine manners but in the knowledge that they had done great things when there were still great things to be done.

What was left for their sons to achieve? What remained for them to do but languish on the plantations carved out of the forests by their more energetic forebears? How could they appear anything but weak and undeserving of the sacrifices made on their behalf?

Throughout his life, Richard's mother had told him that he could never repay this debt, and in time he felt wretched about it and found himself drawn to women like Anne Bingham, who offered much but expected little. Although Jack insisted that his brother was "neither debauched nor dissipated," Richard seems to have seized whatever opportunities for indulging his appetites that came his way. By the time he went north, he had discovered that women found him attractive, and he made the most of it. Before leaving for Princeton, he read for the law with the learned George Wythe in Williamsburg and managed to seduce Betsy Talliafero, who was Wythe's niece, in Wythe's own house. In New York, Richard took as one of his lovers a girl named Kitty Ludlow, and while the extent of his activities in Philadelphia is unknown, it is certainly suggested by the company he kept—and that kept him.

In the months before she died, his mother had fretted over Richard. When she learned that he had disobeyed her by attending more balls than she thought good for a college boy, Richard confessed to misleading her. He had done so only because he could not bear to confess to any act "which I knew directly opposite to your wishes, and opinions which I knew would incur your highest displeasure and ridicule." He nevertheless denied consorting with the "idle, dissipated young men" of the college and insisted that "in those hours which are by some taken up in dissipation and debauch," he could be found in his room studying. He said he would disappoint her not only because he could never live up to the achievements of the men who had raised him but also because his nature was "of the warmest kind." He was prey to "sudden gusts of passion" that, he confessed, he could not "govern or resist."

CHAPTER SEVEN

The summer of 1788, when Nancy was approaching her fourteenth birthday, was a busy one in Richmond and at Tuckahoe. In June, Patrick Henry, Edmund Randolph, James Madison and other orators and statesmen from all parts of Virginia converged on Richmond to debate whether the state should ratify the new federal Constitution drafted the previous year in Philadelphia. People from the other colonies came to observe the Virginians in their deliberations, including Gouverneur Morris of New York, who had also arrived to oversee shipments of tobacco, in which he had an interest, to France. Morris rode out to Tuckahoe to visit Nancy's father, "a gentleman possessing one of the best fortunes in this country," though hard pressed by British creditors. Morris found Mrs. Randolph to be an "amiable woman," though "not in much good health."

Morris left no record of his impression of the Colonel's sons and daughters, although by the time of his visit, Nancy had blossomed into a lovely girl, who was not only beguiling but alarmingly bright. One admirer spoke with affection of her "little upturned nose," and the young men who danced the quadrille with her discovered that she read books. She liked to use such words as "tautology" and "eclaircissement," and she sometimes used them properly. Young men and old also discovered that when teased Nancy responded in kind. Many people seemed to find her bantering manner amusing, and her brother William, putting one prig's disapproval into proper context, said that Nancy "offends only the unamiable."

The annual Jockey Club races were held the same week as the debates. On the last Friday of the month, Colonel Randolph took his daughters to the racecourse, where they encountered their cousin Richard Randolph, who had returned from New York for the debates. He was soon spending afternoons and evenings at Tuckahoe. The household seemed especially merry in August, when Nancy's brother Tom returned from Scotland, followed a few weeks later by John Leslie, his friend from Edinburgh. The Colonel had agreed to employ Leslie as tutor to the younger children. After a few weeks at Tuckahoe, the Scotsman began to feel for Judith "a burning affection tinctured with tender melancholy," but she did not feel the same for him, and by the time the October rains had soaked the tobacco fields, the brokenhearted scholar was on a boat home. Judith, he had been told, was in love with her cousin Richard, who had asked the Colonel for her hand.

Richard and Judith were determined to marry, but their parents were reluctant to give their consent. St. George Tucker told Colonel Randolph that although his stepson's choice was an estimable young lady, Tucker wished that Richard had waited a few years before proposing marriage to anyone. He had hoped that Richard would complete his education so he could take up a profitable profession. While the Randolph boys' late father had been rich in land and slaves, all the property was now mortgaged to London financiers, and when Richard turned twenty-one, he would inherit not wealth but debt. He would not yet be able to provide for a wife, and it was impossible to know when he would be able to do so. Tucker had warned the Randolph boys that much of their inheritance would go to pay their father's debts. Once their inheritance was exhausted, they would be forced to rely on their own "personal abilities and exertions," but Richard showed little inclination to exert himself in any way. His choice of Judith, however, suggested sound judgment, and Tucker told Colonel Randolph he could offer no reason other than the question of money "for deferring a union which would have met my warmest approbations at a future day."

Judith's mother also had misgivings about the marriage. She had wished to "keep my Daughters single, till they were old enough to form a proper judgment of Mankind," she told Tucker. Since a woman's happiness "depends entirely on the Husband she is united to," marriage requires "more deliberation than girls generally take, or even Mothers seem to think necessary." The risk "is doubled when they marry very young; for at sixteen and nineteen we think everybody perfect that we take a fancy to; the Lady expects nothing but condescension, and the Gentleman thinks his Mistress an Angel." Young people "are apt to sour when the delirium of love is over, and Reason is allowed to reascend her Throne." If Richard and Judith were to marry, she hoped that they "will never repent of the choice they have made."

Married at sixteen, Mrs. Randolph had borne thirteen children, three of whom had died in infancy. The illness Gouverneur Morris had noticed the previous summer worsened, and in March of 1789, at the age of forty-four, Anne Cary Randolph died, leaving Judith free to follow her desires. On the day of their mother's death at Tuckahoe, Judith and Nancy used a diamond ring to scratch onto a window words that would remain for two centuries:

JUDITH RANDOLPH
NANCY RANDOLPH
MARCH 16, 1789

It was one of the last times they would act like any two sisters who still loved each other and between whom no serious strife had ever come.

Nine months passed. On Christmas Day, Colonel Randolph had thrown open the gates of Tuckahoe, and scores of Carys, Harrisons, Carters and Blands drove up the lane to the house in their finest coach-and-fours as streams of domestic servants hauled platter after platter of steaming victuals from the kitchen to the house. Drivers acknowledged each other with great solemnity, while the gentlemen seated inside nodded to old friends as their carriages came into view. Riders on horseback tipped their hats to the ladies, then slipped their mounts between the phaetons and chariots that bowled merrily up the hard-packed lane, some emblazoned with coats of arms.

At noon on December 25, 1789, Judith Randolph, seventeen, and Richard Randolph, nineteen, were united in marriage following the liturgy of the 1669 Book of Common Prayer. The pastor reminded the young couple that marriage vows were not to be taken "unadvisedly, lightly, or wantonly, to satisfy men's carnal lusts and appetites," but "reverently, discreetly, advisedly, soberly, and in the fear of God." Marriage was ordained "for the procreation of children," as "a remedy against sin, and to avoid fornication," and "for mutual society, help, and comfort." Richard promised Judith he would "love her, comfort her, honour and keep" her, "forsaking all others," and she pledged to "obey, serve, love, honour and keep" him. He slipped a ring on her finger, and after issuing the standard admonition to any who might threaten their marital harmony, the pastor pronounced Richard and Judith "man and wife."

The guests applauded, and the festivities began. Tables throughout the house were laid for a feast of chicken, roast beef, pork, mutton, ham, venison, duck, goose, rabbit, pheasant, partridge, quail, eels and oysters. The guests ate mince pies, custards and plum puddings, and washed them down with pitchers of wine, ale, lemon punch and cordials. When the guests were properly stuffed, the dining tables were dismantled, and dancing began. There were hunting parties and riding parties, card playing and more dancing, until the guests collapsed onto makeshift beds crammed into every room. At some point in all this merrymaking, the guests gave Judith and Richard a suitable send-off. As the men fired their guns in salute and everyone cheered, the driver started the horses, and the carriage disappeared down the lane. They would spend their wedding night at Presquile plantation. Then they would go on to Matoax, where they would live.

Within the first weeks of their arrival, the household ran through its last barrel of flour. Nonetheless, Richard insisted on furnishing the house with the finest tea tables and carpets, which he bought on credit, and by spring, Petersburg merchants were pressing for payment. A storekeeper from whom Richard received a table and chest of drawers approached him on the street, demanding money, which "mortified" him. Day after day, Richard dispatched his servant Toney to borrow cash from the Randolphs' agent. Whenever Richard needed money for the market ("a dollar or two") or wanted new carpets, furniture, harness leather, or beef cattle, he would requisition it from one of the family's other plantations or tell his agent in Richmond or Petersburg to get it from a merchant and "charge as before." That summer he tried to sell some of his saddle horses to his own overseer.

There were moments in the first months of the marriage when Judith displayed a temper that Richard seems not to have noticed during their courtship. There had even been some misunderstanding on their wedding night, or so Richard's new sister-in-law Nancy claimed. How she came by this information is unclear, but she would later allege that Judith had made Richard sit up all night, refusing to let him get into bed with her. This Judith had done, Nancy said, "to shew her power."

CHAPTER EIGHT

~~~~~~~~~~~

*By the summer of 1790, when Nancy was six-*teen, Jack and Richard's brother Theodorick, whose college career had ended about the time of Richard's wedding, began to pursue her. So did cousin Archibald Randolph, Benjamin Harrison VI of Berkeley and Genlo Lee, who found excuses to linger with Nancy among the boxwoods, gallop across the meadows with her and compliment her father on the quality of his horses.

While gracious to these young men, Colonel Randolph had not been happy since Nancy's mother had died. In late September, eager for companionship, the Colonel announced his intention to marry the daughter of a prosperous friend, Gabriela Harvie, who was not much older than Nancy. The two young women quarreled from the moment Gabriela married the Colonel and moved to Tuckahoe.

Nancy's inability to get along with her new stepmother did not surprise the former Patsy Jefferson, who had married Nancy's brother Tom in 1790 and also found Gabriela difficult. When Patsy told her father that Gabriela was deliberately sowing discord between the Colonel and his children, Jefferson advised his daughter to strive to see good in the Colonel's bride. Colonel Randolph should not be expected to live out his days as a widower, Jefferson reminded her. Colonel Randolph was a "good man, to whose temper nothing can be objected but too much facility, too much milk." Gabriela's disposition should be considered as nothing more than "one bad stop in your harpsichord." Patsy should "avoid what is rough" in Gabriela's character and strive to be "the link of love, union and peace for your whole family."

Soon after her arrival at Tuckahoe, Gabriela began maneuvering to get Nancy married just to get her out of the house. Nancy resisted, and more quarrels ensued. Gabriela told people that Nancy had thrown herself at Richard and that Colonel Randolph had found it necessary to "tear [Nancy] from Dick's arms." Life under the same roof with Gabriela became intolerable, but Nancy did not know where she could go.

A few months earlier, Judith and Richard had concluded that they could no longer afford to live at Matoax and had moved to Bizarre, where the soil was not yet worn out and there were fewer lawyers, should Richard start a practice. They set out for Bizarre in the fall of 1790, when the first cold drizzles began to soak the ground and dead leaves made the carriage trails slippery and soft.

Judith was determined to impose order, and the "smokey Cabbin" where the Randolph boys had taken refuge during the war was soon spotless. "Not one drop of water was ever suffered to stand on her sideboard," Jack Randolph recalled, "except what was in the pitcher; the house, from cellar to garden and in every part, [was] as clean as hands could make it." Even the chamber pots "were as sweet and clean as the teacups." Richard planted trees in the yard, whose growth through the years could mark the progress of their lives together. Although far removed from family and friends, Judith was "much happier here than where we saw more company." Within months of their arrival, she was pregnant.

When Judith and Richard heard of Nancy's difficulties, they agreed to let her live with them at Bizarre.

With its tree-canopied carriage trails and boundless seclusion, Nancy found Bizarre enchanting. She would remember it years later as "that dear, sequestered spot," though this response may say more about her romantic sensibility than the charms of the old house and its rugged setting.

Theodorick, who had turned twenty in January 1791, returned to Virginia about the time Nancy came to Bizarre, followed her there—and stayed. When Richard learned that Anna Bland Dudley, a widowed aunt with two small children, had fallen on hard times in North Carolina, he brought them to live at Bizarre. Richard's hospitality also extended to Judith and Nancy's aunt Mary Cary Page, who came for long visits. As the household grew and expenses mounted, Richard remained as nonchalant about money as he had been at Matoax. He continued to order Scottish carpets and mahogany furniture but exhibited little interest in the tobacco operations that would pay for them.

He also resisted Tucker's encouragement that he practice law. "What inducement have I," he asked Tucker, "to leave a happy and comfortable home to search for bustle, fatigue and disappointment? I have a comfortable subsistence, which is enough to make me happy."

He was surrounded in his fiefdom by family and friends and had servants to wait on him and field hands to work his farm. He had fine horses to ride and game to shoot and a library well stocked with the classics as well as such contemporary works as Chateaubriand's *Atala*, Chesterfield's *Letters to His Son* and Rousseau's *Émile*. Judith would soon give birth to his first child, and if she was not as attentive to him as she had been before her pregnancy, Richard found that he could turn for amusement to his wife's lively little sister.

Although Theodorick was pursuing Nancy, Richard treated her as he treated any attractive young lady. He kissed her when he felt like it, and in the weeks leading up to Judith's confinement, he began to spend more time with her than he did with his wife, who seems to have thought nothing of the affection Richard showed her sister.

Nancy and Theodorick soon announced to the other members of the household—though they appear to have told no one else—that they planned to marry. The secret of their engagement caused some tension in the family, however, because Jack had begun to write letters to Nancy from Philadelphia and did not know of their plans. She had no interest in Jack, but he seemed insistent on courting her, and when his attentions "pestered" her, Richard told him that she had become engaged to Theodorick. Jack was angered by the news, and one day, when he and Nancy were together at Presquile, he led her to the portico and leaned her up against one of the pillars. He told her what Richard had said about her plans to marry Theodorick, which he "hoped was not true," because Theodorick was "unworthy" of her.

Richard was delighted by the news of Nancy's engagement to his brother, or he professed to be. But one morning in the last months of Judith's pregnancy, Nancy's maid brought a pitcher of water into her room and found her alone with Richard. He was on his knees and looked as if he had been weeping; Nancy appeared distraught, too. The consequences of her father's remarriage, and her leaving Tuckahoe and coming to live at Bizarre, were suddenly becoming clear to her. Life had become more complicated than she had ever imagined it could be.

"Polly," Nancy said to her maid, "I wish my mother had lived."

Richard stood, composed himself and hurried from the room. Without saying a word, Polly put down the pitcher and left.

CHAPTER NINE

Richard had indeed been weeping. He had slipped into Nancy's room that morning, thrown himself on his knees and, Nancy said, "begged that I would listen to him and not to alarm anyone." Richard said he was miserable with Judith, who he claimed did not love him. He had known she cared nothing for him since their first night together at Presquile, when she had made him sit up until daybreak in a corner of their room. Weeping, Richard implored Nancy never to marry, saying the idea was unbearable to him, and "endeavored to shake [her] principles."

"I am engaged," Nancy replied, "to your brother."

It was then that Polly entered the room and Richard fled.

Judith was now entering the last months of her pregnancy, when she was no doubt less attractive to Richard than she had been in the early days of their marriage. She was probably tense and distracted as well. Childbirth, Thomas Jefferson liked to tell his daughters, "was no more than a jog of the elbow," but women who had to endure it knew better. Many never survived it, and all women feared it. Dr. William Buchan, whose *Domestic Medicine* could be found in the libraries of the big plantations, warned that many women brought on their own deaths "by excess fear" of it. "Very few women die in labor," Buchan said, "although many lose their lives after it."

After delivery, Buchan continued, a woman will frequently find herself "weak and exhausted" and immediately assume "she is in danger; but this fear seldom fails to obstruct the necessary evacuations upon which her recovery depends. Thus the sex frequently fall a sacrifice to their own imaginations, when there should be no danger, did they apprehend none." Calomel was recommended for most ailments arising from pregnancy. Taken to excess, however, calomel could cause a woman's teeth and hair to fall out. To remedy convulsions, bleeding or shaving the head and applying cold water to the scalp were recommended. By avoiding raw onions and eating "immature meats" like veal and lamb, Dr. Buchan believed a woman could achieve regular evacuations, which were vital to her recovery.

Judith was fortunate that she would give birth in the winter, when the likelihood of hemorrhage would be lessened. Should "flooding" ensue, a bag of snow should be inserted to stanch the flow. To ease the pain, a woman should take opium. There were risks in winter, too, of course. "Above all things," Dr. Buchan advised his readers, "beware of cold." Women "who quit the bed too soon, often contract diseases from cold, of which they never recover."

In the spring of 1791, Judith gave birth to a "fine son," as Patsy Jefferson Randolph told her father, but that did not mean the danger had passed. Dr. Buchan and the other medical authorities said an infant required constant care, and Judith would take no chances with little St. George Randolph, named for Richard's stepfather. As soon as a baby was born, it was to be cleansed with lard or egg yolk. The infant's nipples would need to be squeezed "to draw off the milk," and since a child was known to be ravenous at birth, he would be force-fed a "pap," consisting of bread mixed with milk or wine, chewed first by one of the attending women. If mere bread and water did not perk a child up, a "comforter" or "cordial" of butter, sugar and wine or stronger spirits was recommended. "Daffy's Elixir," sold in most apothecaries, also contained alcohol, to which infants were thought to respond favorably. "Godfrey's Cordial," also given to infants, relied heavily on opium.

Most diseases were brought on by breathing "bad air," which the bottomlands at Bizarre produced as surely as tobacco. Emetics and purgatives were employed to cure fevers and agues, but these ailments, which a later generation would call malaria, were frequently fatal. Bleeding was also recommended. Whooping cough, which could last for six to ten weeks, claimed many young lives; to treat it, bleeding was encouraged, with generous applications of melted hog's lard to suppress the cough.

There was only so much a conscientious mother could do to safeguard a child's health, however. Some things went wrong no matter what a mother did, and Judith had other responsibilities, which she performed with her usual dedication. By the end of the day, she would be worn out, which may explain why Richard continued to exhibit so much affection for Nancy. He kissed her in the presence of others, and Judith seemed not to notice or, if she did notice, not to care. Whether Theodorick suspected that his brother's affection for Nancy was more than that of any other man for his sister-in-law is not known, but there is no evidence that Nancy complained to him about Richard's behavior toward her.

Nevertheless, pursued simultaneously by Theodorick, Richard and Jack, Nancy tried to flee the increasingly awkward situation. She begged her father to let her come home, but Gabriela, answering for Colonel Randolph, said that Nancy would have to remain at Bizarre because the horses were "too lame to travel."

By this time, other friends and relatives began to feel that Richard's attentions to Nancy were improper. They had also come to suspect that his feelings were returned and that any desire Nancy might once have felt for Theodorick was gone. Convinced that Judith was too trusting, Aunt Mary Page began to flutter about outside Nancy's bedroom, listening for sounds that would confirm her suspicions.

Judith may well have been too preoccupied with the baby to notice things that others found suspicious. Little St. George, though healthy in many ways, seemed to need more care than other children his age. The older he got, the less he seemed to hear what those around him were saying, which added to mounting anxieties in the household. The effect on Judith was soon apparent. She was prone, Jack said, to "constant wrath" that he felt was taking its toll on her marriage. But her impatience and irritability may well have been manifestations of suspicions she felt about her husband but refused to acknowledge, even to herself.

Throughout the fall, the family had an additional cause for concern. An illness that Theodorick had been unable to throw off for most of the year grew more worrisome. He had not been able to walk since midsummer, and by autumn his "bones had worked through his skin." When winter came on, he was reduced to "a mere skeleton." Patsy and Tom Randolph visited Bizarre, traveling through the deepest snow anyone could remember. Trees along the Appomattox bent low under the weight of snow and ice, and when the snow melted, the river rose and flooded the bottomlands.

On February 14, 1792, twelve days after his twentieth birthday, Theodorick died, and Patsy and Tom set off, through rain and hail, for Monticello. "I have never seen the end of anything," Patsy told her father upon their return, "with more pleasure in my life."

CHAPTER TEN

By late summer of 1792 the tobacco was ripening in the fields, and Nancy began to worry about her figure. She seemed unusually reluctant to undress in the presence of other women in the household, and Aunt Mary Page said Nancy had become so plump so quickly people might suspect she was pregnant.

There were other reasons for suspicion. In September, Patsy was again at Bizarre and noticed that Nancy was not feeling well and had lost her characteristic joi de vivre. Nancy, Judith and Patsy diagnosed Nancy's condition as "hysterics" from "cholic," the symptoms of which, Dr. Buchan said, included pain in the abdomen and bowels, constipation, flatulence and a "great sinking of the spirits, with dejection of mind." Bleedings, purgings and clysters were recommended. Opium or laudanum in a glass of cinnamon water was known to ease the symptoms, if followed by a plaster of laudanum spread upon soft leather and applied to the belly. Gum guaiacum, which was concocted from the resin of trees, was also prescribed for colic as well as for rheumatism, gout and venereal disease. Patsy, who benefited from her father's interest in science and Monticello's superior supply of medicines, recommended gum guaiacum but warned

MARTHA (PATSY) JEFFERSON RANDOLPH

Nancy that it was a "dangerous medicine" known to "produce an abortion." After Patsy returned to Monticello, Nancy asked Aunt Mary Page to obtain some of the medicine for her. A few days later she wrote to Patsy and the medicine arrived.

Toward the end of September, Richard, Judith, Nancy and Jack took their carriage to Glentivar, the plantation of their cousin Randolph Harrison and his wife, Mary, about thirty miles northeast of Bizarre. Mary's brother Archibald Randolph, who had resumed his courtship of Nancy after Theodorick's death, would meet them there.

The Randolphs arrived at nightfall. The leaves had just begun to turn, but it was still warm. Randolph Harrison met the carriage, and when he offered to help Nancy, he noticed she was wearing a heavy winter coat, buttoned up tight. She did not feel well and was not hungry, so Mary suggested she rest in the Harrisons' downstairs bedroom while the others ate. When Mary had finished eating, she took Nancy upstairs to get her settled. The second story had only two rooms. Nancy would sleep in the smaller room, which could be reached only through the larger one. A door, secured by a lock, led into the larger room, where Richard and Judith were to sleep.

Mary went downstairs; later, she and Judith went up to see how Nancy was doing. After a short visit, Judith went to bed, and Mary Harrison went back downstairs. Sometime later, when the men went to bed, Richard joined Judith. The house grew quiet and outside, the temperature dropped, bringing the first frost of the year. The Harrisons slept soundly until late in the night, when someone's screams echoed through the dark rooms of their house. The screams seemed to come from upstairs.

There would be rancorous disagreement in the years that followed about precisely what was occurring upstairs and even about what happened next. This much seems evident: alarmed by the unsettling noises, Mary Harrison concluded that Nancy was in some distress and took laudanum to the room where she was staying, but Richard did not allow her to enter. Sometime after Mary returned to her room, the Harrisons heard heavy footsteps descending the stairs, which they assumed were those of Richard Randolph, who had presumably gone to order one of the slaves to call for a doctor. They heard the footsteps go back

upstairs a few minutes later. Except for the movement of servants, the house fell silent.

The next morning, Richard Randolph and Randolph Harrison went into Nancy's room to get a fire going in the fireplace.
(For reasons neither of them would ever be asked to explain,
they took this task on themselves rather than leave it, as one
might expect, to the household slaves.) While Nancy stayed in
bed, Richard took Judith and Mary Harrison to shop at a
nearby store. The next day, all the Randolphs rode back to
Bizarre, and some weeks later, the Harrisons visited them there.

There seems to have been little subsequent discussion
among the Randolphs or Harrisons about the peculiar events of
that night at Glentivar. The matter, some of them would insist,
was of such little significance that it was quickly forgotten. A
more persuasive explanation may be that the subject, being far
too painful for any of them to discuss, was deliberately dropped.

CHAPTER ELEVEN

The Randolphs may have chosen not to talk about what had happened that night, but by early October, rumors about their visit to Glentivar were spreading throughout Virginia. Jack first heard the story in Williamsburg, where a friend told him the Harrisons' slaves had discovered the corpse of a white baby. They had tried to show Randolph Harrison where they'd made their grisly discovery, but he would not listen. People said the baby was Nancy's and that Richard, knowing he was the father, had killed it. Because they were in-laws, they were also guilty, under Virginia law, of incest. Richard was a murderer and should hang. Some said Nancy should hang, too.

When Richard heard the rumors, he was furious. His honor had been impugned, and although he doubted that he would be prosecuted, he might have to fight a duel, which he had never done. A duel would allow him to restore his honor, but he would have to find out who was making the accusations before he could issue a challenge. Uncertain how to respond, he took Judith and Nancy to Williamsburg in the first weeks of 1793 so he could confer with St. George Tucker, who was now a judge of the General Court. Urging Richard to do nothing, Tucker told his stepson to trust that the talk would run its course. To react to the gossip of field hands and blacksmiths would be to descend to their level. Should he discover anyone of higher rank making accusations against him, however, he could reconsider his course of action. The test would be whether he was still welcome at the great plantations, and he would go to Tuckahoe first, presumably to see how he was received. If he were welcomed, he had nothing to fear. All the Randolphs, he seems to have believed, would close ranks behind him, people would tire of the story and life would go on as it always had. Richard agreed, and Judith extracted from her husband a promise never to mention the matter again.

Before leaving Williamsburg for Tuckahoe, Richard met secretly with Nancy, who wrote a statement for him to use if arrested. What the statement said is not known, and exactly what happened at Glentivar must also remain a matter of some conjecture. But her comments years later suggest that the document probably contained a formal acknowledgment—whether true or not—that she had given birth that night but that the baby—which the statement would claim was Theodorick's and not Richard's—was stillborn. Richard did not think he would need the statement, but he was prepared to use it if he had to. What such an admission from Nancy would do for Richard was clear enough. What it might mean for her reputation, Richard seems not to have considered.

He did not receive the hearty welcome at Tuckahoe he had expected. Hoping to find a family united in its opposition to his accusers, he discovered one that was deeply divided. The former Gabriela Harvie, whose quarrels with Nancy had driven her from Tuckahoe, appears to have been openly hostile to Richard.

Nancy and Judith's brother Tom, who was still at Monticello, blamed Richard for the scandal. Whether or not he believed Richard had committed any crime, Tom nonetheless held him responsible for bringing shame on his sisters. So, apparently, did Nancy's brother William. William no longer lived at Tuckahoe and was not there when Richard visited, but Richard soon learned that William had complained long and loud about Richard, even to strangers, which prompted Richard to demand that William be called to account for his behavior, perhaps through the courts. For a time, Richard considered settling the dispute as gentlemen. He even insulted William in front of the Tuckahoe household, hoping one of them would pass along the insults, provoking a duel. No one knew where William was, however, or if they did, they refused to say.

Richard decided to go forward with a plan he and Tucker had discussed in Williamsburg. He had hoped, he reported to his stepfather, to find at Tuckahoe that the truth "had prevailed over the dark & little calumnies of cowardly enemies." When he learned that the word of these "enemies" carried more weight than his own, he had no choice but to proceed "in the most public manner." He would write to *The Virginia Gazette*, defying his accusers to come forward. If they did, he would be able to produce proof of his innocence—in Nancy's own handwriting.

Richard believed that as soon as the letter was published the plot against him would collapse; even so, the "horrid and malicious lie" so wounded Richard's feelings that the idea of remaining in Virginia was unbearably painful, and he feared what he might do "in a moment of passion." Staying home would be dangerous to himself and to others he loved. Nancy's plight was "worse than mine on account of the delicacy of her sex & sentiments," so he would need to take her with him.

He would take Judith, too. What troubled him most, he added, "is the situation of my beloved wife." In Williamsburg, Judith had made Richard promise "not to say anything more or make any further inquiry into the abominable story," but he had decided to break that promise. What Judith's response would be, Richard did not know. She was pregnant again, and he wished to shield her from strain. To remain in Virginia in her "present situation" might be "fatal."

CHAPTER TWELVE

Richard's letter, published in The Virginia Gazette, and *General Advertiser* on April 17, 1793, read:

My character has lately been the subject of much conversation, blackened with the imputation of crimes at which humanity revolts, and which the laws of society have pronounced worthy of condign punishment. The charge against me was spread *far and wide* before I received the *smallest notice* of it—and whilst I have been endeavouring to trace it to its origin, has daily acquired strength in the minds of my fellow citizens.

To refute the calumnies which have been circulated, by a legal prosecution of the authors of them, must require a *length* of time, during which the weight of public odium would rest on the party *accused*, however *innocent*—I have, therefore, resolved on the method of presenting myself before the Bar of the public. . . .

I do therefore give notice, that I will on the first day of the next April Cumberland Court appear there and render myself a prisoner before that *court,* or any *magistrate* of the county there *present,* to answer in the due course of law, *any charge of crime which any person or persons whatsoever shall then and there think proper to allege against me.*—Let not my accusers pretend an unwillingness to appear as prosecutors against me in a criminal court. The *only* favor I can *ever* receive at *their* hands is, for them to stand forth and exert themselves in order to [secure] my conviction.

Let not a pretended tenderness towards the supposed accomplice in the imputed guilt, shelter me. That person will meet the accusations with a fortitude of *which innocence alone is capable.*

If my accusers decline this invitation, there yet remains another mode of proceedure which I am equally ready to meet. Let them state, with *precision* and *clearness* the *facts* which they lay to my charge and the *evidence* whether *direct* or *circumstantial* by which I am to be proved guilty, in any of the public papers.—Let *no circumstance* of *time* or *place* nor the *names* of *any* witnesses against me, be omitted. The public shall then judge between me and them, according to other rules than the strict rules of legal evidence.

If neither of these methods be adopted in order to fix the stigma which has been imposed upon me, let candor and impartiality acquit me of crimes which my soul abhors, or suspend their opinions of my guilt until a decision thereon can be obtained in some other satisfactory mode.

RICHARD RANDOLPH, jun.

MARCH 29, 1793

The VIRGINIA GAZETTE, and GENERAL ADVERTISER.

ol. VII.]   *RICHMOND:* WEDNESDAY ... 1793 ... [Numb. ...

To the PUBLIC.

MY character has lately been the subject of much conversation, blackened with the imputation of crimes at which humanity revolts, and which the laws of society have pronounced worthy of condign punishment. The charge against me was spread far and wide before I received the smallest notice of it—and whilst I have been endeavouring to trace it to. its origin; has daily acquired strength in the minds of my fellow-citizens.

To refute the calumnies which have been circulated, by a legal prosecution ot the authors of them, must require a length of time, during which the weight of public odium would rest on the party accused, however innocent—I have, therefore, resolved on this method of presenting myself before the bar of the public.

Calumny to be obviated must be confronted—If the crimes imputed to me are true, my life is the just forfeit to the laws of my country—To meet and not to shrink from such an enquiry as would put that life in hazard (were the charges against me supportable), is the object of which I am now in pursuit.

I do therefore give notice, that I will on the first day of the next April Cumberland Court appear there and render myself a prisoner before that court, or any magistrate of the county there present, to answer in the due course of law, any charge or crime which any person or persons whatsoever shall then and there think proper to alledge against

me.—Let not my accusers pretend an unwillingness to appear as prosecutors against me in a criminal court. The only favor I can ever receive at their hands is, for them to stand forth and exert themselves in order to my conviction.

Let not a pretended tenderness towards the supposed accomplice in the imputed guilt, shelter me. That person will meet the accusation with a fortitude of which innocence alone is capable.

If my accusers decline this invitation, there yet remains another mode of proceedure which I am equally ready to meet. Let them state, with precision and clearness the facts which they lay to my charge and the evidence whether direct or circumstantial by which I am to be proved guilty, in any of the public papers.—Let no circumstance of time or place nor the names of any witnesses against me, be omitted. The public shall then judge between me and them, according to other rules than the strict rules of legal evidence.

If neither of these methods be adopted in order to fix the stigma which has been imposed upon me, let candor and impartiality acquit me of crimes which my soul abhors, or suspend their opinions of my guilt until a decision thereon can be contained in some other satisfactory mode.

RICHARD RANDOLPH, jun.

March 29, 1793

THE VIRGINIA GAZETTE

Tom Randolph was furious that Richard would offer up Tom's sister to public scorn to save his own neck, and hoping to prevent such an outrage, he galloped off to Tuckahoe to confront his brother-in-law. Richard showed him the statement Nancy had written, and Tom warned Richard that he would use the statement at his own peril. Their duty was to protect Nancy, and he would not allow Richard to coerce her into any admission that would soil her reputation. Richard was on his own, to be hanged if that is what his neighbors decided to do with him, but any man of honor would destroy Nancy's statement and never speak of it again. Richard flung the paper into the fire.

THOMAS MANN RANDOLPH, JR.

Back at Bizarre, he received a letter in which Tom was even more explicit: if Richard even intimated that Nancy and Theodorick had been lovers, Tom would take revenge: "I defy you to transfer the stigma to your deceased brother." If you do, he added, "I will wash out with your blood the stain on my family."

Only Nancy seemed untroubled by the scandal swirling

about her. In the days after the family's return from Glentivar, she was up and about and riding horses again. She seemed happier than ever. Judith, however, was miserable. It had been a dreadful year for her. Her second pregnancy did not progress as smoothly as her first, and sometime in 1793, Judith lost the baby. This sad event seems almost lost in the turmoil of the family's ongoing crisis. Nancy seems hardly to have noticed her sister's heartache, the family's distress over the scandal or its consequences for her reputation, prospects and personal safety.

Patsy Randolph felt there was something odd about the way Nancy was responding to the crisis. Patsy was so troubled that, in April of 1793, she sought advice from her father, who was in Philadelphia, serving as George Washington's secretary of state. Jefferson had read Richard's letter to the newspaper, and he assured Patsy that people are "too rational" to blame one person, much less an entire family, for the acts of another. He hoped she felt no uneasiness "but for the pitiable victim, whether it be of error or slander." He saw "guilt in but one person, and not in her. For [Nancy] it is the moment of trying the affection of her friends, when their commiseration and comfort become balm to her wounds." Patsy should be kind to Nancy, "regardless of what the trifling or malignant may think or say."

By now Patsy also blamed Richard. Early on, she had "doubted the truth of the report," but ultimately she began to distrust him more than his accusers. "I would to heaven my hopes were equal to my fear," she admitted, but her fears prevailed. "As for the poor deluded victim," she concluded, "I believe all feel much more for her than she does for herself.

Amidst the distress of her family she alone is tranquil." All Nancy seemed to worry about was whether she would be separated "from her vile seducer."

That separation soon took place.

Richard rode to Cumberland Court House, as promised, "on the first day of the next April Cumberland Court," convinced that his own daunting demeanor would carry the day. His slanderers would look upon his noble countenance, realize the outrage they had committed upon a gentleman of honor and slink away. To his surprise, High Sheriff Henry Skipwith was waiting for him, armed with a magistrate's warrant.

He arrested Richard on charges of "feloniously murdering a child said to be borne of Nancy Randolph" and locked him up in Cumberland jail.

CHAPTER THIRTEEN

On the morning of April 29, 1793, seven days after
Richard's arrest, everybody who had ever made enough money
to pretend they were as good as the Randolphs arrived at the
courthouse in their gaily painted phaetons, riding coaches and
post chaises, tipping their hats and calling to one another as if
they were at the races. Then came small farmers, blacksmiths,
shopkeepers and idlers. The "trial" promised to be the most
sensational entertainment in Cumberland County history. No
one could remember so many people streaming into Cumberland, or so many strange faces. They milled about the scrubby
green, crowded onto the porch at Effingham Tavern and filled
every seat in the courthouse, where Judith, Nancy, Jack and the
other Randolphs were on display, like so many chained bears at
a raree-show. Six toughs hired by the county to guard the gaol
had hauled Richard over to the courthouse, where Randolph after Randolph would testify before the gentlemen justices. Virginia law prohibited blacks from appearing as witnesses against
white men charged with felonies, so none of the household
slaves would be heard from. The Randolphs could be thankful
for that.

Shortly after the proceedings began, Randolph Harrison of

RANDOLPH HARRISON

Glentivar sat impassively in the witness chair, his big jaw thrust forward, and glared at his interrogators.

Will you tell the court what happened on the night of September 31, 1792, at your plantation, called Glentivar, after you retired for the night and defendants Richard Randolph and Nancy Randolph and Mr. Randolph's wife, Judith, had retired to their rooms?

"We were waked," Harrison replied.

And by what were you awakened?

"By loud screams."

Whose screams were they?

We didn't know.

What happened next, sir?

A slave girl told us the screams "proceeded from Miss Nancy," so we [the Harrisons] got laudanum for her.

And then?

"Mrs. [Mary] Harrison soon went up and remained in the Room some little time and then returned, Miss Nancy being easier."

And were you not, sir, roused from sleep some moments later?

We were.

By what cause?

We "heard some person come down stairs."

Did you have any idea who it might have been?

We assumed "from the weight of the step" that they were Mr. Randolph's footsteps, going to send for a doctor. But the servants "frequently passed up & down stairs during the night," too.

To the best of your knowledge, Mr. Harrison, what happened in that room that night?

Miss Nancy "had probably had an hysteric fit, to which she [is] subject." She had had such a fit "two or three days before."

What happened the next day?

I was told Nancy "probably had an hysteric fit" in the night.

Anything else?

Nothing, really. That morning, while Nancy remained in bed, "Mr. Randolph and I went into her room to lay the Hearth."

And what did you observe then, sir?

Nothing "remarkable, except considerable paleness, and a disagreeable" odor.

Did you reach any conclusion about the source of that odor?

Only that it could be attributed "to a cause totally different from childbirth."

And you have nothing more to report on this matter?

No, sir. The next day, "Mrs. Harrison, Mrs. Randolph & Mr. Randolph rode out to a store." Then they all went back to Bizarre.

But did you not obtain additional information regarding this matter after the Randolphs went home?

No, sir.

But were you told nothing that might prove relevant to this inquiry?

Whatever he might or might not have been told, Harrison said, he saw no reason to suspect that anything had happened on the night in question. Despite the lurid rumors, he had detected no unpleasantness between Judith and her sister. The "behaviour of the Ladies while at [Glentivar] was the same as usual."

And how did Mr. and Mrs. Randolph treat each other when the Harrisons visited them later at Bizarre?

"The behaviour of Mr. & Mrs. Randolph to each other was as usual except . . ."

Except?

". . . except that Mr. Randolph seemed somewhat . . . crusty."

Is there not some explanation, sir, for that "crustiness"? Will you tell the court what you were told had happened the night Nancy awakened you with her screams?

I was told "she had miscarried."

And who had told you that?

"A negro-woman."

Something else happened, did it not, to revive your memory of that Negro woman's claim?

Some time after the Randolphs left, I "heard a Report among the negroes that the Birth . . . had been deposited . . ."

Where had the birth been deposited, Mr. Harrison?

". . . on a pile of shingles . . . between two Logs . . ."

Did the witness find anything to support that story?

About "six or seven weeks afterward," he was shown "such a place, where there was a shingle which appeared to have been stained."

Have you ever witnessed familiarities between Mr. Randolph and Miss Nancy that went beyond those of sister-in-law to brother-in-law and brother-in-law to sister-in-law?

I "observed . . . familiarities" that might have been "imprudent."

The gentlemen justices were ready to dismiss the witness when Patrick Henry asked Harrison if he had drawn any sinister conclusions from the foul odors, the screams, the alleged murder of an alleged newborn whose corpse was supposedly hustled down the stairs and tossed into a woodpile.

None whatsoever, sir, for I have "too high an opinion of them both to entertain any suspicion of criminal correspondence."

Thank you, sir. That will be all.

* * *

When Randolph Harrison of Glentivar described the bad odors, the screams, the hushed conversations at midnight, and the bloodstains in the shingle pile, the crowd shuddered and gasped and waited with ill-concealed excitement for even more lurid revelations.

The next witness did not disappoint. Randolph Harrison's wife, Mary Harrison, testified that soon after they were awakened by Nancy's screams, she went upstairs with the laudanum and found Judith Randolph sitting up in bed. Judith, who was alone, told her that Nancy "had the hysterics [since] she did not think the colic could make her scream so." Mrs. Harrison found the door to Nancy's room locked from the inside. Richard opened it but told her she had to leave her candle behind because the light would hurt Nancy's eyes.

Through the darkness, Mrs. Harrison could see Nancy and two slave girls. Richard took the laudanum, and Nancy told her she could go, so she went back to bed. The next day, she noticed "some blood" on Nancy's pillowcase. It looked as if "an attempt had been made to wash it, but it was still stained." Mrs. Harrison also discovered bloodstains on the stairs but drew no conclusions from the presence of the stains beyond the obvious fact that Nancy was sick. Mrs. Harrison insisted she "entertained no suspicion which was unfavorable to Miss Nancy" until several days later, when a slave woman told her Nancy had "miscarried." Mrs. Harrison considered that unlikely, since Judith showed no anxiety that "might be expected if she supposed her sister were about to be delivered of a child, or that resentment which would arise from suspecting her husband of being the father of it." Judith "only appeared uneasy at the illness of her sis-

MARY HARRISON

ter." At Glentivar and later at Bizarre, Mrs. Harrison saw nothing but "entire harmony between Mr. Randolph & his lady."

Mary Harrison's brother Archibald Randolph testified that
he often felt Nancy and Richard "were too fond of each other."
One night at Glentivar, Nancy appeared "extremely weak" and
asked him to help her climb the stairs. When they arrived at the
top, she rested on his arm, and "a disagreeable smell" emanated

from her bedroom, though it meant nothing to him at the time. Sometime later their kinsman Peyton Randolph told him Nancy had had "a child or miscarried."

Cousin Peyton Randolph testified that the defendants exhibited a "fondness for each other" that he found unseemly. Peyton had also been told by a servant that Nancy had "miscarried," and, bound by "friendship," told Archy the story. Carter Page, the husband of Aunt Mary Page, told the court he had seen Richard and Nancy "kissing." Even so, he had no reason to believe she had been pregnant, other than an "apparent alteration in her size," which he had first noticed the previous May.

Ann Randolph, another cousin, said she thought Richard had been "very attentive to Miss Nancy, rather more so than to Mrs. Randolph." Nancy wore a gown "without any loose covering to conceal her shape," and her belly seemed "encreased [*sic*]." At Bizarre a few weeks later, Nancy seemed thinner, though the "removal of her ill Health might have produced the change in her size." Randolph Harrison's mother, who had come to Glentivar to look in on Nancy, "discovered no mark (either by milk, fever, or otherwise)" to indicate that Nancy had given birth, and she had never before seen Judith "with a more chearful [*sic*] countenance."

Patsy Randolph told the court how, five months earlier, she had talked to Judith and Nancy about gum guaiacum and warned the sisters that it was a "dangerous" medicine that could cause abortion, but Nancy had asked Aunt Mary Page for it anyway. This had not surprised Patsy, she said, because she had long suspected that "Miss Nancy was pregnant."

CHAPTER FOURTEEN

*Patrick Henry had looked forward all day to cross-*examining Mary Page, who was a daughter of Archibald Cary of Ampthill, a longtime political foe. Henry still seethed over the Old Bruiser's insults and had no use for him or his haughty family.

Aunt Mary Page had been a frequent visitor to Bizarre, she said, and during her visits, she had become suspicious of the affection Nancy and Richard showed each other. She seemed eager to air these suspicions, and Henry sat quietly throughout her testimony. Mrs. Page once heard Judith say, "Mr. Randolph and Miss Nancy were only company for themselves," and there was such "fondness" between the defendants, in fact, that by April or May of 1792, she began to suspect "a criminal intercourse between them." About this time, she also began to observe "Miss Nancy's shape to alter." Nancy became defensive about her appearance and "unwilling to undress" when Mrs. Page was present.

Had Mrs. Page discussed these concerns with Miss Nancy?

She had indeed. Shortly after Nancy was said to have given birth, Mrs. Page learned of the rumors and brought them to Nancy's attention. When Nancy insisted she was innocent, Mrs. Page offered to examine her and put the matter to rest.

Nancy refused. If her denial was not good enough, Nancy replied, she would "give no further satisfaction."

At this, Henry moved slowly toward the witness. With much courtliness, he said that Mrs. Page seemed more certain of the defendant's pregnancy than had earlier witnesses—more knowledgeable about the girl's physical condition despite Nancy's refusal to disrobe in her presence. Henry asked her when she had first become convinced of Miss Nancy's pregnancy.

One day at Bizarre, Mrs. Page overheard a conversation between Nancy and Polly, her maid. Nancy asked Polly whether "she thought she was any smaller; the maid replied she thought her larger." Another time, Mrs. Page saw Miss Nancy "look down at her waist, & then cast her eyes up to Heaven in silent Melancholy." On yet another occasion, Mrs. Page heard Nancy and her maid discussing Nancy's figure. Already, "suspicious of her situation and, on that account, desirous of hearing what passed," Mrs. Page tried to enter the room but found it locked. Peering through a crack in the door, she could see that Nancy was naked. And with all her clothes off, Nancy certainly *looked* pregnant.

Henry fixed the witness with his piercing stare and asked so that everyone in the courtroom could hear: "Madam, which eye did you peep with?"

The courtroom rocked with derisive laughter, Mrs. Page flushed with indignation and Henry boomed: "Great God, deliver us from eavesdroppers!"

* * *

JACK RANDOLPH

Richard Randolph's younger brother Jack took the stand. He was nineteen, a "tall, gawky-looking, flaxen-haired stripling" with a complexion "of a good parchment colour, beardless chin, and as much assumed self-consequence as any two-footed animal" in captivity; he was, by far, "the most impudent youth" some people had ever encountered.

Jack's long legs and short torso gave him a marked resemblance to a well-dressed heron, and he spoke in high-pitched tones rather like a woman's. His manner was almost flippant, yet he appeared so disarmingly sure of himself that he inspired a peculiar sort of confidence. His testimony, moreover, put the events in question in a new and somewhat more exculpatory light.

Jack began by explaining how he often stayed at Bizarre. People were mistaken if they believed Richard was the only candidate to have impregnated Nancy, if she had indeed been pregnant, which he did not believe was the case. If she had been pregnant, it would have been by Theodorick, to whom Nancy had been engaged, not Richard. But Theodorick had died in February, which accounted for Nancy's melancholia. Richard and Judith once warned Jack never to mention Theodorick's name in Nancy's presence. The only time he forgot, Nancy "burst into tears."

Except for the obvious sadness at her betrothed's passing, how were relations in the household?

"The most perfect harmony subsisted in the family."

Did Judith Randolph appear to resent her sister's presence?

Not at all. Jack "often observed how much fonder Mrs. Randolph was of Nancy than any of her relations."

Had those feelings changed in any way?

No, the "fondness had increased."

Had Miss Nancy's appearance changed to indicate pregnancy?

Surely not. If she had been pregnant, Jack would certainly have noticed. She never wore stays, so it would have been impossible for her to conceal from him any significant alteration in her size and shape. Jack "frequently lounged on the bed both with her and her sister, & never suspected her of being pregnant."

JOHN MARSHALL

Was there any reason, other than rumor, for the defendants to be in court here today?

None whatsoever.

When all the witnesses had been heard, John Marshall delivered the closing argument for the defense. Although he was neither a fiery orator nor a clever debater, Marshall had a subtle grasp of the evidence and its implications. He took up where Henry's cross-examination left off, offering alternative explanations for the facts that had been introduced in the day's proceedings.

"Let us examine the evidence without favour or prejudice." As for Richard's fondness for Nancy, "there is no man in whose house a young lady lives who does not occasionally pay her attentions and use fondnesses, which a person prone to suspicion may consider as denoting guilt." Such courtesies were particularly likely in Richard's case, since Nancy had been driven from her home by her stepmother and had then suffered the loss of her betrothed. "Is it wonderful," Marshall asked, "that the attentions of Mr. Randolph should be somewhat particular?"

Circumstances that to others suggested guilt were, to Marshall, evidence of innocence. Had Richard and Nancy been guilty, they "would have suppressed any publick fondness and would have avoided all publick intercourse." Yet the affection they showed for each other "was under the eye of Mrs. Randolph, and never produced suspicion in her mind." Nancy's appearance of pregnancy—observed by some witnesses but not by others—could also be attributed to innocent causes. Those who testified that her belly had gotten larger observed this change in May. If she had been pregnant, "she must have been advanced three or four months" by that time. That would have made her eight or nine months pregnant by the time of the Glentivar visit and "the size of a woman about to be delivered." Could this be? Obviously not, since other witnesses who had seen her at the time reported no alteration at all.

Gum guaiacum could indeed be dangerous to pregnant

women. The time of Miss Nancy's request for it, however, proved that she wanted it for some purpose other than to cause miscarriage. If Nancy had been determined to induce an abortion, "she would have taken it at home where the event would have been concealed, and not . . . where discovery was inevitable." Had a baby been born and destroyed, Marshall argued, "no person on earth would have deposited the birth on a pile of shingles!"

Nancy's refusal to submit to examination by the meddlesome Mrs. Page could also be explained. "The most innocent person on earth might have acted in the same manner," Marshall argued. A "heart conscious of it's [*sic*] own purity resents suspicion; the resentment is still stronger when we are suspected by a friend." Had Nancy known then that she would someday need a witness to her virtue, she might have submitted to such a humiliating ordeal. In the absence of such prescience, however, "the pride of conscious innocence was sufficient to produce the Refusal."

Nancy's friends, Marshall admitted, "cannot deny, that there is some foundation on which suspicion may build." But her enemies could not disagree that every circumstance might be accounted for, without imputing guilt. "In this Situation," he concluded, "Candor will not condemn or exclude from society a person who can be only unfortunate."

The justices reached their verdict with little deliberation, and Thomas Jefferson learned of the decision from his nephew John Eppes. The reports "so injurious to the reputation of Miss Randolph, which has for some time engaged the public attention," Eppes wrote, "are now found to be absolutely false." The defendants were "acquitted with great honour." The court-house crowd "unanimously cried out shame on the accusers after the evidence was heard." Jefferson told Judge Tucker he was delighted by the outcome. "No person on earth," he wrote, "heard with more sincere regret" that Nancy had been accused of any wrongdoing. No one "lamented more the torture thro' which their victim must have passed" or rejoiced more sincerely in her acquittal.

The Randolphs left Cumberland Court House in an atmosphere of triumph. Richard had business in Williamsburg; Nancy, Judith and Jack returned to Bizarre. What was said during the carriage ride no one knows, and Nancy's version of the Glentivar episode would not be heard for years. In Jack's account of the trip, he recorded only these words: "The trial. Return. *Quarrels of the women.*"

CHAPTER FIFTEEN

Although the charges against the Randolphs had been dismissed, and their immediate legal difficulties appeared to have ended, their financial problems continued to mount. On July 28, 1794, Richard Randolph appeared a second time before the gentlemen justices of Cumberland County. Patrick Henry claimed that Richard had not paid him his fee, and the court ruled in Henry's favor.

Judith continued to insist on Richard's innocence and allowed a letter she had written to Richard's stepfather, St. George Tucker, to be published as a public circular. In it, she stated that Richard had never gone downstairs that night at Glentivar. He had entered Nancy's room only after Judith repeatedly asked that he check on her sister's condition, which was "a trifling complaint in the stomach." The disturbances in the night had "made no impression" on her at the time. The birth of a child "could not possibly have taken place."

Despite Judith's insistence that Richard was innocent, she was unable to put out of her mind the evidence presented in court, and she began to wonder about Richard's feelings for Nancy and about what might have happened between them. In a rambling and sometimes confusing letter to Mary Harrison, she said she had been in a "perfect state of misery" since hearing the evidence. She no longer knew "whether I should have suffered so much had I doubted my husband's innocence, for then, I shall confess my esteem for him would have been so diminished that I should not have felt what I did on his account." Her resentment toward Nancy would intensify in the months to come until she found it hard to fend off "those corroding reflections which in secret prey upon my mind."

Despite these suspicions, Judith continued to sleep with her husband, and by January 1795, she was pregnant again. In September, when St. George was four, she gave birth to a boy the family named Tudor, who was healthy, with no signs of the peculiar lack of responsiveness that continued to afflict his big brother. The older St. George got, the less he seemed to hear, which added to Judith's anxieties. After giving birth, she felt so weak she sometimes feared she would die, leaving two small children. Should that happen, she told Mary Harrison, "you alone, except my husband, I can call upon to befriend my dear little innocents," whom Judith hoped Mary would raise. For reasons she did not disclose, Judith had decided she did not want Nancy taking care of them.

Part Two

CHAPTER SIXTEEN

BENJAMIN LATROBE

The English-born engineer, architect and amateur painter Benjamin Henry Latrobe sailed out of Norfolk, Virginia, on April 1, 1796, bound for Hampton, where he hoped to board a mail coach to Richmond. Along the banks of the Elizabeth River, he could see grim evidence of the war that had ended fifteen years earlier: responding to British offers of emancipation, slaves by the thousands had gathered, hoping to board ships to take them to freedom in England. The ships had never come, and wagons filled with "the bones of Men women and Children, stripped of their flesh by Vultures and Hawks which abound here, covered the sand for a most considerable length."

Latrobe had arrived in Virginia from England after four months at sea. He had left his home almost two years to the day after his wife died in childbirth and after he had recovered from a spell of grief-induced insanity. The ambitious thirty-one-year-old hoped to seize the boundless professional opportunities that America seemed to offer and begin life anew. He soon discovered that the New World offered no haven from mental distress: just outside Williamsburg, one of Latrobe's fellow travelers "went mad" and had to be chained to the floor of the coach. The deranged man was given a quart of stiff grog, and after he drank it, "his reason by degrees returned, and he behaved tolerably well" the rest of the way to Richmond.

Over the next four weeks, Latrobe explored the Virginia capital and its surrounding countryside. He spent ten days at the races at Petersburg, where the crowd included respectable gentlemen and their ladies, "young puppies waiting to be pilfered, sharpers ready to do their business, and whores all agog to drain the Sharpers." Many racegoers stuck around afterward to gamble at loo, whist, faro and roulette. One evening, a Lieutenant So-and-So called a General What's-His-Name as "great a fool as myself," and six men "swore, bauled, cursed, damned, blasted, drank punch" for nine hours "without settling the important matter."

Most of the men Latrobe met sported military titles, though

these honorifics seemed rarely to reflect actual service under arms. The keeper of Richmond's Eagle Tavern was "often Captain, sometimes Major, and now and then Colonel Radford." The "Multitude of Colonels and Majors" reminded Latrobe of the Polish aristocracy, except that "instead of Count Borolabraski and Leschinski and Zetroblastmygutski and Skratchmypolobramboloboski, and Saradomschittiguttelkowski, we have here Colonel Tom, and Col. Dick, and Major Billy, and Col'n. Ben, and Captain Titmouse, General Rattlesnake, and Brigadier General Opposum."

On the plantations, Latrobe could have "fancied myself in a society of English County Gentlemen (a character to which I attach everything that is desireable as to education, domestic comfort, manners and principles) had not the shabbiness of their mansions undeceived me." The sorry condition of their houses was no fault of the planters who owned them but a consequence of the distance of the plantations from the towns where workmen lived. That windows were frequently missing and the houses were drafty were not the planters' fault, either. "An unlucky boy breaks two or three squares of Glass," Latrobe noted. "The Glazier lives fifty miles off. An old Newspaper supplies their place in the *mean time*. Before the *mean time* is over the family get used to the Newspaper, and think no more about the Glazier." Mail delivery was uncertain, and newspapers were a fortnight old. Roads were often impassable, and rivers were too shallow for the transport of tobacco.

Hoping to improve these waterways, the trustees of the Upper Appomattox Navigation Company had asked Latrobe to advise them, and in early June, he set off on horseback to meet them in Cumberland County. He reached Tuckahoe on the morning of June 7, exchanged his tired mount for a fresh one and five miles farther west caught the ferry across the James. Then Latrobe planned to ride on to Hopkins Tavern to spend the night and continue to the Appomattox to meet his employers.

South of the James, his troubles began. Setting off down a muddy road, he promptly got lost. An old Negro slave plowing a cornfield directed him to his overseer's house, a half mile down the road. Latrobe rode for ten miles without seeing either the house or another human being.

He had to retrace his steps through the woods twice more, until he finally reached a fence. In a clearing he could see a small shack. There a man, "apparently dying of a consumption," sat with his head in the lap "of a very beautiful young woman who was crying over him." Several children, white and black, played in the yard. Latrobe remained on his horse, wondering what to do. The sick man managed to rouse himself and invited his visitor "to alight and refresh myself," but Latrobe begged off, finding the scene "too distressing."

The English simply "trample on each others sufferings," but among Virginians, like the dying man who tried to put his hale and hearty visitor at ease, "there is hospitality and neighbourly feeling to assist and alleviate" discomfort in others. This extraordinary sense of hospitality, evident among rich and poor alike, was no doubt another consequence of these people's isolation. Their habit of intermarriage seemed "also to result from a great degree of separation from the rest of their fellow citizens." Latrobe saw "nothing *morally* wrong" in this practice, though "old ecclesiastical regulations may have prejudiced the minds of many of us. Nothing seems to me more natural than a sexual affection founded on family intercourse." Nature "indeed seems to have implanted in us an instinctive abhorrence of connexions between Brothers and Sisters," though Latrobe rather favored the idea.

Society, he felt, should be as closely knitted together as possible. It "ought to be like a coat of Mail composed of rings, in which none can be strained without dividing and communicating the force throughout the whole texture. Its strength, and its flexibility depend upon it." Latrobe did not say what might result when the armor is pierced and the soft tissue beneath it is exposed.

CHAPTER SEVENTEEN

An hour after leaving the sick man's cabin, Latrobe reached Hopkins Tavern. He was exhausted, but he found the tavern so noisy he decided to push on rather than spend the night. He fed his horse, drank a cup of tea and rode on. The drizzle of the last few days became a steady downpour that lasted throughout the night. He slept at Horsdumonde Plantation in Cumberland County and awoke in the morning to find it was still raining. The sky was dark, the heat oppressive and the branches of the Appomattox so swollen that they could scarcely be crossed. By early afternoon on June 12, it thundered almost incessantly, and as a black cloud in the southwestern sky rolled toward him, Latrobe urged his horse forward. At half past two, he arrived at Bizarre.

When he reached the house, the Randolphs greeted him with the graciousness he had come to expect from Virginians, but there was no gaiety in their manner. Were it not for the presence of children and the mistress's pretty sister, the atmosphere in the house would have been unbearably somber. Richard Randolph had suddenly taken ill. An "inflammatory fever" had taken over his body since his recent return from Petersburg, where he had visited his brother Jack, who was also sick. A doctor had been called. Richard remained lucid, however, and insisted that the visitor stay.

The Randolphs told Latrobe that the men he hoped to meet had passed by that very morning, waited for him and left, which rendered his entire journey a horrendous waste of time. Latrobe stayed the night, trying to sleep despite almost incessant thunder and lightning.

In the morning, the rain finally ceased. Around noon the doctor arrived. He examined Richard and, couching his explanation in "a long string of hopes and technical phrases," said he doubted if Richard would recover. Latrobe stayed for dinner, and although Richard was "much worse" by the afternoon, Judith and Nancy showed their guest "every attention and kindness in their power."

Soon after Latrobe left, Richard slipped into a delirium and was unable to recognize his own wife. Judith was frantic, and she and Nancy administered medicine as well as they could under the harried circumstances.

In the hours before Richard's delirium he had struggled to put his affairs in order, which included arranging a last hushed meeting with Nancy. He appears to have been concerned that his two sons be spared as much as possible the shame of the scandal, and Nancy vowed never again to speak of the events at Glentivar, "a promise which I held sacred." Richard would take their shared secrets to his grave. There was much that Nancy had wanted to say to him, but she resisted the temptation to speak freely. What Nancy wished to tell Richard is not possible to know, though she believed that she would be doing Judith a great service by her silence. For that alone, Judith "can never [again] quarrel with me." Richard's own refusal to divulge family secrets at Cumberland Court had been "noble," Nancy told Judge Tucker the night Latrobe left, "and will be rewarded in Heaven, where his physician thinks he will shortly be."

Nancy hoped Tucker would know where Jack was and send him home. "Our poor dear Richard," she wrote, "is on the brink of the grave. Never was there a scene of more wretchedness. He is the perfect Bedlamite with a most violent fever. He does not know a creature." Before long the candle was guttering, and Nancy could scarcely see to write. Judith, she reported, "is quite overwhelmed." Bizarre had become a scene of "perfect madness . . . Jack, come or it will be too late."

Jack was still in Petersburg. Why Richard had failed to tell the family where his brother was is unclear, though by the time they had begun to look for him, it may be that Richard was unable to speak. In any case, the family's efforts to contact Jack proved futile. On the third Sunday in June, Jack set off for Bizarre, having no inkling that his brother had even been sick. When he was riding through Amelia County, one of Richard's slaves caught up with him and told him that Richard was seriously ill and he should hurry home. By the time he reached home, it was all over. At four o'clock on the morning of June 14, 1796, Richard had died. A funeral service had already been conducted, and he was buried near Theodorick, with a boulder rolled into place to mark the grave.

Jack was incredulous. His brother had been in perfect health when they parted in Petersburg. He demanded to know everything that had happened, but Judith and Nancy could only explain that he had suddenly been brought low by a raging fever, followed by severe pain in the stomach. Not even the doctor seemed to know exactly what was wrong with him. They had given him medicine that seemed to be called for and mixed it themselves, including something toward the end to induce vomiting. Richard had groaned horribly, then died.

Nothing they said satisfied Jack, who was not only distraught by the death of the brother he adored but angry.

CHAPTER EIGHTEEN

Summer passed. Tobacco that had been green when Richard died was drying in the barns, and still Judith mourned. For months after his death she wore black, and the household at Bizarre remained gloomy, especially when she learned of "the deranged state" of the family's finances. Richard had left her more deeply in debt than she had imagined, and it was up to Jack, who would assume responsibility for the plantation, to put things right. He had shown as little interest in agriculture as his brothers, but Judith insisted that her expectations were minimal. All she wanted now was enough for her and "her help- less and destitute little ones" to live on. To meet the children's needs and feed and clothe the seventy-two slaves would mean the plantation must be made profitable as quickly as possible. Until then, everyone would have to sacrifice.

Judith fretted constantly about her elder son, St. George, who at five had not learned to speak. The family was forced to conclude that he was a deaf-mute. He was an intelligent boy but, considering his condition, his prospects in life were not good, and special care would need to be taken to ensure that he was provided for in adulthood. Her younger son, Tudor, was a healthy child, and at ten months he could already walk. Judith remained worried about her own health and about what might become of St. George if she, too, were to die. Nancy, who turned twenty-three in September, loved her nephews and felt some compassion for Judith and the family, but she also seems to have considered her sister too young to give in so early and so completely to life's misfortunes.

The family did not get out as often as it once had, and there were fewer visitors at Bizarre than there had been in the years before the scandal and even fewer since Richard's death. Nancy was not allowed to visit friends as frequently now, and it is doubtful if she was still welcome at the plantations to which she had once been regularly invited. She was not yet a spinster, but her reputation was so badly soiled that her prospects for marriage were increasingly remote. And she seemed to feel that Judith had come to treat her like one of the servants, assigning her to do needlework for hours, which she did not enjoy.

Judith's affection for Nancy, which had begun to deteriorate by the conclusion of the trial, if not earlier, was steadily giving way to a resentment she was unable to disguise. Sometimes Judith behaved toward her with "utmost ingratitude and horrid inhumanity," Nancy said. If Judith believed Nancy had used poor judgment in her affection for Richard, Nancy seemed to feel that her sister should try to understand why she had acted as she had.

Judith's resentment angered Nancy, who had begun to hope that Judith would someday receive the punishment she felt her sister deserved for judging her harshly. "Were our trials here to arise solely from our own errors or vices," Nancy said, "one should imagine that we might submit with patience, to the penalties thus voluntarily incurred." But Nancy believed her "keenest sufferings" had resulted from indulging her "most virtuous affections."

Nancy could endure such treatment for one reason only: She was sure "the time of retribution" would come.

While Judith and Nancy spent hours at their needlework, their cousin Jack took over the farm operations at Bizarre and proved a more competent plantation master than anyone might have predicted. Until Richard's death, Jack, by his own admission, had been a "mere lounger," a devotee of the racetrack who gambled frequently, spent his money foolishly and often found himself dogged by creditors. Four years earlier, while a student at the College of William and Mary, Jack had fought his first duel. His opponent was a friend with whom he had disagreed over the pronunciation of a word. Jack had wounded his opponent in the "fleshy portion" of the backside but was unharmed himself. Since the college forbade dueling, Jack had had to leave. After that, he had traveled aimlessly, sought amusement, and imposed on the hospitality of others, including Richard.

Now acutely aware that he was the sole surviving son of John Randolph of Matoax, Jack took the painful measures necessary to shore up its rapidly dwindling fortunes. When the family had taken refuge at Bizarre during the war, his mother had admonished him never to sell any of his father's land. She had taken him on a carriage ride to the plantation at Roanoke and shown him the broad fields he would inherit.

"Johnny," she said, "all this land belongs to you." When he grew up, he was not to sell any of it. "It is the first step to ruin for a boy to part with his father's home," she said. "Be sure to keep it as long as you live. Keep your land, and your land will keep you."

One sign of manhood, however, is the ability to make difficult decisions, and Jack proved fully capable. He immediately sold the old homeplace at Matoax, where he had grown up and where his parents were buried, and made sure the remaining lands were productive and profitable. Richard's will made his job considerably more challenging, however. Written a year before he died, the will was as eloquent a denunciation of slavery as anything from the pen of a Yankee abolitionist.

Expressing an "abhorrence of the theory as well as the infamous practice of usurping the rights of our fellow creatures, equally constituted with ourselves to the enjoyment of liberty and happiness," Richard seemed to pronounce judgment on the slaveholding society into which he had been born. Wishing "to impress my children with a just horror" of slavery, Richard ordered that the slaves be freed as soon as the mortgage held by the "British harpies" could be paid. Once the Randolphs held title to the slaves, 400 acres on the south side of the Appomattox were to be distributed among the heads of the slave families as his widow saw fit. They were to work the land as free men, and Judith was to help them get established. In that way, he would "yield them up their liberty basely wrested from them by my forefathers and beg, humbly beg, their forgiveness for the manifold injuries I have too often inhumanely, unjustly, and mercilessly inflicted on them."

The plan, while noble, obligated Judith to manumit the slaves as soon as possible, which would deprive her of her property and means of support. To provide for her and her family when the slaves were gone, Jack would have to work them doubly hard until their release. Jack took his new responsibilities to heart—and to bed. He scarcely slept. On mild, moonlit nights, he would call for his horse to be saddled, and he would ride madly over his land with two loaded pistols at the ready. On other occasions, he would wake the rest of the household as he paced the floor, muttering, "Macbeth hath murdered sleep, Macbeth hath murdered sleep. . . ."

An unlikely patriarch, Jack was driven by the fear that, under his authority, his once-illustrious family was "verging toward extinction." Even if he could restore the family fortunes, it seemed increasingly unlikely that the descendants of John Randolph of Matoax would carry on much beyond Jack's own lifetime. Richard had been the only one of the three sons to produce heirs, one of whom was a deaf-mute, the other a mere child who might not live to see his twenty-first birthday.

By now Jack might have begun to wonder if he would ever have children of his own. In 1792, he had suffered an attack of scarlet fever—that was what he called it—in Richmond that he believed was the cause of physical peculiarities that would become more noticeable as he aged. As a young man in Philadelphia, he had shaved regularly, but there would be no need of it in later years. Jack's voice never changed, and he observed that his skin remained "more tender than many infants of a month old. Indeed I have remarked in myself from my earliest recollection a delicacy or effeminacy of complexion that but for a spice of the devil in my temper would have consigned me to the distaff or the needle."

Although he had been a handsome boy, Jack looked much younger than his twenty-four years, and if he were interested in women, they did not seem interested in him. His one stab at courtship ended badly. Her name was Maria Ward, a Chesterfield County girl whom Jack had courted after the war. For a time he thought they would be married, but she broke off the engagement without explanation. The last time he rode up to her father's house, she refused to see him. Furious, he stalked out of the house—or so the story went—and slashed his horse's tether with his knife and galloped away.

Except for writing to Nancy, Jack was never again to court any woman. It no doubt hurt him that Nancy had preferred Theodorick's attentions, then Richard's, though he was surely too proud to admit it. But he was not the sort of man to forgive or forget.

CHAPTER NINETEEN

⌇⌇⌇⌇⌇⌇⌇

By the summer of 1798, as the farms at Bizarre began to prosper under Jack's management, Creed Taylor approached him about running for Congress. At first Jack did not take the suggestion seriously, but as the most prominent politician in the county, Taylor was someone the Randolphs respected, and Jack was an ambitious young man.

The Seventh District's congressman would soon retire, Taylor told him, and their neighbors had seen Jack turn Bizarre into one of the most admired plantations along the lower Appomattox. Jack was becoming a man of consequence; his neighbors would look to him for leadership.

Taylor was aware that Jack knew the classics of political economy, could express his opinions eloquently and was well acquainted with developments in Philadelphia that distressed the Virginia planters and, increasingly, the agricultural interests of the entire South. For nearly a decade, throughout the presidencies of George Washington and John Adams, the planters had watched these so-called Federalists enact mercantilist policies that they believed betrayed the ideals of the Revolution and threatened hard-won liberties. Led by Jefferson, the Virginians had been building an informal opposition political party to counter the Federalist faction of Adams and Hamilton. The party, to be known as the Democratic-Republicans, opposed the creation of the Bank of the United States, the imposition of excise taxes and involvement by the United States in the war between France and Great Britain. Their ideology opposed not only the administration, the policies of which seemed increasing to favor the merchants and stockjobbers of the mercantile North, but increasingly the national government itself.

The Jeffersonians valued liberty above everything else, and they believed it could be secured only by restraining the power of government. Although the Virginians considered themselves more genuinely "democratic" than their northern adversaries, they held that the only stable basis of a free society was an agricultural economy, presided over by a landed aristocracy of freedom-loving "gentlemen" like themselves. The greatest threat to their liberty was the consolidation of power in the national government, which could usurp the privileges and prerogatives of the states that composed it. They saw the Constitution as a compact of sovereign states, which retained all powers not explicitly relegated to the national government. The states, they believed, could rule on the constitutionality of federal laws—and, if need be, could secede. Public debt, taxes, protective tariffs, paper money, government banks and projects of national "improvement" the Virginians viewed with extreme suspicion.

They believed that the greatest threat within the national government was posed by the executive branch, followed closely by the federal courts. Any enlargement of presidential power was to be opposed; titles, levies and other trappings of executive power smacked of "monarchy." Presidential patronage, which the gentlemen planters considered tantamount to "corruption," should be abolished. Foreign wars were to be opposed. Standing armies should never be allowed to supplant state militias.

The simmering conflict between the Federalists and Democratic-Republicans came to a boil over the war between the British Crown, which the Adams administration supported, and Republican France, favored by the Jeffersonians. In the spring of 1798, the details of the so-called XYZ Affair, in which French agents attempted to extort a bribe from the United States, were made public, and Adams asked Congress to authorize preparations for war. By early summer, it had suspended commerce with France, authorized U.S. warships to seize French merchant vessels, created a new Department of the Navy and raised a 10,000-man army. By July, the Federalists in Congress had passed four laws, called the Alien and Sedition Acts, that not only gave the president the power to expel foreigners he deemed dangerous but made it illegal for citizens to criticize their own government. The fourth act made the publication of "any false, scandalous and malicious writing" punishable by fine and imprisonment.

Such repressive measures, Creed Taylor and the other Jeffersonians believed, rivaled those of George III and must be opposed. The independence for which the gentlemen of Virginia had sacrificed so much was being threatened by the "monarchists" of the North. The financiers of Philadelphia, New York and Boston had no respect for the southern states, whose independence was under siege. Some Virginians were calling for the freedom-loving men of the state to take up arms against the national government. The cause of liberty, Taylor said, needed new men.

Although Jack shared Taylor's view of the Federalist menace, he had been so deeply immersed in running the plantation that he had not given as much thought to politics as he otherwise might. Now Jack turned his attention to the national scene, where conditions were suddenly bleak. In July, George Washington came out of retirement to lead a new army, whose second-in-command was Alexander Hamilton, a man the Virginians detested. Washington declared publicly that if he had to march his men from the Schuylkill to the James to put down dissent, he would do so. In September, Benjamin Franklin's grandson Benjamin Franklin Bache, editor of the pro-Jefferson Philadelphia *Aurora*, was jailed under the fourth of the Alien and Sedition Acts on charges of libeling Adams; Jefferson himself, the Virginians said, might be next.

Jack shared his neighbors' alarm, and now that the farms were doing well, he could ponder new possibilities. His mother often said he could be as great a speaker as Edmund Randolph. Perhaps it was time for a new Randolph to strike a blow against tyranny.

CHAPTER TWENTY

GOUVERNEUR MORRIS

At dusk on a Friday in early January 1799, one of the richest men in New York arrived at his Harlem River home after living abroad for more than ten years. He was forty-seven and at the height of his powers.

Gouverneur Morris had served from 1792 through 1794 as U.S. Minister to France. Ordered out of Paris by the Revolutionary French government, he remained on the Continent for four more years, managing his business interests. Of French Huguenot descent, Morris had been born into great wealth at Morrisania, his family's estate, in 1752. A graduate of King's College at sixteen, he was admitted to the bar at nineteen and served as a delegate to the Continental Congress at twenty-two. At the Constitutional Convention of 1787, his fellow delegates thought so highly of his supple prose style that they asked him to write the final document, which he did. Morris had nevertheless been a reluctant revolutionary who dreaded the prospect of a "democratick" government. "I see, and I see it with fear and trembling," he wrote before independence was declared, "that if the dispute with Britain continue, we shall be under the worst of all possible dominions . . . the dominion of a riotous mob." Morris knew something of riotous mobs. He had braved the bloody streets of Paris, where he had remained throughout the Reign of Terror. In its darkest days, the story went, his elegant carriage was blocked by a gang of angry Parisians who shrieked that it contained "an *aristocrat*." Morris flung open the carriage door and brandished his wooden leg. "An *aristocrat?*" he bellowed. "Yes, truly, who lost his leg in the cause of American liberty!"

The story was nonsense, but Morris did not object if people were foolish enough to believe it. Some people even said he had been shot by a jealous husband. The truth was that his carriage had toppled over in Philadelphia years before the American Revolution, and his left ankle had been caught in one of the turning wheels. His leg had required immediate amputation. After a friend came to console him, Morris told him, "You argue the matter so handsomely and point out so clearly the advantages of being without legs that I am almost tempted to part with the other one."

John Jay wrote to Morris, reporting that he had learned "that a married woman after much use of your legs has occasioned your losing one." Jay told Robert Morris that their womanizing friend's loss of leg made him "almost tempted to wish he had lost *something else.*"

Morris was a man of the world who never pretended to be anything else. A cosmopolitan by instinct, he cut a fine figure in the salons of Europe, where he enjoyed the company of Tallyrand, Lafayette and La Rochefoucauld and their aristocratic ladies, including Madame de Staël, Adelaïde de Flauhaut and Maria Cosway, with whom Thomas Jefferson had fallen in love.

This world, considerably more broad-minded than the one he had left behind, would accept the Count de Narbonne, known to be the product of the incestuous union between the late King Louis XV and his daughter. Madame de Flauhaut, a fashionable novelist who was also Tallyrand's mistress, told Morris of the count's parentage one night after they made love. She also liked to entertain Morris while in her bath, where, he explained, "milk is mixed with water, leaving it opaque." In October 1789, fearing she was pregnant, Madame proposed marriage, which Morris declined, preferring to live "in his own way—as a bachelor." A rationalist in philosophy and Christian deist in religion, Morris was a congenitally happy soul, at peace with himself and the world.

When his ship docked in New York Harbor at two in the afternoon of December 23, 1798, friends surged on board to meet him. He found lodgings in New York City, and he dined with Alexander Hamilton, who told him of the sour relations between Adams and the Democratic-Republicans, how desperate matters were and how ardently he wished Morris would lend his talents to the embattled Federalist cause.

"Hamilton tells me I *must* take an active part in our public affairs," Morris wrote to a friend in Europe, "for the Anti-Federalists are determined to overthrow our Constitution." Just before he had arrived in New York, the legislatures of Virginia and Kentucky had responded to the Alien and Sedition Acts with a series of defiant resolutions, written by Jefferson and Madison, that claimed the constitutionality of federal laws could be determined by the states. The Virginians were said to be arming themselves, and true patriots should resist this threat to federal authority and, perhaps, to national survival.

Morris shared Hamilton's views but wished "to lead a private life." After a decade in other people's houses, he looked forward to inspecting his estate and, as Voltaire might recommend, cultivating his garden.

Within days of his arrival at Morrisania, Morris was visited by well-connected Federalists whose interests, he discovered, were not exclusively political. Senator Philip Schuyler and his wife showed up, "bringing their unmarried daughter to dine." John Dickinson of Pennsylvania came and talked to him "about my supposed gallantries and seems desirous of knowing whether I intend to marry." Dickinson had a daughter, and friends said that Dickinson's family "wish me to espouse her."

People were forever doing this sort of thing. They would lecture Morris on his shortcomings—his reputation as a roué, his lack of gravitas, his blunt and racy conversation—and then ask him to help them. He would perform whatever service they sought, extraordinarily well most of the time, then blithely go on behaving exactly as before. He drew the line, however, at marrying their daughters.

The one man in all of America who had been able to chastise Morris and make any kind of impression on him was George Washington. Morris had idolized Washington since Valley Forge, where Morris had labored mightily to secure provisions for the general's bedraggled troops. Washington came to appreciate his character and competence when others did not. When he named Morris minister to France, Virginians opposed the nomination, for they considered Morris a monarchist, an Anglophile and a foe of slavery. Roger Sherman, a Connecticut Federalist, opposed it on other grounds. Acknowledging the nominee's "spritely mind" and "ready apprehension," he called Morris "an irreligious and profane man."

Washington stuck by Morris but took the opportunity to examine, for the nominee's edification, aspects of his character others found troubling. "Whilst your abilities, knowledge in the affairs of the country and disposition to serve it were adduced and asserted on one hand," Washington wrote, "you were charged on the other hand with levity and imprudence of conversation and conduct." Morris's "habits of expression indicated *hauteur*, disgusting to those who happen to differ with you in sentiment." The "promptitude with which your lively and brilliant imagination is displayed allows too little time for deliberations or corrections." To succeed as a diplomat, he must restrain his cleverness. His frequent resort to ridicule "begets enmity not easy to be forgotten but which could easily be avoided if it were under the control of more caution and prudence." A greater "circumspection should be observed by our representatives abroad."

Morris comported himself admirably in France, and his countrymen proved grateful. He returned home triumphant, and Hamilton spoke for almost all Federalists when he urged his friend to help the party. After all, they said, he had no wife, no children, and nothing to keep him at Morrisania forever.

Still Morris demurred. He had returned to find his ancestral home "leaky and ruinous," so, "in total defiance of expense," he went to work on the house, grounds, orchards and farms. He laid out new roads and inspected the stones brought up from his own quarries. He added rooms and even wings to the mansion and within weeks "laid out 50 to 60 thousand dollars in buildings and alterations," including a "bath room $50." The result was a "pretty good house, not a castle," with a 130-foot-long terrace roof overlooking the Harlem River. From it, one could breathe "the most salubrious air in the world."

A household staff, including an imported chef, was assembled. An experimental agriculturist from Scotland saw that the farms and orchards benefited from the most progressive methods, and a huntsman looked after the dogs. The grounds came to resemble a private park, with smooth walkways winding through well-tended gardens and groves of shade trees. Game was plentiful. Morrisania became a scene of "great society added to splendor in the extreme," Jonathon Mason of Massachusetts reported. Morris "is a real aristocrat and lives literally like a nobleman." He had everything required for human happiness except "a good wife and amiable children." This lack, Mason believed, saddened his otherwise jolly friend, who "laments the fact that he did not, twenty years ago, unite his talents with some corresponding female mind to make each other happy." Morris did indeed say such things but only to mollify well-meaning friends who believed he could not be happy as a bachelor.

CHAPTER TWENTY-ONE

In February 1799, while Judith and Nancy were visiting St. George Tucker and his new wife, the former Lelia Carter, in Williamsburg, they were invited to a ball at Bassett Hall, one of the most fashionable houses in the town. Almost three years had passed since Richard's death, yet Judith remained reluctant to go into society. But Tucker insisted that an evening out would do her good, and in time Judith consented. In a nod to her protracted mourning, she affixed a black ribbon to her white bonnet, which she wore "only a *very little* to one side," not as "some fair Damsels of *2 & 3* & thirty" wore theirs.

Nancy showed no such restraint. She chose a "little pearl-colored taffin hat," wearing it at a saucy angle, the way fashionable ladies did, and a muslin dress with balloon sleeves. When the servants helped her into it, and she gazed into the mirror, Nancy "could not credit her own eyes." Even Judith enjoyed her sister's transformation. "You are not to suppose that I TOO metamorphosed into a fine Lady," Judith told Mary Harrison, though the dress she wore to Bassett Hall was "much finer than you are accustomed to see me in." Nancy and Judith danced "many a joyous dance" with the gallant captains, colonels and majors who came to drink their host's whiskey, wine and rum punch. The night flew by, and the sisters' "hearts [were] light as air."

Back at Tucker's house, Judith again felt "the keen dart of misfortune." By the time they had returned to Bizarre, her feelings for Nancy had soured once again, and she resumed her "oppression" of her sister. Fanny Tucker, the last child of Richard and Jack's mother, was now ten years old, and Nancy liked Fanny, but Judith would not allow her to visit if Nancy was there. Nancy promised to "keep my room constantly" if Fanny came, but still Judith refused. About this same time, Judith accused her of "having transgressed the bounds of decorum" in her behavior toward Jack. Nancy, who was not the least bit interested in him, was baffled by the charge.

Nancy no longer understood Judith's attitude toward Jack. For a time, Judith seemed to think he was not to be trusted. Although Bizarre was soon prospering under his supervision, Judith sometimes wondered if this new prosperity would ever benefit her or her boys, and she felt that her own interest was "endangered by [Jack's] uncommon attention to his own." Then, just as Nancy would begin to think Judith and Jack were enemies, they seemed to join forces against her. The constant shift in alliances was enough to drive her mad.

Week followed week in tense if monotonous succession, and the spring rains came. By the time the slaves were hustling the tobacco plants from the seedbeds into the muddy fields, the sisters returned to Tucker's house in Williamsburg, one of the few places either of them still felt welcome. Nancy was comfortable in Mrs. Tucker's company, but Judith appears to have disliked it when the two of them spent time alone. Once Nancy told Mrs. Tucker how, when they were younger, she and Judith had selected a certain bush at Bizarre where they would meet to tell secrets. When Mrs. Tucker mentioned the conversation to Judith, she marched off to find Nancy and said, "So, you have begun to blab," then turned away. Nancy burst into tears.

Judith was also losing patience with her neighbors. Bizarre had been turned into a veritable highway, she said. Day and night, strangers would traipse onto the property on their way to Allen's Mill or to the ferry at Sandy Ford, which would take them to Farmville, the little settlement that was growing up across the Appomattox on land that had once belonged to the Randolphs. Leaving the gate flung wide open, they invited other trespassers.

The plantation already resembled a walled city. A sawed-plank fence, eight feet high, now enclosed the mansion and dependencies. All these buildings were locked, and Judith kept the keys. She did not encourage strangers to feel welcome, and she did not venture out much herself, except to church. When the roads were good, she would take the carriage to the Cumberland Presbyterian Meeting House, just up the Cartersville road. The Presbyterians had obtained a license to start a dissenting church in Cumberland County years before Judith was born, and their meetinghouse now drew members from both sides of the river. The "simple piety" of the Presbyterians, as Judith called it, attracted farmers and slaves as well as big planters.

Unlike the Anglicans with whom Judith had been raised, the Presbyterians seemed to take their faith to heart. They studied their Bibles, examined their souls for evidence of sin and prayed earnestly for its removal. They faced with Christian fortitude the fact that life on earth could be pitiless, found joy in submission to its hardships and put their hope in redemption through Jesus Christ. The other Randolphs were Church of England people, deists, or even outspoken nonbelievers like Jack. They seemed to think contentment could be found in this life, on their plantations. The last Anglican church in the neighborhood, abandoned during the war with England, now lay in ruins, but this did not trouble the Randolphs. Like other families who paid for their pews in the Anglican churches, they expected sermons to be short, perfunctory and reassuring. They preferred homilies in which the rector issued a tactful reminder to his well-dressed parishioners to give thanks to a benevolent Providence astute enough to reward so fine a people so handsomely.

If Nancy felt any attraction to the dissenters and their Calvinist theology, there is no evidence of it. While Judith at twenty-six frequently spoke as if her life were already over, Nancy seems never to have given up hope. Nancy continued to believe—against mounting evidence—that she and her sister could be friends again, that the rupture in their feeling for each other could be healed.

She also believed she could find happiness again, though she might have to flee Bizarre, just as she had fled Tuckahoe, to find it. Nancy felt a "sincere affection for Judy," notwithstanding her "aversion to me," which was increasingly evident. Sometimes

Judith lashed out at Nancy, just as she had at Richard. Once, probably in the first weeks of 1799, she told Nancy that she had always harbored a "despicable opinion" of her, which the passage of time had done nothing to mitigate. On another occasion, she called Nancy "the blaster of my happiness."

Nancy did not deny that she had made mistakes, but she believed her "errors were those of the heart." Neither Judith nor Jack believed that, however, and by February, Nancy told Tucker, "my being obliged to leave Bizarre is very probable."

CHAPTER TWENTY-TWO

When the crowd at Charlotte Court House caught its first glimpse of the old man climbing down from his carriage, they made such a fuss that a Baptist preacher felt moved to reprimand them.

"Mr. Henry," the clergyman intoned, "is not a god."

"No, indeed, my friend," Patrick Henry replied. "I am but a poor worm of the dust, as fleeting and unsubstantial as a shadow of that cloud that flies over yon fields, and is remembered no more."

It was March Court Day of 1799. The proud citizens of Charlotte County had painted their plank courthouse in patriotic colors, and a platform had been built out front. But there were so many people eager to hear their hero's speech, which they feared might be his last, that they urged Henry to speak from the tavern where he had gone to rest.

Henry was sixty-one years old. He had agreed to seek public office again only because George Washington had urged him to run. When Virginians had passed the resolutions condemning the Alien and Sedition Acts and said they were willing to take up arms against the federal government, Washington had come out of retirement to put down the talk of insurrection and expected other patriots to do the same.

Pausing until the crowd was quiet, Henry began in a voice that barely rose above a whisper. The passage of the Virginia and Kentucky Resolutions, he said, had troubled his sleep. That Virginia felt it possessed the authority to rule on the constitutionality of federal laws "planted thorns on my pillow." His native state courted her own destruction by such presumption.

His voice "rang loud and melodious," and his features "glowed with the hue and fire of youth." Defiance of federal law would require a military response, which would in turn "probably produce civil war," from which "there could be no retreat." General Washington himself had consented to lead a new national army, "numerous and well appointed," which could descend on Virginia itself and bring the rebellious state to heel. "Where are [Virginia's] resources to meet such a conflict? Who will dare lift his hand against the father of his country, to point a weapon at the breast of a man who had so often led them to battle and to victory?" Lowering his voice and clasping his hands, Henry implored his neighbors to reconsider their folly. "United we stand, divided we fall. Let us not split into factions which must destroy the union upon which our existence hangs."

People were weeping when Henry sank into the arms of the dignitaries on the platform and disappeared into the tavern to rest. The dignitaries had promised a debate, but the crowd, having scant interest in anything anybody else might say, had already begun to disperse when the man who was to refute Henry stepped forward.

He was a long-legged, reed-slender sapling who looked about fourteen, dressed in a blue frock coat, buff-colored shirt and fan-top boots. Recognizing Jack Randolph, some of the people lingered, but even the county clerk seemed unimpressed. Turning to Creed Taylor, the clerk asked, "Mr. Taylor, don't you . . . mean to appear for that young man to-day?"

"Never mind," Taylor said, "he can take care of himself."

As Jack got up to speak, he was not so sure he "could take care of himself" at all. That he had agreed to debate the great man now seemed the height of presumption. That he had offered his name as a candidate for Congress suddenly seemed laughable. At least he had not presumed to run against Henry, who was a candidate for the state legislature. Jack's opponents for Congress were Powhatan Bolling and Clem Carrington, who were not nearly so formidable as Henry. Still, if Jack disgraced himself in his debate with Henry, he would surely lose to both of them.

Jack persisted, and before he knew it, it was all over. Beyond referring to Henry as "Father," a man whom he "admired . . . more than any on whom the sun had shone," he could not remember what he had said. He spoke for three hours and, Taylor said, acquitted himself nobly. He managed to keep people's attention, and before long, some cheered. When he stepped down, an old farmer clapped him on the back, telling his neighbors, "He's no bug-eater now, I tell you."

Henry, who had received reports of his opponent's oration while resting in the tavern, met Jack at the door and invited him to dinner. "Young man," he said, taking Jack's hands, "you call me father; then my son, I have something to say unto thee—

keep justice, keep truth, and you will live to think differently."
Before they sat down to dine, Henry turned to a friend and said
sotto voce: "I haven't seen the little dog since he was at school;
he was a great atheist then."

Over the next four weeks, Jack gained confidence, and as the
election approached, he began to think he might win. He rode
to Buckingham Court House for the balloting, in which Bolling
was winning so handily that Jack no longer entertained "the
slightest expectation" of being elected. But when the ballots in
the other counties had been counted, Jack had defeated Bolling
by five votes and had achieved an even a greater margin of victory over Carrington—and a seat in Congress.

Patrick Henry won his race, too, though the old man never
made it to Richmond when the legislature convened. After his
speech at Charlotte Court House, he returned to his plantation,
Red Hill, and was so weak that people said he never again ven-
tured out of the house. Henry's doctor diagnosed a blockage of
the bowels and acute inflammation of the intestines and tried
every known remedy. Finally, he gave Henry a vial of liquid
mercury and declared that it would either relieve the patient or
kill him. Henry sat in an armchair he found more comfortable
than his bed, said a prayer and swallowed the medicine. He
watched his fingernails turn blue, then lost consciousness. On
June 6, 1799, at the age of sixty-two, he died.

CHAPTER TWENTY-THREE

The summer after Jack was elected to Congress, Nancy was invited to visit Monticello. All her Jefferson cousins were reuniting for the first time in years, and she was eager to go. Her brother Tom Randolph, husband to Patsy Jefferson, was living there while a house of his own was being completed, and Patsy was pregnant with the couple's fourth child. Patsy's sister Maria, who had married her cousin John Eppes, was also visiting with her husband from their plantation near Petersburg. Thomas Jefferson himself had returned in March from his vice presidential duties in Philadelphia and would remain in Virginia for the rest of the year.

Spring had come late to Albemarle County in 1799. The peach trees had not bloomed until early April, and the cherry trees had not put forth their pink blossoms until the middle of the month. In the mountains, the air seemed more like spring than summer, but with none of the "unwholesome chilling mists" like those Nancy had come to know at Bizarre. The gardens, orchards and farm fields at Monticello stayed green deep into July and August, by which time the sun had parched the countryside at Bizarre. The Appomattox would have slowed to a trickle. The lightning bugs would have long vanished, and the cicadas would have already begun screeching in the trees.

But in the mountains of Albemarle, Monticello was like an enchanted world. Mount Alto rose to the southwest, and to the north the Blue Ridge mountains rolled agreeably toward the western territories. A smoky haze would drift through in the late afternoon, enshrouding the mountains. The Rivanna River flowed lazily through the valley.

In stark contrast to the surrounding countryside, Jefferson's own mansion, Nancy discovered, was in a "terrible state of dilapidation." For some years, Patsy's father had been tearing up his original house and replacing it, in fits and starts, with an even grander one. The banging of hammers and the billowing of dust were unceasing. Grand columns were pulled down, exposing wooden beams eaten away by dry rot. Bricks were piled in unsightly heaps.

Much of the mansion had no roof when Nancy was there. Many rooms had not been plastered; some had no flooring; none were painted. People slept wherever they could, some in unfinished rooms. The food was excellent, however, and the whole family's presence, plus the "constant succession of company," made for lively dinners. Jefferson mostly kept to himself, supervising the renovations, riding across the plantation or engaged in relentless correspondence with his political allies.

Relations between President Adams and Vice President Jefferson had broken down completely. Although Nancy's cousin Jack had won election that spring as a Democratic-Republican, the Federalists had triumphed in other races, picking up four of nineteen seats in the Congress. John Marshall, whom Washington and Henry had endorsed, was elected to Congress as a Federalist. These setbacks for the "cause of republicanism" surprised Jefferson, who had begun to speak of the day when the southern states might need to "sever ourselves" from the federal union.

Determined to resist the Federalists, he spent much of the summer writing letters, unaware that the tide was already turning irretrievably against Adams, even among the Federalists. Gouverneur Morris believed that with the irascible Adams at the helm, the party had squandered its opportunity. The Federalists had done their share of "foolish things as a party, over and above the many wild ones from which we are indebted to the unsteady temper" of the president, who was sure to be replaced.

Jefferson, of course, hoped to succeed Adams and devoted much of his time at Monticello to that end. "Mr. Jefferson's presence imposed on me the reserve which I should feel in yours," Nancy told Judge Tucker, "were I less acquainted with your heart." She had grown more cautious. She would turn twenty-five in September and could ill afford to make any more mistakes.

CHAPTER TWENTY-FOUR

In December 1799, Jack Randolph presented himself to Theodore Sedgwick, the Speaker of the House. The Massachusetts Federalist glanced at the stripling before him, turned to his colleagues with an expression of amused incredulity and pretended not to understand what Jack wanted. He repeated that he wished to be sworn in as a representative from Virginia, and Sedgwick demanded to know if he were old enough to serve.

"Go ask my constituents," Jack snapped.

The members of Jack's party were delighted by his spirited riposte, and before the month was out, he rose to make his first speech. Preparing for war, the Federalists in Congress had increased expenditures for defense, raising taxes on houses, property and slaves. They had established a standing army, and standing armies, Jack declared, have been "the downfall of every free state," riveting the "fetters of despotism." It was time to reduce the size of this army, which would "remove a considerable cause of irritation." Soldiers could be seen on every street, and their slovenly deportment was an insult to every man and woman in America. The citizens "feel a just indignation at the sight of loungers who live upon the public," consuming the fruits of honest industry "under the pretext of protecting them from a foreign yoke." Americans "put no confidence, sir, in the protection of a handful of raggamuffins."

Loungers? Raggamuffins? Congressmen who were talking among themselves, smoking, spitting and ambling into and out of the House chamber suddenly began to listen to their new colleague with the high-pitched voice, whose words were repeated in the streets and taverns.

The following Friday night, Jack attended a performance of *The Stranger* and *Bluebeard, or Female Curiosity* at the Chestnut Street Theatre with a party of other congressmen. Before the orchestra began to play, a Marine officer in the crowd shouted to the musicians: "Play up, you damned ragamuffins!" He then squeezed into the box with Jack and his friends. The orchestra played, the curtain rose and actors portraying Turkish soldiers appeared onstage. The officer asked a companion if he did not believe they "acted very well for mercenaries," and the companion said he "presumed from their color that they were Virginians." Another Marine said they must be "black Virginia ragamuffins."

The performance ended and Jack and his friends prepared to leave, when there was a commotion in their box. He cried out: "Who was that that pulled me by the coat?" Whoever it was, was "a damned puppy." As the group descended the stairs, someone shoved them, "jostling one gentleman and striking another's foot." The soldiers followed them up Chestnut Street until they turned at Fifth and disappeared into the night.

The next morning, Jack fired off a letter to President

Adams, which was conspicuously lacking the customary diplomatic niceties. Reminding the president that they both held "the honorable station of servant to the same sovereign people," Jack recounted how he had been "grossly and publicly insulted." The "independence of the Legislature has been attacked and the majesty of the people, of which you are the principal representative, insulted." He demanded that a "provision, commensurate with the evil, be made" to discourage others from "future attempts to introduce the Reign of Terror into our country." By addressing Adams "in this plain language," Jack offered "the best proof I can afford" of the esteem in which he held the presidency. He signed the letter, "your fellow citizen."

Adams referred the impudent letter to his cabinet, which recommended that the "contemptuous language therein adopted required public censure." Adams then sent the letter to the House, saying the issues it raised concerned the privileges of the House and required a congressional, rather than presidential, response. The House appointed a select committee to investigate the matter, take testimony from the Marine Corps officers, and hear Jack's side of the story. In a written statement, Jack claimed he was the victim of a premeditated assault. One of the officers "suddenly, and without requesting or giving time for room to be made for him, dropped with such violence as to bring our hips into contact." The collision caused "a slight degree of pain on my part," for which the culprit would have apologized had the act not been intentional. The Marines professed complete innocence. One claimed he did not know that Jack planned to attend the performance and would not have recognized him, anyway. "From his youthful appearance and dress," the officer testified, "I had no idea of his being a member of the House of Representatives."

Far from vindicating Jack, the committee in its report expressed regret that a congressman would address the president in such "improper and reprehensible" language. Finding no evidence that the officers had acted "with a design to insult Mr. Randolph," the committee resolved that no further action was warranted. The Federalists prevailed, though *l'affaire* Randolph remained the talk of Philadelphia for days. "This stripling comes full to the brim with his own conceit and all Virginia democracy," Abigail Adams declared. "He chatters away like a magpie." This arrogant *"youth* will find that the old birds are not caught with the chaff." The Democratic-Republicans, however, were delighted with Jack's debut. He acted "with great splendor and approbation," Vice President Jefferson wrote. Although Jack "used an unguarded word in his first speech, applying the word ragamuffin to the common soldiery," he "conducted himself with great propriety" and would emerge from the controversy "with increase of reputation."

CHAPTER TWENTY-FIVE

Jack's constituents were thrilled by his actions.
A family friend, Will Thompson, who looked after the household at Bizarre in Jack's absence, wrote him that the language of his letter to "Citizen" Adams was not only proper but also heroic. "Had you addressed the President in courtly style they would forgive the contents of your letter." Addressing Adams as he did, he proved "there is one man left us whose principles and whose manners stand uncorrupted in these corrupted times." He spoke "the language of [his] State." His "persecutions" made Jack "more dear" to the people he represented.

Judith would have written, too, Thompson said, but the admirable woman—a "pattern for her sex"—had worn herself out the last two nights, sewing the children's clothing by candlelight. Judith's sons were healthy and happy. Eager for Jack's return, everyone "is cheerful."

The household was not as cheerful as Thompson would have had Jack believe. The winter had been unusually harsh, and snows as late as March kept the Randolphs indoors. Their confinement no doubt exacerbated tensions that Thompson neglected to mention, which were made worse by what Judith admitted was her "gloomy disposition." Nancy's "bad health and worse spirits," Judith said, imposed "an additional burthen."

It rained heavily that spring and the rain continued into the summer, damaging the corn and wheat at Bizarre. At Roanoke, "one of the most promising crops of Tobacco" Jack had ever seen was destroyed.

In August, reports from Richmond added to the family's anxieties. On a plantation northwest of town, nearly nine hundred slaves, carrying knives, clubs, scythes, spears, pikes, bayonets and muskets, assembled, planning to march into Richmond. They were to arrive in darkness, burn the warehouses on the riverfront, capture the armory, kidnap Governor Monroe and free all the other slaves. A wholesale slaughter of whites was to follow. When a sudden storm washed out the roads into town, the slaves interpreted the downpour as an ill omen. As they waited for a more promising sign, one slave warned his master, who alerted other slaveholders. Governor Monroe called out the militia, and some forty of the leaders were rounded up, tried and hanged. He claimed that "most of the slaves" in and around Richmond had been in on the plot. Had the conspiracy not been foiled, the town would have been burned, with "its inhabitants butchered." All Virginia would have been a "scene of horror."

Jack attended the trials, where one conspirator had the audacity to claim he had attempted to do for his people only what George Washington had done for his. The leaders "manifested a sense of their rights and a contempt of danger and a thirst for revenge which portend the most unhappy circumstances," Jack reported. This spirit, allowed to spread, would "deluge the Southern country in blood."

Aware of Richard's desire that they be freed, the slaves at Bizarre grew impatient. Since Judith would not be able to retire the mortgage on them for at least ten years, it was not in her power to release them, even if she had wanted to. Her reluctance stemmed, she believed, from Christian charity. She tried to "soothe and conciliate these unhappy people" and to ease "the hardships of their situation," but she also believed they would be unable to take care of themselves. She felt she could live more comfortably by selling her land or leasing it to other planters, but "no selfish consideration" could tempt her to release the slaves, and she considered "fallacious" their belief that they would be happier fending for themselves. Judith cared about the slaves but feared them, especially after learning of the planned insurrection at Richmond. She began to worry that they would kill her, a fear she knew to be "groundless and absurd." In time, she seemed to surrender to a "conviction of impending ruin," as Nancy put it.

Nancy, by contrast, seems not to have been afraid of the slaves, with whom she enjoyed easier and more amiable relationships than her sister. In her letters, she expressed affection for them, a sentiment Judith's correspondence lacks. Nancy was especially fond of two of the maids. One was Priscilla, "an incomparable servant," who complained when Judith would not allow her to work for Nancy. The other was Polly, who had walked in on Nancy and Richard that morning in 1792 and with whom Nancy had discussed her thickening figure. She also seems to have enjoyed some sort of friendship with one of the black men on the plantation, the nature and propriety of which, in an episode of astonishing ferocity some years later, she would be called on to explain and justify. He was a carpenter on the plantation, and his name was Billy Ellis.

Perhaps because of these friendships Nancy did not fear the slaves as Judith did, although Nancy seems not to have given in to her fears at any period of her life. In the years after Richard's death, when she had much to be discouraged about, she fought bravely against the hopelessness that threatened to engulf her, and she fought alone. Judith had begun to treat her more as another servant than as a sister, and she found this treatment increasingly difficult to endure. She was to labor all day at "some species of drudgery," and Judith forbade her to drink wine with the other adults and discouraged her from talking. Nancy had little time left for reading, which was the one pastime that allowed her lively imagination to roam free.

"I could not ask of heaven an exemption from sorrow," she told St. George Tucker in Williamsburg, "because I am conscious of not meriting it." All she desired was "to elude those violently agitating emotions which have sometimes threatened a total deprivation of reason." She cherished news from Williamsburg. A kindly word from friends in that "Beau Monde" enabled her to cast off for a moment the gloominess of life at Bizarre and rekindle "the long lost hope of negotiating ascendancy" over her despair.

CHAPTER TWENTY-SIX

The new federal city, Gouverneur Morris discovered upon his arrival in November 1800, was a marvel. "We want nothing here," he told a lady friend in France, "but cellars, kitchens, well-informed men, amiable women and other little trifles of this kind, to make our city perfect." Appointed to the U.S. Senate when one of New York's Federalists retired in midterm, Morris found Washington ideal—for those keen on mud, hunting or political intrigue. Most legislators slept two abed in wooden shacks, with "endless forests up to the very doors" of their lodgings. Those seeking more civilized lodgings built mansions two miles away in George Town and took carriages to the unfinished Capitol. Near the Capitol were a few row houses, a tavern, an oyster market, a grocery store, a washerwoman's establishment, a shoemaker, a tailor and a print shop. The only industry in town was a brewery; past the brewery, in a swamp, were gravel pits, worked by slaves. A muddy lane called Pennsylvania Avenue connected the Capitol to the president's house and several federal buildings that had been gutted by fire before their completion. Pennsylvania Avenue was bisected at Second Street by a ditch that the legislators, with no apparent irony, called the Tiber. To a man, the lawmakers seemed to regard themselves as Catos and Ciceros, and Morris tried to conceal his amusement at their presumption. "I busy myself here at the trade of a senator," he told his Parisian *amie,* "and amuse myself lazily watching the petty intrigues, the insane hopes, the worthless projects of that weak and proud animal they call man."

These unseemly traits were on gaudy display as 1801 dawned. The Democratic-Republicans, with Thomas Jefferson and Aaron Burr as their candidates, had defeated Adams and his running mate, Charles Pinckney, in the presidential election in December, but many of Jefferson's followers feared that the Federalists would not relinquish power in March as the Constitution required. Hotheads in Virginia were said to be arming themselves, fearing that Adams would try to use the new army to cling to office. To make matters worse, when the ballots were counted in February, Jefferson and Burr had received an equal number of votes. Although everyone knew that Jefferson was his party's presidential candidate and Burr the running mate, the election would have to be decided in the House, where Federalists still enjoyed a majority. Convinced they would fare better with Burr as president, many Federalists began to support the New Yorker. This was most unfortunate, Morris wrote to Hamilton, since it was "evidently the intention of our fellow-citizens to make Mr. Jefferson their president." Both parties were too busy with their schemes to listen to reason, however. "You who are temperate in drinking," Morris said, "have perhaps noticed the awkward situation of a man who continues sober after the company are drunk."

Although still in New York, Burr had agents in every

Washington boardinghouse, and he was busily offering to cut deals to ensure his election, while Jefferson, in the very seat of power, would not lift a finger to advance his own cause. One day in February, Morris met Jefferson on the steps of the Capitol and tried to elucidate for the vice president what seemed a fairly simple matter. The Federalists opposed him, Morris explained, out of fear that he would abolish the navy, replace all Federalist officeholders and repudiate the public debt. If he would simply reassure the Federalists on these three matters, the prize would be his.

"I believe it my duty to be passive and silent during the presidential contest," Jefferson replied. "I shall certainly make no terms, and shall never go into the office of President by capitulation, nor with my hands tied by any conditions which will hinder me from pursuing the measures which I shall deem for the public good."

A man like that Morris simply could not understand.

By the time Speaker of the House Sedgwick called for the twenty-sixth ballot, Jack Randolph had not slept in two days. A wet snow was falling over Jenkins Hill, and an impatient crowd had gathered outside the Capitol. Every time a congressman entered the chamber, he would bring in snow, which mixed with the tobacco juice and melted in pools on the floor.

Jack had not wanted to sleep. Too much was at stake for the supporters of Jefferson, for Virginia and for the country. Candles, blankets and pillows were brought into the Capitol, and

Jack's colleagues dozed wherever and whenever they could. With each vote, they rushed into the meeting rooms, nightcaps still on their heads. Confined to bed with a fever, Joseph Nicholson of Maryland allowed himself to be carried to the anteroom, where his wife stood by, medicine in hand. Ballot after ballot, Nicholson's wife would place a pencil in his fingers and guide his hand as it formed the word "Jefferson."

Each time, the lawmakers gathered around the New York delegation, expecting it to defect from Jefferson to Burr. But New York held firm. James Bayard, Delaware's one representative and a Federalist, said he would vote for Jefferson if he would agree to four conditions: he must remain neutral in the war between England and France; maintain the navy; keep some of the lesser Federalists on the government payroll; and not repudiate the debt. Jefferson refused. Burr's supporters expected their man to arrive at any moment, make his case to the delegations from Maryland and Vermont and claim the prize. To their consternation, Burr was no closer than Baltimore, and before the thirty-fourth vote was taken, Bayard of Delaware lost patience and shortened his list of conditions. He had two friends, both minor Federalist jobholders. If Jefferson would agree not to replace them, Bayard would deliver Delaware. Again Jefferson refused, but Samuel Smith of Maryland, speaking for him, made it known that Jefferson did not think such jobholders should be dismissed "on political grounds only."

When the House met on Tuesday, February 17, 1801, and Burr still had not arrived, Bayard called the Federalists into caucus and told them that they could continue to deny victory to Jefferson only "at the expense of the Constitution." To "vehement reproaches," he announced his intention to vote for Jefferson, igniting a chain of events Jack recounted to St. George Tucker.

"On the thirty-six ballot there appeared, this day, ten States for Thomas Jefferson; four (New England) for A. Burr, and two blank ballots (Delaware and South Carolina). This was the second time we balloted to-day," Jack reported. "The four Burrites of Maryland put blanks into the box of that State; the vote was, therefore, unanimous. Mr. [Lewis] Morris of Vermont left his seat, and the result was, therefore, Jeffersonian. I need not add that Mr. J. was declared duly elected."

At sunset, candles in the windows of the row houses along New Jersey Avenue were lit in the new president's honor. At nine o'clock, jubilant Democratic-Republicans gathered to celebrate their "glorious revolution," as Jack called it. By the time they stopped counting, they had offered sixteen toasts. There were huzzahs to Thomas Jefferson, to George Washington and to Patrick Henry. Before the exhausted legislators trudged home through the snowy streets, there were even toasts to "Little Johnny" Randolph.

When Congress adjourned in the spring, Jack returned home in high spirits. A holiday was in order, so he took Judith across the Blue Ridge to spend the summer in the cooler elevations of Warm Springs. She left her sons and Nancy at Bizarre.

While Jack and Judith enjoyed the mineral waters of the mountains, a severe drought parched the lowlands at Bizarre. When the travelers returned in September, they found that a whole year's crop of tobacco had wilted in the fields.

CHAPTER TWENTY-SEVEN

In January 1802, two weeks after the first Congress
under Jefferson's presidency convened, Jack moved to abolish
the new federal judgeships and other lesser governmental positions that John Adams had created in his last hours in office. He
argued that the Federalists, rejected by the people, had tried to
cling to power by creating positions beyond the reach of the
voters who had turned them out of office. This process would
bleed the treasury. But it was not because of the "paltry expense" of the new positions that Jack wished them eliminated.
What was intolerable was the effort to turn the judiciary into a
"hospital for decayed politicians."

People repeated that phrase much as they had quoted his
words two years earlier about "raggamuffins," but much had
changed since then.

When the Democratic-Republicans took power, Jack had
been made chairman of the new Committee on Ways and
Means. Within days, President Jefferson began to deal directly
with his young kinsman, expressing to Jack, and sometimes to
Jack alone, his administration's legislative goals. It became
Jack's job to move Jefferson's legislation through the House,
which he did with alarming skill. He proved frighteningly adept

at instilling discipline among the Democratic-Republicans and was willing to use whatever tactics were called for. He wheedled, cajoled, bullied—and ridiculed.

The administration wanted to repeal the Hamiltonian commercial platform erected by the Federalists, and bad laws, Jack understood, were not overturned by cleverness alone. Hard work was required, and he worked very hard indeed to master the intricacies of public finance. By the time of his hospital speech, his Democratic-Republican colleagues had shredded whole libraries of Federalist laws. By spring, they had repealed the midnight-judges laws, killed every internal tax levied by the federal government and reduced the size of the military. The appropriations bill that emerged from Jack's Ways and Means Committee and sailed through Congress was the smallest in years.

At twenty-eight, Jack had become the most effective legislator in the House, and his alliance with the president, strengthened by blood, was advantageous to both—and disconcerting to their enemies. The Federalist *Richmond Examiner* accused the president's protégé of "adulation and toad-eating" surpassing that of British courtiers.

Jack did not mind making enemies; sometimes he seemed to revel in it. One day, he met one of them on Pennsylvania Avenue. Seeing Jack approach, the man stepped directly in his path.

"I don't get out of the way of puppies!" he declared.

"I always do," Jack replied, stepping aside. "Pass on."

The ridicule Federalists heaped on Jack often masked their fear of him. He had established himself not only as the wittiest and most eloquent orator in the House but also as its foremost legislative tactician. How high he could climb in politics, and at what cost to Federalist policies, was a constant subject of discussion in anti-Jeffersonian circles. So, apparently, was his virility—or lack thereof. Congressman Tristam Burges of Rhode Island said the shrill-voiced Virginian was "hated of men and scorned of women." Senator Plumer of New Hampshire wondered how long the Democratic-Republicans would be willing to be led by someone "who has the appearance of a beardless boy more than a full grown man." Samuel Taggart of Massachusetts had never seen a "human figure whose appearance is more contemptible." He never "had a razor on his face, and has no more appearance of a beard than a boy of 10 years old, and his voice is the same." He seemed "either by nature, or manual operation fixed for an Italian singer." There are "strong suspicions of a physical disability." (Jack's response to such assaults on his manhood also gave rise to derisive laughter: "You pride yourself," he once told one of his boasting antagonists, "upon an animal faculty, in respect to which the negro is your equal and the jackass infinitely your superior.")

When his fellow Federalists ranted on, Gouverneur Morris of New York bade them be patient. A few weeks of legislative reversals should not discourage them. No leader, not Randolph, not even Jefferson, could keep a party together forever, especially one as full of combustible elements as the Democratic-Republicans. "We have indeed a set of madmen in the administration, and they will do many foolish things," he told the members of his party. But the Federalists had done "some foolish things as a party, over and above the many wild ones" Adams himself had committed.

Morris found all the frantic politicking of the last few months unseemly as well as futile. When Congress adjourned on May 4, he visited Jefferson (he is "cold as a frog," Morris said after their dinner), then set off for Morrisania, where agriculture made it possible to "forget, as fast as I can, that there is in the world any such thing as politics. This even course of life is not unpleasant to me who have toiled in the storms of the world."

As usual, he continued to fend off the well-meaning efforts of his friends to find him a wife. One business associate seemed determined to match him up with a woman Morris described only as "that enchanting Yankee," but, if they should meet, he vowed "to oppose the power of reason to the fascinations of the enchantress." A tapestry in his drawing room, he reminded his friend, depicted Telemachus "rescued from the charms of Circe by the friendly aid of old Mentor." He hoped his friend took the hint. Morris was now past fifty, and marriage "especially at my time of life should be more a matter of prudence than of passion. Good sense and good nature are of more importance than wit and beauty and accomplishments. Everybody here says I must marry, and, indeed, they seem determined that it shall be done whether I will or no."

Morris already had a companionable woman to his liking—and one who was safe because she was already married. Her name was Sarah Wentworth Apthorp Morton, and she was forty-four years old. Some years earlier, she had become the wife of Perez Morton, a rich Bostonian. Early in their marriage, Morton had seduced Sarah's younger sister, and when the seduction was exposed, the girl had killed herself. Still, the marriage had managed to endure.

When Morris began to woo Sarah, she professed to be "indisposed (this is *en règle*)." In time, she succumbed to his blandishments, perhaps because, having had ample opportunity to enjoy the purely physical charms of other women, Morris was sincere in his desire for intelligent female companionship, which Sarah, an accomplished poet, offered in abundance. Jealous at first, her husband—a "sensible" man, in Senator Plumer's words—in time offered little resistance to the *affaire de coeur.* When business took Morris to Boston in July, he dined with the Mortons, and "*monsieur* was cordial all things considered." Where his friendship with Sarah would lead, Morris did not know, but it would not result in marriage, for which he was grateful.

In the fall of 1802, Morris's Senate term expired, and the Democratic-Republicans, led by the wily Burr, seized control of the New York legislature and put up DeWitt Clinton as their candidate. When the votes were counted, Morris showed characteristic good cheer in defeat. "My political enemies have had the goodness to relieve me," he wrote, "and although from their motives I cannot be thankful, yet I must be permitted to rejoice in the event."

Free of the burdens of political office, Morris could stay home at Morrisania and solve at long last the problem of proper household help. He wanted his friends in Europe to find him a good *chasseur* who could fish and a new cook.

"No good domestics can be had here," he lamented, "not even women."

CHAPTER TWENTY-EIGHT

*In the spring elections of 1803, the Democratic-*Republicans won handily. They increased their majority in Congress, which now included Tom Randolph and John Eppes, Jefferson's two sons-in-law, elected in April to represent Albemarle and Chesterfield Counties, respectively. No one had dared oppose Jack in the Seventh District, and he felt confident that Jefferson would be eager to reward him for his hard work during the previous session. Jack hoped for an illustrious diplomatic post, probably Paris, where he could help his fellow Virginian James Monroe, who had been sent to France in January to resolve the dispute over trade on the Mississippi.

It was with these dreams of a diplomatic assignment in mind that Jack made his offer to Judith. He suggested that, when Jefferson gave him his assignment and he left for Europe, he would take St. George with him. The boy was ten. He could read and write but still could not speak. He was intelligent enough to be frustrated by his limitations, and the older he got, the more difficult he became. Jack believed they had done everything they could for him at Bizarre, and the day would come when he and Judith would be too old to look after him. He must be trained to take care of himself.

Although her worries about St. George left her "insensible to every other consideration," Judith opposed any plan that would take him away from her. "A mother need not blush to affirm," she told Jack that spring, "that she values the society of her children above every other good." While she wanted the best for her unfortunate son, she nevertheless found it unbearable "to resign to others the performance of those duties which constitute the chief duties of life. . . . [W]hen I consider the probable diminution of his attachment to me & to his brother, my heart revolts at the idea of a separation from him."

Jack would not be deterred. There were no schools for the deaf in Virginia, but such institutions had been established in England and France. He would enroll the boy in one of them as soon as he received his diplomatic post, which he was sure would be a glorious one. His spirits soared at the possibilities before him, and he wore out the household with what Nancy saw as increasingly grandiose imaginings.

"Soon, my boy," he crowed to St. George, "we shall be sailing across the Atlantic."

But the diplomatic appointment never came.

Bitterly disappointed, Jack remained in Congress, where, from May 1803, when the United States signed with France the treaty for the Louisiana Purchase, until October, when the Senate ratified it, he continued to put his considerable ingenuity to work in service of the administration. As chairman of the Ways and Means Committee, he made sure the House came up with

the money to pay for the territory and concocted tortured jus-
tifications for the deal, which under a Federalist administration
he would surely have opposed. The purchase, for which there
was no constitutional provision, doubled both the size of the
nation and the debt Jack had worked so hard to reduce. By an-
nexing the territory, Jefferson had broken irrevocably with the
old American republic and the constitutional theory on which it
was based. The addition of millions of acres would shift power
from Virginia and the other original colonies to untold num-
bers of new states in the West.

If the implications of the Louisiana Purchase troubled Jack,
he was too immersed in securing ratification to let his misgivings slow him down. Certain the deal would be immensely
popular, he believed—correctly—that it would solidify the
Democratic-Republicans' popularity and secure Jefferson's reelection in November 1804. His kinsman's first years in office,
he had once proclaimed, represented the republic "in the full
tide of successful experiment! Taxes repealed; the public debt
amply provided for, both principal and interest; sinecures abolished; Louisiana acquired; public confidence unbounded." In
1808, there would be another presidential election, and ambitious Democratic-Republicans were already beginning to position themselves to succeed Jefferson, who seemed to favor
Secretary of State James Madison.

Jack considered Madison a closet Federalist, insufficiently
committed to true Jeffersonian principles. To secure Madison's
position as his heir apparent, Jefferson had maneuvered to give
credit for the Louisiana Purchase to him instead of to Monroe,
where Jack felt it belonged. Convinced that the president was

elevating Madison at Monroe's expense, Jack wrote to the former Virginia governor, then in London, in November 1803, hoping to ingratiate himself and alert Monroe to the machinations of his ersatz friends.

The acquisition of Louisiana, Jack told Monroe, was a "monument of wisdom" that would sweep the Democratic-Republicans to victory. He should know, however, that his detractors were whispering that he had made a botch of the negotiations, paying more for the territory than he had been authorized to offer. Jack was in a position to pass along "intelligence" of this kind, since he continued to work with both Jefferson and Madison and could "faithfully report to you the opinions of the leading men of the day."

Once he assured Monroe of his loyalty (while planting doubts about the loyalty of others), Jack changed the subject from one of a public nature to one that was decidedly personal: "I must request a favor of you, my dear Sir, to inquire whether a Mr. Braidwood, a celebrated teacher of the deaf & dumb, yet lives, & practices his profession?" If Monroe did not know Braidwood, could he inform Jack where a young person "in that unfortunate circumstance" might be placed? "Can I venture farther to recommend to your good office an unhappy son of my late brother who will cross the Atlantic in the Spring, for the purpose of acquiring that education which his own country cannot afford him? I shall say no more on this subject—but leave you to judge of my feelings towards this unfortunate offspring of the best of brothers & of men."

There is nothing in Judith's correspondence to indicate that she had agreed to part with St. George, but Uncle Jack may have taken matters into his own hands, since his nephew's situation, in Judith's own words, was "becoming each day more calamitous," and she had grown increasingly morose. Her existence, she had decided by the summer of 1803, was nothing but "one continued series of affliction." At thirty-one, she felt she was growing old "very fast" and lived "only in the hopes of deserving a happier fate in a better world."

Until then, she was exercising what Nancy called "the last paroxysm of tyrannic power" over her sister. "My presence now operates like a reproachful conscience" on Judith. "Heaven," Nancy decided, "cannot sanction such oppression."

Judith was aware of how Nancy felt. "Poor Nancy cannot be less satisfied with any of her friends than she is with me," Judith wrote. "She is unfortunate, & she is my sister. While I can call anything my own, she shall continue to share it with me, perhaps at a distance she will think more kindly on me." Judith's use of the words "at a distance" suggests that she was contemplating Nancy's departure—whether Nancy knew it or not.

CHAPTER TWENTY-NINE

Jack had been Jefferson's greatest champion in the
Congress and the administration's most vociferous propagan-
dist. But in the fall of 1803, his support for the president began
to disintegrate as Jefferson, perhaps wary of Jack's volatile nature, looked to other legislative allies. Two of his new confi-
dants were his sons-in-law, John Eppes and Tom Randolph,
who had been elected to Congress the previous spring. In November, a few days after Congress convened, Eppes offered
what seemed an innocuous resolution asking Jack's committee
to report on the budgets of the various departments of government. Taking great umbrage, Jack opposed the measure, announcing that he would form his opinion of any matter before
the House *"without any consideration of the quarter from which a*
motion comes."

The newspapers reported this insult to Eppes, and Jack
wrote to Jefferson, denying any intention to offend his congressional colleague or the president. Jefferson accepted the explanation and said he understood how people might assume
"that what comes from [his sons-in-law] comes from me." In
fact, he and his sons-in-law rarely talked politics, and then only

"historically." Whether or not Jack believed him, he let the matter drop.

As Jack predicted, Jefferson won a rousing reelection in November and was now as adored by the country as Jack was disliked in Congress. The Federalists had never cared for him, but even some of his Democratic-Republican colleagues now admitted that they, too, found him obnoxious. Senator Plumer reported that members of Jack's own party confessed in the presence of Federalists that they thought him "very assuming & very arrogant & that they hated him."

Jack's reputation was further damaged in early 1805, when the Senate impeached Samuel Chase, the gouty, blustering and wildly partisan Maryland Federalist whom George Washington had appointed to the U.S. Supreme Court. The Democratic-Republicans wanted "Old Bacon Face" off the court, but the Federalists feared that his removal would embolden their opponents to lay siege to the rest of the remaining justices and, in time, to the judiciary itself.

Chase's trial was held in the first week of February. The Senate chamber was done over for the solemn occasion, with red baize benches for the senators and a special gallery constructed for female spectators, who came in their most fashionable clothes. Vice President Aaron Burr, still under indictment for the murder of Alexander Hamilton, would preside. Jack, who had never practiced law in his life, served as chief prosecutor for the House, facing several of the country's most capable lawyers, who had been recruited for Chase's defense.

His performance was a disaster. Confessing himself "physically and morally incompetent" to the task at hand, Jack apologized repeatedly for the weakness of his arguments. As bored and distracted senators ate apples, Jack made speeches "with as little relation to the subject matter as possible; without order, connection or argument . . . mingled up with panegyrics and invectives upon persons." His orations, which went on for hours, were "weak, feeble, and deranged." He "cried like a baby with clear, sheer madness," Congressman Manasseh Cutler of Massachusetts said. Finally, he broke down altogether, proclaiming, against all evidence, that the prosecutors "have performed our duty. We have bound the criminal and dragged him to your altar. The nation expects from you that award which the evidence and the law requires. It remains for you to say whether he shall again become the scourge of an exasperated people." When he had finished, he sat down and threw his feet upon the table in front of him in a posture "as disgusting as his harangue."

At half past noon on March 1, after deliberating for two hours, the Senate acquitted Chase of all charges. When Jack heard the verdict, he immediately left town. The disappointments and defeats of the past two months had taken their toll, and by the time he reached Bizarre, he was ready to lash out.

Nancy had also returned from one of her few trips away from Bizarre about the time Jack arrived. She was full of stories about a new friend she had made, but Jack was in no mood to find them amusing. Sarah Maria Theresa McKean D'Yrujo was the spirited wife of Don Carlos Martínez D'Yrujo, Envoy Extraordinary and Minister Plenipotentiary of his Catholic Majesty to the United States of America. Three years younger than Nancy, the former Sally McKean was the daughter of Governor Thomas McKean of Pennsylvania. Sally had converted to Catholicism to become the Marchioness de Casa Yrujo, and the wedding of the politician's daughter to the Spanish don invited the derision of the enemies of both of them. William Cobbett entertained readers of *Porcupine's Gazette* for more than a year with satiric pieces on the marriage, claiming Governor McKean was a drunkard who had allowed his daughter to convert so he could call himself the "father of a nobleman" and win Catholic votes. He also said that D'Yrujo's "Dulcinea" was no better than her mother, whose own son called her a "bitch."

Sally possessed "vast affability," Nancy said, and it is easy to see why the two women, both of whom had absorbed their share of abuse, liked each other. In their brief time together, the more sophisticated of the two took it upon herself to remake her less fashionable friend's appearance. Declaring that Nancy's hair was hopelessly passé, the marchioness promptly "made an attack" on it. She implored Nancy to discard her cap, calling it "the most ridiculous thing in the world to dress in such a style." If she did not get rid of the silly cap, Madame threatened to snatch it from her.

How readily her protégée accepted Madame's counsel is not clear, but the attention did her a world of good. Nancy's correspondence during the early months of 1805 shows she was able to laugh at herself and her situation and enjoy the fact that others found her amusing. She had apparently been so passionate in her support for Jefferson that her enthusiasm made others laugh, which Nancy did not seem to mind. She, too, found it comic when Senator Wilson Nicholas asked if she "retained her veracity unimpaired," and her sister Virginia said she was more outspoken than ever, calling her "the most serious moralist of the age." She had been blamed for many things, Nancy said, but never "of saying what I did not think."

She remained an avid reader. If she could find a few hours to herself, she hoped to read William Godwin's novel *The Adventures of Caleb Williams*, which was very popular that year. She asked Judge Tucker if he would let her borrow his copy and an edition of Collins's poems. Nancy had been a great admirer of Collins years before, and her interest in poetry was rekindled, though her taste had improved. "I am indeed metamorphosed in many respects," she reported.

There would be little leisure for reading, however. For reasons that are not altogether clear and seem not to have been discussed in any detail even then, Jack and Judith's patience with Nancy finally ran out. A decade or more of grievances had taken their toll, and what happened next perhaps had as much to do with Jack's volatile frame of mind as it did with any specific actions by Nancy. Jack and Judith could take no more of what they regarded as Nancy's unrelenting frivolity, her blithe refusal to help Judith with household chores, her utter lack of gratitude for their indulgence and her colossal indiscretion.

Exactly what precipitated the sudden rupture it is not possible to know and seems to have baffled Nancy herself, though she does not appear to have been especially surprised by their action or even to have asked either of them to explain themselves. The last conversation on the night of the final break seems almost perfunctory.

One evening shortly after Jack had fled Washington, he met privately with Judith and then announced to Nancy with chilling finality that she was no longer welcome at Bizarre.

"Nancy, when do you leave this house?"

Surprised, she replied: "I will go as soon as I can."

She had better get out as quickly as possible, he went on, because she had been taking "as many liberties" at Bizarre as she would "in a tavern."

Part Three

CHAPTER THIRTY

TUCKAHOE

In late winter of 1805, Nancy, thirty-one, unmarried, penniless and reduced, in her own words, to a "condition of total despair," headed home to Tuckahoe. What she discovered when she rode up the rutted lane to the old mansion could not have lifted her spirits. After Nancy's father had died, her stepmother, Gabriela Harvie Randolph, had married John Brockenbrough, president of the Bank of Richmond. He had built a brick mansion and Gabriela had moved to town, leaving the old house at Tuckahoe empty and the fields and outbuildings showing signs of neglect.

Using a key she had borrowed from Brockenbrough, Nancy let herself into the house. She carried the few belongings she had been allowed to take with her to the upstairs bedroom that had been her mother's and where she had been born. There was nothing in the once-sumptuous room but an old trunk and a pile of books. Using aspen boughs to construct a pallet, she spread out a blanket and tried to sleep.

How long Nancy stayed at Tuckahoe is unclear. She was soon moving from house to house, imposing on friends but never staying more than a few nights at a time. She stayed one night at Wilton, an old Randolph plantation on the James, but decided she would not accept favors from family. Although she spoke at one point of going to Curles Neck, another Randolph plantation, and of moving to Williamsburg, there is no evidence that she went to either place. She stayed at Grovebrook, the Amelia County plantation of Captain William Murray and his wife, in March and July.

Sometimes her brothers Tom and William would send her money, but these acts of kindness were most certainly sporadic for at least two reasons. First, both Tom and William had serious financial problems of their own, and second, there were long stretches in which nobody knew where Nancy was. The one person who tracked her movements, or tried to, was Jack. As soon as he had ordered her to leave Bizarre, he began to justify his decision to others, and when he found out where she had gone, he would spread stories about her behavior. When he learned she had been at Grovebrook, Jack said she had thrown herself at another of the Murrays' guests, a Doctor Meade, and that her "advances became so immodest" she had been asked to leave.

He more than once claimed that he had ordered Nancy off the plantation upon discovering her "love letters" to one of the slaves, the carpenter named Billy Ellis, whose "concubine" she had become. That Jack took no action against the slave he said had engaged in sexual relations with the mistress's sister—in that place and time tantamount to rape—suggests that he did not believe the story himself and that the charge was "folly," as Nancy insisted. Slaves had been killed for less, and Jack was not known as a kind master.

The most explosive allegation concerned the sudden death, almost ten years earlier, of Richard Randolph. Jack began telling people Nancy had killed him—and that Judith had come to believe it herself.

Before the year was out, Nancy moved to Richmond. Six thousand people now lived in the town, and every day, wagons, ox-carts and carriages wheeled down Broad Street, bringing still more restless souls eager to work in the flour mill, tobacco warehouses and ironworks. On the noisy docks, broad-backed black men unloaded crates of goods from England and rolled barrels of flour and hogsheads of tobacco up ramps and onto boats. There were churches and taverns and a new prison, designed by Benjamin Latrobe, who, at President Jefferson's behest, had gone to work on the U.S. Capitol in Washington City.

Mansions like Brockenbrough's loomed over the wooden shacks that had made up the town when Nancy was a girl. John Marshall, now chief justice of the Supreme Court, had built a brick house near the courthouse. Closer to the docks, David Meade Randolph, who had married Nancy's sister Molly, had built his house, which—playing on his name and Molly's—he called Moldavia. When John Adams was president, David Randolph was the U.S. Marshal of Virginia. The post had paid handsomely, enabling him to maintain their plantation and their house in Richmond. When Jefferson took office, the couple remained outspoken Federalists, and David lost his post. The plantation was sold, and Moldavia was turned into a boardinghouse.

Fortunes could be made and lost with dizzying speed in Richmond, the streets of which were full of professional gamblers, would-be gentlemen, women of easy virtue and sharp operators of every description. Games of chance, although illegal, were played in scores of establishments, and a small industry developed solely to meet the mounting demand for entertainment. There were taverns, a theater that specialized in farce and, by the docks, a large, sometimes rowdy carnival grounds called the Hay Market Gardens. The park surrounded a large house where the owners of the establishment, Major John Pryor and his wife, lived and conducted their business. Pryor's, as people called it, was the scene of public entertainments of all varieties, including masquerade balls considered by some to be "dangerous to virtue." It had a music hall, replete with organ, and offered nightly concerts, fireworks displays and exhibitions by ropedancers. Beer and rum punch were sold from stalls on the terraced grounds near the proprietor's mansion, where, sometime after leaving Grovebrook, Nancy came to live.

Her rented room had barely more than a bedstead in it, over which she stretched a burlap sack and spread her blanket. She seems to have had almost no contact with members of her family during this period and very little money. Once, when she learned that her nephew Tudor, who was eleven, was attending school in Richmond, she wrote to Jack to ask if Tudor could visit her. Jack refused. He came instead and, there being no chair in the room, sat on the bed. A few days later, Tudor brought her $100, saying Judith wanted her to have it. Nancy refused to take it. It would be some years before she would see either Jack or Tudor again.

By now Jack had come to certain conclusions about how Nancy was managing to support herself, but this time—for reasons known only to himself—he was not going to tell anybody what he had concluded. At least not yet.

CHAPTER THIRTY-ONE

Early in 1806, as England and France were seizing American ships, Jack broke with the administration in a fiery speech opposing a ban on British imports. Convinced that any such prohibition would make the southern states dependent on northern manufacturing, Jack declared that talking sense to the measure's advocates was futile.

"It is a mere waste of time to reason with such persons. They do not deserve anything like serious refutation. The proper arguments for such statesmen are a strait-waistcoat, a dark room, water, gruel, and depletion." Do they really intend to provoke the British? Do they seek war? Do they wish "this great mammoth of the American forest [to] plunge into the water in a mad contest with the shark?" If so, let the mammoth "beware that his proboscis is not bitten off in the engagement."

As the seizure of Americans ships and sailors continued un-challenged, Jefferson supported an embargo as energetically as Jack opposed it. Jack denounced the administration, the Democratic-Republican leadership and, in many ways, the American experiment itself. As long as Jefferson and Madison were in the saddle pursuing policies that strengthened the fed-eral government at the expense of the states, Jack could no longer ride with them. Until new leaders, like Monroe, took the reins, he would oppose the Democratic-Republicans as ardently as he opposed the Federalists. He would lead a third faction, the quids, from *tertium quid,* or "third thing." Only when the Democratic-Republicans returned to the principles on which they had campaigned against Adams and Hamilton would he come back to the fold, and he held little hope that they would ever again embrace the ideals of limited government and state sovereignty. What Jack had feared ever since witnessing George Washington's vow to uphold the Constitution almost two decades earlier was coming to pass: the consolidation of power in a war-mad, expansionist federal government, which would mean certain death for the states. "The Constitution was in its chrysalis state," he would recall of his visit to Federal Hall in New York eighteen years before. "I saw what Washington did not see . . . *the poison under its wings.*"

On April 21, 1806, on the last day of the first session of the Ninth Congress, Jack proposed a repeal of the salt tax that Jefferson had planned to use to purchase Florida. Jack wanted to reduce government expenditures and to end the administration's relentless effort to acquire new territory. He also wanted to thwart Jefferson, whom he had come to despise. Tempers flared, and in a gesture galling to his enemies, Jack lamented the "contumely and hostility" of the debaters and suggested that the bad feelings of the session be put aside.

For some reason, Tom Randolph thought the remarks were directed at him. He sprang to his feet and accused Jack of launching a personal attack "behind the shield of the dignity of the House, which he would not venture to make use of elsewhere." He told Jack he should watch his mouth, because "lead and even steel [were] proper ingredients in serious quarrels" and stalked out of the room.

Since his marriage to Patsy Jefferson, Tom had proved to be an impulsive, impractical, bullying man as consumed by self-doubt as Jack was by pride. Tom was also an abusive husband, an indifferent father, an inept plantation manager and a wearisome son-in-law. Perhaps Tom felt that attacking Jack might please his father-in-law, whose considerable patience with his former floor leader had long since worn out.

Within hours, Jack had sent an emissary to demand an apology and, failing that, said he would seek satisfaction in a duel. Tom accepted the challenge, but his friends persuaded him that he could withdraw his remarks with no loss of honor, and the next day he did. That would have been the end of it, but the newspapers reported the quarrel in terms that antagonized both camps. The anti-Jefferson *Aurora* supported Jack, the pro-Jefferson *National Intelligencer* backed Tom, and everyone waited for the two Randolphs to "cut each other's throats."

Before things escalated further, Jefferson intervened and in so doing revealed his contempt for Jack. He counseled Tom to "suppress all passion" and consider how different were the responsibilities he and his opponent would carry into their duel. Jack was "unentangled in the affections of the world, a single life, of no value to himself or others." But Tom had "a wife, and a family of children, all depending for their happiness and protection in this world on you alone." Women were fragile creatures, he reminded his son-in-law. Patsy had been ill lately, and if her "frail frame" were to sink under the weight of added burdens, what would become of their children? "Seven children, all under the age of discretion and down to infancy, could then be left without guide or guardian, but a poor broken-hearted woman, doomed herself to misery the rest of her life."

Heeding his father-in-law's warnings, Tom mumbled a perfunctory apology on the floor of the House and let the matter drop. His wife and children were safe. So, for now, was Jack.

CHAPTER THIRTY-TWO

The cold weather came early to Cumberland County in the fall of 1806, and Judith feared that the winter would be "a very severe one." She was thirty-five now but said she felt much older. Each year brought "some yet untasted ingredient in the bitter cup of adversity," which "blasted [her] youth and now consign [her] to premature infirmity & old age."

Just after Christmas she parted with St. George. At fourteen years of age, the boy sailed with his manservant, Essex, for England, where James Monroe was minister to Great Britain. Monroe and his family promised to care for him "as if he were [their] own son" and enrolled him in Braidwood's school near London. Jack wrote to him there, explaining how important it was that he learn a trade and be able to support himself.

"Your mother's resources are heavily burthened with the expense of your own & your brother's education. You cannot wish to continue to divide with her the moderate income which should make her old age easy when you shall be in a situation to provide for yourself:—& your principles—I might say your instincts,—will spurn with contempt the bread of dependence." He hoped St. George would become a physician. But if "your misfortune preclude you from the science of medicine, or the art of surgery,—and your inclination not lead to them—mechanics and agriculture are open to your pursuit." Jack would rather see his nephew "fixed to a work-bench, or following the plough than leading a life of unprofitable & discreditable idleness." Above all, he must be a gentleman, and gentlemen never lie. Of all the virtues, "none is so important as Truth." A liar "is at once the most odious and contemptible of the human race:— and to reveal a secret is the most base & detestable species of lying, since it involves breach of confidence."

Judith had no news of St. George until the following June, but it was extraordinarily encouraging. The boy was "in good health," Monroe reported, and doing well in his studies. His professor "thinks he will be able to teach him to speak intelligibly, and as his genius is spritely, and his mind well organized, that his improvement in every line will do credit to the school." Monroe, his wife and his daughters found him a delightful addition to their household, in which he "holds the relation of a child and with others of a brother."

But a few months later, Monroe reported that the school had given up hope of teaching St. George to speak. His "conduct continues to merit highly everything that I have hitherto said of it. He improves, but owing to his natural defect, not so fast as he otherwise would do."

Judith could not have taken the news well. With Tudor in school in Richmond, her expenses were mounting, and the slaves would soon need winter clothes. "They are really in a miserable plight," she told Jack, "and I am unable to do anything but listen to their well founded complaints." She asked him to lend her money, which she would pay back with the proceeds from the sale of flour ground at the plantation. She would ship it to Petersburg as soon as she could, along with an order for winter coats, blankets and other items for the slaves.

For a time, Judith had tried to stay in touch with her sister, but before long, she no longer knew where Nancy was.

Nancy was not in Virginia.

She had headed north, but exactly when she crossed the Potomac is difficult to determine. Leaving the state where she was born and raised had been difficult for her, and she would never forget how miserable she had been the day she left. "In quitting Virginia," she told Judge Tucker, "every chord in my heart burst asunder."

One of her last acts before departing was to leave a statement similar to the one she had prepared for Richard in Williamsburg more than fifteen years earlier. What that document said, like the one that preceded it, is also lost to history, as is Nancy's exact itinerary. For a time, she lived in Rhode Island. Some have speculated that she taught school there, but that does not explain why, if employed, she found it necessary to write a letter to Jack from Newport that suggests that she was desperate. Sick and without funds, she asked him for money. She wanted only a small sum—perhaps fifty dollars. She would repay it as soon as she was able. Jack received the letter but refused to answer it or send the money.

In time, she went to Fairfield, Connecticut, where she befriended Mrs. Pollack, a widow who owned a boardinghouse in New York City. Mrs. Pollack had a niece in Stratford, Connecticut, and she and Nancy planned to visit her on their way to New York. Despite the happier circumstances, gossip had followed Nancy all the way to Connecticut.

The likely conduit was someone she considered a friend but should not have trusted, Lewis Sturges, a Federalist congressman from Fairfield. "Sturges loves wine and women more than business," Senator Plumer said, and "is often intoxicated" by both. Sturges appears to have told Jack what he knew about Nancy and received information about her from him. People in Fairfield, as ignorant of the facts as most gossips, were soon saying that Nancy had been ordered to leave Bizarre when Richard died. She had been allowed to live there, they claimed, only because Richard had forbidden Jack and Judith to turn her out. The persistence of such stories made Nancy wish she could leave the country for good. Once during this period, she asked Tucker if he knew of any lady who would be going to Europe and might need a traveling companion. He did not, and nothing came of the idea.

When they reached New York, Nancy moved into one of Mrs. Pollack's rooms, and things seemed to be looking up. Nancy had a friend she could depend on, a respectable place to live in and an end to her wanderings.

New York was surely big enough to allow a woman of soiled reputation to find anonymity and, perhaps, to start over. Speculators were dividing the entire island into lots in hopes of building a grand city, which they planned to call Manhattan.

Roads were being built through the estates along the Harlem River north of the island, and visionaries were planning to throw bridges across the rivers.

Before Nancy arrived, she wrote to the one person in the state to whom she felt she could appeal. This was Gouverneur Morris, whom she had met at Tuckahoe so many years before, when Richard had first come calling.

CHAPTER THIRTY-THREE

~~~~~~~~~~~~~~~~

The summer of 1807 was one of the hottest, driest and most contentious anybody in Richmond could recall. Accused of the perhaps treasonous act of leading a private army in an invasion of Spanish territory in the West, Aaron Burr was about to go before a grand jury in a federal court, which would be presided over by Supreme Court Justice John Marshall. Strangers flocked to Richmond eager to witness the spectacle. And when the taverns were full, people camped in the open air near Pryor's or slept in wagons. Despite the charges against him, the former vice president was still popular, especially among the Virginians who had hated Hamilton, and he was ably represented by Edmund Randolph, the former U.S. attorney general. Confined to the state prison that Latrobe had designed, Burr received gifts of pineapples, oranges, raspberries and apricots. One of the town's leading citizens hosted a fancy dinner in his honor, which even John Marshall attended. People were outraged. From the roof of a grocery store near the state capitol, an energetic young Tennessean named Andrew Jackson harangued passersby about the treachery of Jefferson and the innocence of Burr.

Jack Randolph, who had even less admiration for Burr than

he had for Jefferson, believed the rascal was guilty and said so publicly. Such bias against the defendant was no reason to bar a man from serving on the grand jury, Marshall said, and made Jack its foreman. After days in closed session, Jack led his fellow grand jurors into the hall of the House of Delegates to announce that they had agreed to indict the prisoner for treason. This unpleasant duty was not without its compensations. Among the other grand jurors was John Brockenbrough, who had gone to school with Richard and Theodorick, and he and Jack immediately became fast friends. For years to come, Jack would stay with the Brockenbroughs while in Richmond, forming a close alliance with the former Gabriela Harvie Randolph. Jack thought her an exemplary woman with "manners a queen might envy." She also had information about Nancy that he was only too happy to hear.

After Burr was acquitted in the fall of 1807, Jack resumed his political duties, which, to his extreme annoyance, had been considerably circumscribed. Power within the Democratic-Republican party had shifted to the members from the North. When Joseph Varnum of Massachusetts became Speaker of the House, he promptly stripped Jack of the chairmanship of the Committee on Ways and Means. Jack disliked being a mere spectator, but he played the role of unperturbable obstructionist with almost sinister glee. He would saunter into the House chamber and nonchalantly drape his long legs, encased in sleek white riding boots, over the bench in front of him. He would study his gloves or gaze at the ceiling or peruse a book of verse or even affect sleep. Sometimes he had his dogs with him, and he would pay more attention to them than to his colleagues. But when someone said something that grabbed his attention, he would throw himself into the debate with an astonishing ferocity. He would awaken from what appeared to be utter self-absorption and go on the attack, quoting his adversaries at length. He had heard every word they had said and could recall it with greater precision than they could.

Throughout the fall and early winter, he railed against Jefferson's plan to prohibit trade with France and England. By January 1808, when the embargo went into effect, tobacco was piling up, unsold and rotting, in the warehouses of Richmond, Norfolk and Fredericksburg. When cotton prices fell, the South's economy went into decline, just as Jack had warned. By creating a shortage of British goods, the embargo boosted northern manufacturing, and southern farmers who had seen the market for their crops collapse moved to town to work in factories—or struggled to hang on to their plantations. Judith's brother William was ruined, and when the sheriff came to seize his slaves for nonpayment of debts, William hid them in his house. Archy Randolph, who had courted Nancy before the Glentivar scandal, also lost everything and moved his wife and children in with his father because they had no place else to go.

Jack believed that Jefferson was waging a war against his own countrymen to avoid one with England and enforcing the embargo with the zeal of the village snoop. "[E]very shipment of provisions, lumber, flaxseed, tar, cotton, tobacco, &c." was to be considered suspicious, and Jefferson took it upon himself "to decide personally how much bread, and with what degree of whiteness, the American people could eat during the Embargo." He regulated the nation "down to its table fare," and people said a baby "couldn't be born without clearance from a government customs house."

Jefferson's presidency had become as tyrannical, Jack believed, as Adams's, and just as foolish. Madison, who could be expected to carry forward the policies that were destroying the agricultural South and spurring the country toward war, would have to be stopped. To that end, Jack urged Monroe, who was still in London, to seek the Democratic-Republican nomination. He believed Monroe was committed to the principles of limited government that Jefferson and Madison only pretended to uphold and campaigned for him throughout the fall. Monroe did not return to the United States until late December 1807, when the campaign was all but decided.

In late January 1808, the Virginia General Assembly voted on which candidate the state's congressional delegation would support, and Madison crushed Monroe. When party leaders convened in Washington later in the week, Madison again won handily, and by the time he had won the general election in November, most of Monroe's supporters had come back into the fold. Monroe persuaded Jefferson that, having been overseas much of the time, he had been a mere spectator in Jack's campaign on his behalf.

Jefferson offered Monroe the governorship of Louisiana. Madison would have his turn as president, Jefferson told Monroe, and then his would follow.

Monroe's defeat was worse for Jack than it was for Monroe. Monroe was in line to be president, but everyone blamed Jack for the campaign on Monroe's behalf, and it was increasingly uncertain whether he could even keep his congressional seat.

CHAPTER THIRTY-FOUR

In October 1808, a carriage driven by French servants stopped in front of a boardinghouse at 54 Greenwich Street in New York. Gouverneur Morris climbed out and hobbled into Mrs. Pollack's establishment to call on Colonel Randolph's daughter. He was fifty-six years old; Nancy was thirty-four.

During a pleasant visit, Morris expressed his desire to secure the services of a "reduced gentlewoman" to keep house, since "the lower class of house-keepers" invariably "provoked the servants to a riot in his dwelling." He was going away, he said, and he would not return for six months.

Nancy wrote to her visitor shortly after he left. She appears to have mentioned the scandal that had driven her from Virginia and the hardship that had followed and how, in poverty and ill health, she had been deprived of good books, lively talk and amusing company. She evidently thanked him for his kindness.

"Talk not of gratitude, my dear Madam," he replied, "but communicate so much of your situation as may enable me to be useful. I once heard but have no distinct recollection of events which brought distress into your family. Do not dwell on them now."

There would be time to talk more freely. Until then, he implored her not to trouble herself with the judgment of others. His notion of virtue, he told her, differed from that of most people. He used the word not in "the tea-table sense that calls a woman virtuous tho she has the malice of a dozen Devils, nor yet in the roman sense that applies chiefly to the Courage of a Soldier." Morris used the word to mean "a pure Heart, a chastened spirit, Fortitude, Benevolence, Charity." Nancy had those qualities, no matter what others might say. He also urged her not to exaggerate the charms of witty conversation, which led her to suppose "Existence without Genius to be a World without a Sun." The enjoyment of music and painting is very close to "sensual gratification," after all. Even "intellectual Pleasure is generally obtained by the aid of our senses." The difficulties she had known would find their compensation soon enough. "The Incidents of Pleasure and Pain are scattered more equally than is generally imagined. Let us not quarrel with the order of nature. It is the order of God."

Thinking she might "like these notions better in the loose jingle of Rhyme" than in "stiff and stately prose," Morris enclosed a "scrap" of verse he had written for her:

> *Since Fortune's Favor can't allay*
> *The Soul's distress or Body's Pain,*
> *Then, if she take her Good away,*
> *Should Mortals peevishly complain?*
>
> *Her boasted power the Brave defy*
> *Her wrath or Smiles unmoved they see*

What tho in Chains the Body die,
The gen'rous spirits [sic] flight is free

A heedless World may smile and frown
Capriciously on Worth or Crime,
May Doom to Death or grant a Crown
As suits the Change of Chance or Time,

And feeble insults of a Day
May pine beneath the World's Disdain,
But when that World has past [sic] away
The soul immortal shall remain

Then why, dear Girl, rejoice or mourn
What men approve or disapprove
See, far beyond his mortal Bourne,
The God of Mercy and of Love.

Someday, perhaps, Nancy would trust him enough to share her whole story with him. "If we ever happen to be alone, you shall tell your tale of sorrow when the tear of your cheek may fall on my bosom."

By March 1809, Morris had made up his mind. He had visited with Miss Randolph, as he called her, and they had corresponded for several months. She was not only capable of performing the duties of a housekeeper, she was also an intelligent and lively woman whose company he enjoyed. He wanted her to leave Mrs. Pollack's boardinghouse and come to live at Morrisania. But he realized it might take some effort to persuade a lady of her breeding and background to accept such lowly work. "Pride may proclaim, 'Miss Randolph cannot descend to the rank of a servant under whatever name, or however elevated and distinguished,'" Morris wrote. But pride "is such a wrangling disputant that I have never argued with him."

Nancy would be his employee, but he would treat her with respect and affection and something like equality. "I can only say that our real relations shall be that of friends." He would pay her the same salary he paid all his housekeepers, "because appearances are best supported by Realities." He would even make some provision "for future storms," should he die while she was still in his employ. Nancy told him she received money from her brother Tom, and Morris assured her that her salary, combined with whatever she might receive from Tom, would enable her to live without worry in her old age.

Lest she worry about his intentions toward her, Morris pointed out that his relations with his housekeepers had always been exemplary. One of them, of humble birth and scant education, was nonetheless a "well-made, good-looking woman" whose presence might have invited unseemly speculation, but because his conduct toward her had been proper, there was none. "The numerous Ladies who visit me have never harbored an idea injurious to the Virtue, as they call it, of my Housekeepers: and they are right, for certainly I have never approached either of them with anything like Desire."

In Nancy's case, however, Morris refused to rule out the

possibility that a deeper affection might develop. Even at his age, he warned her, the presence of a beguiling female might have a stimulating effect on him. Would their connection as master and servant become a genuine friendship? They were friends already. Would that friendship develop into something more? "I can only answer," he concluded, "that I will love you as little as I can."

Nancy pondered his offer, and on the morning of April 23, 1809, Morris took his carriage to New York. After breakfast at Armstrong's Tavern, he directed his driver to stop at Pollack's boardinghouse, from which, he wrote in his diary that night, he "brought home Miss Randolph of Virginia."

CHAPTER THIRTY-FIVE

"You have perhaps heard," Morris wrote to John Marshall in early December, "that Miss R., the daughter of our old friend of Tuckahoe, is in my House and has the care of my Family." She may not have been the most efficient of housekeepers, but her employer liked having her around, wanted her to stay and needed Marshall's help. Gossips were circulating "sundry reports respecting this unfortunate young Lady, founded on events that happened when [I] was in Europe." Any scandal with which she was associated was likely to form a "foundation of calumny against me." People might say Morris could not possibly employ "a person so undeserving unless there existed between [them] an illicit connection." They could claim he was defying "not only the Morals, but the Decencies, of Life."

Morris was not so vain as to believe the world cared much about him personally, but the Federalist cause was a matter of public concern. Allegations of misconduct against one Federalist could be leveled against all, and this was a risk Morris did not want to take, considering the political stakes. When Madison took office in the spring, he continued Jefferson's restrictions on trade with Great Britain. War seemed inevitable. Morris found it hard to imagine that Madison would "plunge the country into a situation distressing to all, but ruinous to the Southern states." Morris agreed with Jack Randolph. War would be "downright madness," but without staunch opposition from southern Federalists like Marshall, it could happen. With so much at stake, he had to know the truth. "The object of this letter," he wrote, "is to ask you frankly the Reputation Miss Randolph left in Virginia, and the standing she held in society."

Marshall replied promptly, choosing his words with evident care. He had some vague recollection of Nancy's troubles but insisted that he did not recall them in any detail. The circumstances that had led to the Randolphs' appearance in court were "ambiguous," and "rumor, with her usual industry, spread a thousand [stories that] were probably invented by the malignant, or magnified by those who love to supply any defects in the story they related." Opinion in Virginia had been divided. Many "believed the accusations brought against Miss Randolph to be true, while others attached no criminality to her conduct and believed her to be the victim of a concurrence of unfortunate circumstances." Judith Randolph, "who had the fairest means of judging the transaction and who was most injured by the fact if true," had given Nancy a home long after Richard's death. This alone was sufficient evidence of Nancy's innocence, if that is what Morris sought.

Morris read Marshall's reply and embarked almost immediately on a plan he evidently had been considering for some time.

December 25 dawned. The weather was harsh and roads were bad, but nieces, nephews, cousins and other family members came for dinner. That one of the guests was Isaac Wilkins, the rector of St. Peter's Church of Westchester County, was not unusual. Wilkins was married to Morris's sister and had been to Morrisania many times.

That night, when his stunned visitors had retired to their rooms or returned home, Morris made an entry in his diary. "I marry this day Anne Cary Randolph, no small surprise to my guests." He gave his bride an elegant set of pearls.

To a one-line account of the ceremony she sent to a friend back home, Nancy added a poignant detail: "I glory that I was married in a gown patched at the elbows, one of only two I now own." That gown had served her well, and to cast it aside in favor of a fancier dress would perhaps have seemed ungrateful.

CHAPTER THIRTY-SIX

Three days after the wedding, Morris thanked
Marshall for his "candid" response and described the events of
that memorable week. On Christmas Eve, he had presented to
Nancy a prenuptial contract. It was the first time he had
broached the subject of marriage, "tho' I had perceived in her
manner that Good Will and amusing Conversation had produced that effect on her mind which ought not to be expected
by people of my Age." Nancy had all the qualities Morris
sought in a wife, "good sense, good temper, and cleanliness," as
well as a few others he probably did not feel comfortable sharing with the chief justice. Her housekeeping skills, while "not
ample," had improved during her residence at Morrisania, and
she would, given time, prove competent enough. Morris did not
prize beauty, but if he did, Nancy "has her Share."

His only concern had been her reputation, and he was now
satisfied on that point. No man worthy of the name could hold
against an otherwise exemplary woman the mistakes of her
youth, and Morris was appalled by the treatment Nancy had received at the hands of other Randolphs. Even if one believed the
worst about her, "persons capable of prosecuting a Relation so
young" were of baser character than she. "Malevolent" people

will condemn a person with Nancy's past, but more charitable souls "will, for charity's sake, acquit." Honest and well-meaning persons could draw their own conclusions, but "fifteen years of irreproachable Conduct under circumstances which no common fortitude is sufficient to support" should count for something.

She had been cast aside by her "nearest relations," and her character was "already tarnished," so if she had had any inclination to turn to a life of vice and corruption, she would surely have done so. She had had ample opportunity to show her true colors, if they were indeed the lurid hue of scarlet that others alleged. Yet she had endured her years of deprivation with grace and good humor, and had not once, to his knowledge, degraded herself or compromised her principles in any way. That, he believed, was proof enough of her virtue.

Others were not so sure. Nancy's new set of "nearest relations" were not pleased that their rich uncle had decided, so late in life, to take a bride. Morris had been generous with his nieces and nephews; some were in debt to him and hoped to inherit part of his fortune. Now he had married a woman young enough to give him children. That she was a mere housekeeper, and one with a scandalous reputation, persuaded them of her predatory nature and his obvious folly.

In January, Morris's niece Gertrude Meredith complained to her uncle of his poor judgment. His reply was both ironic and conciliatory: "I received your letter, my dear child, and perceive in it two charges, viz., that I have committed a folly in marriage and have acted undutifully in not consulting you. I can only say to you that I have not yet found cause to repent, and to the second that I hope you will pardon me for violating an obligation of which I was not aprized."

His niece's reaction no doubt reflected the rest of the family's opinion. "If I had married a rich woman of seventy the world might think it wiser than to take one half that age without a farthing, and if the world were to live with my wife, I should certainly have consulted its tastes." But, "as that happens not to be the case, I thought I might, without offending others, endeavor to suit myself, and look rather into the head and heart than into the pocketbook." Gertrude's feelings would change when she met Nancy. She was welcome at his house as always. When "we have the pleasure to see you at Morrisania, it is possible you may approve my choice."

The first months of Nancy's marriage were among the happiest of her life. Heaven had blessed her "with the best of husbands," and, as Morris had predicted, most of her new relatives treated her "with great affection." He continued to entertain on a grand scale, which provided Nancy, as wife and hostess, with new challenges. New York servants, unlike Virginia slaves, were not in the habit of obedience. The household staff was a "motley crew of wild Irish, some French who have fled Napoleon's conscription—a few cutthroat English, a portion of Americans who disdain subordination—also a small number of Germans." The Germans, Nancy decided, "are the best" of the lot.

When the apple trees at Morrisania were in bloom, Morris invited the English artist James Sharples to the estate to paint the newlyweds. He arrived on Friday, May 25, when he was entertained by his hosts' "agreeable conversation" and admired

GOUVERNEUR MORRIS

their extraordinary collection of "pictures, sculptures, tapestry, plate, china, etc." The Morrises and their guest then enjoyed a three-course dinner "on a magnificent service of silver," followed by dessert on the "most beautiful French china." Nancy was "chaste" and "demure." The next day Sharples began the portraits. When they were delivered in early June, Morris paid the painter fifty dollars.

ANNE CARY MORRIS

The New York legislature that year voted to dig a new canal all the way from Albany to Lake Erie and appointed Morris commissioner of the project. This immense undertaking required huge commitments of money. Morris would need to recruit the best available talent, so he wrote to Benjamin Latrobe to see if he would consider serving as chief engineer. Latrobe declined unless given a commission for life. If he were to come to New York, however, he would certainly enjoy meeting Morris and his wife.

"Nothing would give me more pleasure," Latrobe wrote, "than to see at the head of this family a lady whom I had known in Virginia, who may recall my visit" to Bizarre—a comment some observers have interpreted as a subtle attempt at blackmail. If Morris did not give Latrobe the lifetime commission he sought, he might retaliate by exposing his wife. If that was what Latrobe intended, Morris was unmoved by it.

Taking his duties seriously if not solemnly, Morris was eager to inspect the land where the new canal was to be constructed, and he turned a business trip into a holiday by bringing Nancy with him. They left for Albany in June, with a second carriage transporting their French cook and other servants. By late July 1810, they were rattling merrily to Fort Niagara, and from there they crossed into Canada. With the falls still "thundering in [their] ears," they began to make their way home. In August, Morris dined with the other canal commissioners in Lewiston, New York, and in early September, they stopped in New Lebanon to watch the Shakers at worship. After the Shakers sang a hymn to the tune of "Jolly mortals, fill your glasses," an earnest young preacher sought to persuade the newlyweds "to abandon worldly pursuits, pleasures and enjoyments, and, more especially, the conjugal pleasures, for the sake of that pure felicity which attends celibacy." Morris had no intention of honoring such an "unnatural and impious doctrine," especially now.

CHAPTER THIRTY-SEVEN

While Mr. and Mrs. Morris enjoyed the falls at Niagara, the Randolphs of Bizarre sweated through one of the most miserable summers on record. Storm clouds that rolled up over the Blue Ridge dumped torrents of rain that swelled the Appomattox and drenched the tobacco fields. The sun would come out, the temperature would rise, then new clouds would appear, followed by more storms.

On one of the hottest days, Jack and Judith had a fight at dinner. A plate of cold lamb was brought to the table; Jack decided it was spoiled and ordered a servant to take it away. Judith said the lamb was fine. He insisted that it "absolutely stank," but she said it had been boiled the day before and been kept in the icehouse. Her response, he said, proved that her thinking "was truly a woman's," i.e., scarcely thinking at all. "We must reason from facts," he said. In the absence of facts, we may "argue from probabilities," but in this case, the facts were evident to the senses.

"The lamb stinks," Jack stated, "and, therefore, [is] not sound."

Furious, Judith motioned for the servant to put a piece of

the meat on her plate. She cut a bite, put it into her mouth, and managed to swallow it, although under other circumstances, Jack said, she would not have been able to get the morsel down "for a thousand dollars."

In the fall, Jack moved away, leaving Judith to look after the farms, the slaves and her two sons. Exactly what precipitated the break is not clear, but he said later that he decided to leave Bizarre when he learned she was in contact with Nancy. Judith's feelings toward her sister seem to have softened, but Jack wanted Judith to have nothing whatever to do with the woman who had ruined Richard's reputation and, quite possibly, cost him his life. He would no longer live under the same roof with someone who could forgive such behavior.

With Jack gone, Judith began to pin all her hopes in life on her younger son, Tudor, who would turn fifteen in September. He would be ready for college in a couple of years. She wanted him to go to the finest institution possible, but she would have to sacrifice to pay for his schooling. By then, the mortgage on the slaves would have been paid, and she could grant them their freedom, as Richard had intended. They would work their own land, and she would lease the fields at Bizarre to other planters. Until she knew more, she resolved to "stay at home & spin & weave & spend nothing in order to keep out of debt."

St. George had returned from England, and as soon as the boys were old enough to want to live on their own, she planned to divide between them whatever would be left of Richard's property—although she questioned whether St. George would ever be able to enjoy real independence. She assumed that Tudor would marry, a possibility she "never contemplated for poor

St. George." She especially wanted them to have reasonable expectations, since life was sure to disappoint.

Young people, "ardent in pursuit of the phantom which we know to be a vision," often expect more of life than it offered. "My boys are soon to be men," she told Jack, "activated by the same passions, eager in the chase of happiness in some ideal form or other," yet their "fortunes are narrow. Let me if it is not too late, teach them the unestimable art of contracting their wants within its limits."

She knew that Tudor would fulfill her fondest hopes, for he had "seen his mother's difficulties," understood their plight and accepted it without complaint.

Never, she declared, "was there a nobler child."

When he left Bizarre in 1810, Jack moved to Roanoke plantation, a cluster of modest buildings that squatted alongside a dirt road in a thick forest on the Little Roanoke River, surrounded by tobacco fields a half day's ride from Farmville. Red Hill, where Patrick Henry had died, was a few miles to the west, but once you passed Red Hill and reached Danville, there were few towns until you crossed the mountains and entered Kentucky. Randolph slaves had worked the land at Roanoke for at least three generations, but because Jack's progenitors had spent so little time on the property, a proper mansion had never been built. There was an airy summer cabin Jack could use in warmer months and a snug cabin for winter, a kitchen, and several even smaller dependencies. Past the stables, the fields were

ROANOKE PLANTATION

broken up by barns and other outbuildings, creeks and still more forests. Finally, there were the fence rows of other plantations, from whose owners Jack kept a comfortable distance. There were shacks along the trails that meandered through the woods and, every few miles, "some large, bare, rectangular frame structure with no more pretensions to architectural beauty or grace than a dry goods box, where Sunday after Sunday, some dutiful Presbyterian divine expounded the stern dogmas of his creed." Jack avoided them, too.

For weeks, he was the only white man on the plantation, and he found this "savage solitude" very much to his liking. Once his English-made furniture was carted down from Bizarre, along with his china, his wineglasses, his guns, books, prints and maps, all his needs could be met. He had his brandy, horses and dogs, and the hunting was excellent.

Now that he was finally established on his own ancestral lands and no longer living on land that had been bequeathed to Richard, Jack could ask that others call him what he had always preferred to be called: John Randolph of Roanoke. He would expect his colleagues in Congress to refer to him by that name, though his plans for a suitably pompous return to Washington were unhorsed almost as soon as he settled in.

In late October, one of his horses stepped squarely on Jack's right foot, crushing four of the toes "almost to a jelly." For a time, he feared the injury might require amputation. Night after night for several weeks, he woke up shrieking with pain, which only a "large dose of opium" could ease. Before long he was using it every day.

CHAPTER THIRTY-EIGHT

When it came time to hobble back to Washington for the opening of Congress, Jack crossed the Appomattox at Farmville and stopped at Bizarre. He was still in great discomfort, and the reception he got was so unpleasant that, if not for his nephews, he said he might never go back. "Tantrums of Mrs. R.," he wrote in his diary.

He reached the federal city in late January 1811. On his first day back in Congress, he got into a scrap with Willis Alston, a Democratic-Republican from North Carolina and war hawk who had accused Jack of being a British agent. The lawmakers were descending a staircase, Alston leading the way, when Jack took his revenge.

"I have a mind to cane him," he announced to no one in particular, "and I believe I will."

Before Alston could cover his head, Jack began to beat him severely. Alston, who was unarmed, kicked at his assailant, but the blows continued to rain down, and blood began to flow. Alston's friends managed to pull Jack off their man and get him to his boardinghouse, where they dressed his wounds. A grand jury charged Jack with breach of the peace, and the case went to the district court, which fined Randolph of Roanoke twenty dollars. He paid the fine, amused that the court's "appraisement of Alston's head was fixed at a very moderate estimate."

People repeated the jape, as they had repeated so many of Jack's retorts—or attributed other men's jests to him. "All the bastard wit of a nation," he complained, "is fathered on me." Most of these witticisms were of his own coinage, however. "Asking one of the states to surrender part of her sovereignty," he declared, "is like asking a lady to surrender part of her chastity." His kinsman Edmund Randolph did not merely lack the courage of his convictions; he lacked convictions. He is "like the chameleon on the aspen, ever trembling, ever changing." Edward Livingston of New York was "a man of splendid abilities, but utterly corrupt. Like rotten mackerel by moonlight, he shines and stinks." Benjamin Hardin of Kentucky, a rough but energetic orator, sounded like a "carving knife whetted on a brickbat." Tactful, calculating Martin Van Buren "rowed to his object with muffled oars." Governor James Pleasants of Virginia was like one of Jack's blooded horses, "too weak for the plow, and too slow for the turf."

Shortly before Congress adjourned in March, his friends were scrambling to extricate him from another quarrel. John Eppes had accused him of trying to defeat a bill through endless delays, which Jack said was a lie. As snow covered the Capitol, Eppes challenged him to a duel, and a series of formal notes passed between the principals and their seconds. As the negotiations went on, Jack secured the services of a surgeon from Baltimore and spent two hours a day in target practice. An inexperienced shot, Eppes also began to drill and soon became so proficient that people said Jack would surely be killed.

All their preparations went for naught, however. Late in the month, the principals were informed that their friends had met without their knowledge and had drawn up language each could accept. Jack would confirm that "in saying that the opinion of Eppes was untrue, he intended only to repel the insinuation that he understood to have been made by ascribing to him a motive which he had disclaimed." Eppes, in turn, would agree that he "did not intend to ascribe to Randolph any motive that the latter had disclaimed."

The honor of the two gentlemen was restored, though Eppes was not entirely satisfied. Even if he were not to be afforded the satisfaction of killing Randolph of Roanoke, Eppes could destroy him politically, which he quietly resolved to do.

In June, Nancy's husband sailed to Albany with Robert Fulton on his steamboat. Fulton's invention, Morris reported, moved at the astonishing speed of eight miles an hour. Such boats, moving on great canals, could do wonders for American commerce, but the restrictions on trade with Great Britain and the empire's reciprocal interruptions of American trade with France were sapping the nation's economic vitality. War with the mother country, which would only make matters worse, looked inevitable. The people seemed to want it, and Morris wondered if "anything short of that bloody scourge will whip our mad folks into their sober senses."

In early winter, after Nancy celebrated her thirty-seventh birthday, they made plans to go to Washington, where Morris hoped to enlist federal support for the canal. They left on December 4 and traveled through Philadelphia, York, Lancaster and Baltimore, reaching the federal city in mid-month. They took lodgings at Tomlinson's boardinghouse near the Capitol as the lawmakers rushed about with the enthusiasm reserved for old men who are preparing to send young ones to war.

Morris regretted that they had not arrived in time for him to hear a "much-admired" speech by Randolph of Roanoke, whose eloquence in opposition to the war was being drowned out by raucous demands for blood. After a few days, when it was well known that the Morrises were in town, Morris sought Jack out. Setting aside what might have united them politically, he demanded to know if Jack "intended to mortify" his wife by not calling on her. On December 17 or thereabouts, Jack spent the morning with Nancy at Tomlinson's in what appears to have been civil conversation. How she received the man who had driven her from Bizarre is not known, but this must surely have been for her a time of quiet triumph and, perhaps, vindication.

That same afternoon, just two years after she had been reduced to poverty in Richmond, Nancy went with her husband to the president's mansion for a private audience with James and Dolley Madison. She enjoyed a sumptuous Christmas Eve dinner with the French minister at the French Legation, and in mid-January, she celebrated with her husband when the House committee voted its approval of the Erie Canal. They left the distracted capital for home at the end of January 1812, and Morris left almost immediately for Albany to continue his work for the canal commission. By the time he returned, the flowers were blooming, and the cry for war, clamorous and insistent in

Washington, could not be heard in the quiet gardens of Morrisania. Reunited with Nancy, he felt a "renewed spring of life" that even the certainty of war could not discourage.

Morris went back to Albany in late May. The gossips must have been torturing Nancy again, because he felt it necessary to remind her to pay no attention to what others thought of her. "As to other folks," he wrote, "their civilities or the want of them are of no consequence. Estimate such things and indeed all things at their worth."

Three weeks later, on June 23, 1812, Morris returned to his "dear, quiet, happy home." Within weeks, Nancy felt peculiar. She tired easily, and in mid-summer she began going to bed early.

CHAPTER THIRTY-NINE

RANDOLPH OF ROANOKE

Riding through Prince Edward County one morning that spring, Jack Randolph overtook a man on horseback and pulled alongside.

"How do you do?" Jack said, as politely as possible.

The two men exchanged greetings, and Jack reminded his neighbor of his candidacy for reelection.

The man explained that he was sorry, but, owning no land, he was prohibited by Virginia law from voting.

"Good morning," Jack replied curtly and rode away.

Dignified, even imperious, it was the only way Jack knew how to campaign, and it had proved effective for years. His impassioned speeches, his fiery and unpredictable antics and his noble bearing had gotten him reelected for seven terms, often without challenge. Three years before, in 1809, exasperated party leaders had persuaded another Democratic-Republican, Jerman Baker, to challenge the incumbent. "A new broom sweeps clean," Baker said, and Jack conceded the point. "A new broom sweeps clean," he said, "but an old one knows where the dirt lies." Baker was defeated, but Jack's old manner of seeking office seemed to have lost its charm.

In July 1812, the British had fired on the American fort at Sackets Harbor on Lake Ontario, and the war Jack had dreaded for so long finally erupted. By August, victories by the U.S.S. *Essex* and U.S.S. *Constitution* stoked the fires of outraged national honor, and mobs of patriotic citizens in Baltimore, Savannah and elsewhere broke into the offices of antiwar newspapers and smashed the printing presses. People who had dared oppose the war were branded as traitors, and Jack found himself facing more serious opposition than ever before.

This time he was opposed by John Eppes, who had moved to Charlotte County in 1811, for no other purpose, Jack believed, than to run against him. Jack had defeated him handily that year, but Eppes was not discouraged. In the spring of 1813, with the war on and Jack's popularity falling, Eppes announced that he would run again. When British gunboats appeared in the Chesapeake, people said the ships had come solely to keep Jack in office, and Eppes's candidacy gained strength.

Jack stuck to the old school of campaigning, with high-toned speeches at county courthouses, but Eppes was busy rewriting the rules. Descending, in Jack's words, "to the lowest and most disgraceful means" of seeking office, his opponent attended worship services conducted by preachers of the dissenting sects and even went to meetings in the "cabins and hovels of the lowest" enfranchised Virginians.

This method of electioneering seemed to have had an effect on people of the lower orders, who were no longer as respectful of incumbents as they had once been and now felt free to insult their congressman. Toward the end of the campaign, Jack began to take his overseer with him whenever he was to make a speech. He was a huge, hulking man who walked a few steps behind the candidate, brandishing a horsewhip. The campaign was going dismally, and three weeks before the election a family calamity demanded Jack's attention.

On March 21, 1813, Judith Randolph was returning to Bizarre from Sunday services at Cumberland church when she saw an eerie glow in the distance and smoke rising above the tops of the trees. Her house was on fire.

A spark had leapt from one of the chimneys, and the roof had burst into flame. As St. George and the servants tried to stop the conflagration, the support beams of the old house collapsed; the walls of upstairs rooms folded in on themselves. Rafters crashed to the floor.

By the time Judith's carriage arrived, the fire had all but run its course. By dusk, the house was reduced to charred rubble, out of which rose the blackened ruins of chimneys. A bedstead, a table, some chairs and odd pieces of furniture that had been dragged out of the house or thrown from windows littered the scorched yard. Richard and Jack's books were scattered everywhere.

Jack canceled all campaign appearances and, putting aside the hard feelings of the past few months, helped Judith move into a small frame house across from the tavern in Farmville. Tudor, who had been sent to Harvard College the previous summer, was spared the horror of seeing the old house burn down, but his deaf-mute brother had seen it all. The unnerving spectacle made St. George more frantic and distracted than ever.

When news of the fire reached Williamsburg, Judge Tucker sent Judith five hundred dollars. "My once comfortable & peaceful dwelling," she told him, "is now a heap of ruins, a scene of total desolation." The trees Richard had planted when they had first moved to Bizarre, "in the highest perfection but a few days ago," now "exhibit such a sight as my nerves can scarcely bear." The library was gone, and the yard was "strewn with burnt pages." Years of labor on homespun as well as carpets, curtains, blankets, glass, china, silver "and all my hoard of petty comforts and conveniences" were gone. One item rescued from the house that Judith neglected to mention was a portrait of Nancy.

By the time Judith and St. George were settled in Farmville, the day for balloting had come. On the green outside Prince Edward Court House, a man who had been seen laughing in Eppes's presence "undertook to speak impertinently" to Jack. The crowd, which still respected the man who had represented them so passionately for the past fourteen years, turned on the "notorious villain." He was obliged to flee, Jack recalled, "or he would have been beaten to a jelly." The rout of Jack's heckler was the only bright moment in an otherwise miserable day. When all the ballots were tallied, there were 1,110 votes for John Eppes and 936 for Jack.

With Bizarre burned, Matoax sold, and his political career by all evidence over, Jack visited his birthplace at Cawsons plantation, or what was left of it. As his boat neared the water's edge, the soft spray of the tide reminded him—self-pityingly, perhaps—of more peaceful times.

"The days of my boyhood," he wrote to his friend Francis Scott Key, "seemed to be renewed; but at the end of my journey I found desolation and stillness as of death—the fires of hospitality long since quenched; the parish church, associated with my earliest and tenderest recollections, tumbling to pieces; not more from natural decay than from sacrilegious violence!" Jack saw at Cawsons what he had seen all over Virginia, especially south of the James. "What a spectacle does our lower country present! Deserted and dismantled country houses, once the seat of cheerfulness and plenty, and the temples of the Most High ruinous and desolate, 'frowning in portentous silence upon the land.' The very mansions of the dead have not escaped violation. Shattered fragments of armorial bearings, and epitaphs on scattered stone, attest [to] the piety and vanity of the past, and the brutality of the present age."

Jack also learned about this time that Mrs. Anne Cary Morris had begun to send Judith packages of goods. Nancy did so, she said, "to pay for every mouthful I ate because I could not bear to be under obligation to her," but also, it would seem, out of pity, and Jack could not countenance such condescension.

CHAPTER FORTY

Perhaps Nancy sent the gifts out of love. The spring of 1813 must have been one of the happiest of her life. On Tuesday, February 9, she gave birth to a healthy boy they named Gouverneur Morris II.

His parents' joy was not shared, however, by some of the child's uncles and aunts. The arrival of a male heir to the Morris fortune—a possibility its presumptive beneficiaries had dreaded since the pretty housekeeper had shown up—shattered their hopes and embittered their hearts. Nancy managed to keep her sense of humor. She reported with evident amusement that one of her in-laws said the Morrises should have named the boy after the Russian field marshal who had chased Napoleon back to Prussia the previous winter. They might have called him Kutuzoff, Nancy told a friend, since his arrival "cutoff" so many would-be millionaires.

The Randolphs' response to the birth of Nancy's son is a matter of conjecture, though Jack Randolph wrote to the new father, offering his congratulations, "with cordial wishes for Mrs. Morris's speedy and perfect recovery." It seems clear that they were too absorbed in their own mounting problems to think much about events in New York. Judith and St. George were not adjusting well to life in Farmville, and Judith's health had begun to fail. Only forty-two, she now walked with a cane and found it difficult to sleep in the house across the road from the dusty, noisy tavern. The constant comings and goings were also unsettling to St. George.

At Roanoke, Jack claimed to be glad to be free from the "odious thraldom" of public office but confessed to Francis Scott Key that such statements were "sheer hypocrisy, assumed to guard against the pity of mankind." Cursing his fate, he kept to himself for most of 1813, reading Byron, when the British put ashore at Hampton Roads, burning, looting and killing his fellow Virginians. In September, the river overflowed its banks, destroying his crops. Jack believed that victory over the British was unlikely, but whether the invaders were driven back to their homeland or not mattered little. The way of life for which Virginians thought they were fighting was already doomed. "Peace or war," he decided, "the ruin of this country is inevitable; we cannot have manufactures on a great scale" without destroying the South.

Gouverneur Morris had come to remarkably similar conclusions. The country had yet to confront the "awful secret" that "commerce and domestic slavery are mortal foes; and, bound together, one must destroy the other." He did not "blame Southern gentlemen from striving to put down commerce, because commerce, if it survives, will, I think, put them down, supposing always the Union to endure." But the "only means under God to preserve American freedom," he concluded, was in a "union of the Northern states," which would require that they cut themselves free of the slaveholding states, including his wife's beloved Virginia. This would constitute a bloody rupture that Morris opposed.

In October, Morris visited the battlefield at Saratoga, which brought back memories of a more heroic time, when the colonies had triumphed by joining forces. On this same spot, almost forty years ago, the Continentals had turned back Burgoyne's redcoats, in what had been the turning point of the war. Now the British were back, but Americans were far from united in their opposition. The British would soon blockade Long Island, closing all ports south of New London, Connecticut. As things grew increasingly bleak, Morris was eager to see his wife and child. From Stillwater, Nancy received a note from her homesick husband, who enclosed another scrap of verse:

> *Kiss for me, my love, our charming boy*
> *I long to taste again the joy*
> *Of pressing to his father's breast*
> *The son and mother. Be they blest*
> *With all which bounteous Heaven can grant*
> *And if among us one must want*
> *Of bliss, be mine the scanty lot.*
> *Your happiness, may no dark spot*
> *Of gloomy woe or piercing pain*
> *Or melancholy ever stain.*

It was the last letter Nancy would ever receive from him.

CHAPTER FORTY-ONE

The summer of 1814 was "intolerably hot," in *Jack's* words. Once again his tobacco was drenched by seemingly interminable spring rains and wilted in the scorching sun. In late July, flash floods destroyed corn that was to be fed to the hogs, which in turn were to be slaughtered to feed to the slaves. Even the Charlotte County granary was empty, so Jack and the other planters would have to import the corn—or the pork—from the west.

A peculiar sluggishness of spirit, perhaps exacerbated by the opium he continued to take, had afflicted Jack since losing his congressional seat and prevented him from doing anything about his mounting financial problems. Since he owned more than two hundred slaves and thousands of acres, the simple solution would have been to sell all his property and retire on the profits. He and Francis Scott Key, a prosperous lawyer as well as poet, discussed establishing an American literary review. All that kept Jack from going forward with the project was his inexplicable lack of energy and a sense of obligation to the slaves who depended on him. He would dearly love to sell them, he said, but found it impossible to "shut [his] heart to the cry of humanity and the voice of duty." Selling his slaves would mean abandoning them to new owners, which he could not in good conscience do. If he were to free them, they would have to fend for themselves without political rights, and that would mean they would probably be forced to move to the western territories. Who knew what would await them there?

Sometimes Jack thought about joining the growing exodus to the west. Land was cheap and fertile there, and one could live on next to nothing. "In a few years more," he wrote, "those of us who are alive will have to move off to *Kaintuck* or the *Massissippi*, where corn can be had for sixpence a bushel, and pork for a penny a pound." The West "must be the Yahoo's paradise, where he can get dead drunk for the hundredth part of a dollar."

That summer, his deaf-mute nephew decided he wanted to get married. St. George was twenty-three. In April he had asked Jack to get a gold ring for him in Richmond, and in July he proposed to his cousin Jane Hackley. She was a "very amiable, exemplary girl," Judith said, but unlikely to "submit to the inconveniences arising from [St. George's] misfortune." Jane rejected him, as Judith feared she would, and St. George lost his mind.

When Jack learned of his nephew's condition, he took him to live at Roanoke. Looked after by Theodore Dudley, who had grown up at Bizarre and was now a physician, St. George proved "manageable with little trouble." Even so, Dudley entertained "no hopes for his restoration." St. George was calmer at Roanoke than he had been at Bizarre, though his writings—scribbled on scraps of paper and on the correspondence of family members—were the ravings of a madman. St. George lived in "terrors of future punishments" and seemed convinced he was pursued by the devil. He was also "incurably alienated from his mother" and wrote cryptically of her "guilt," though he would never say what Judith had done.

Toward the end of summer, the British put ashore at Benedict, Maryland, within twenty miles of Alexandria and Washington, raiding towns and destroying tobacco. On August 24, they brushed aside the defenses at Bladensburg, Maryland, and marched into Washington. There they burned the Capitol and wrecked the Navy Yard, then crossed the Potomac and captured Alexandria.

Fearing that Richmond would fall, Governor James Barbour called up the Virginia militia. Shaken from his indolence, Jack left St. George in Dudley's care and volunteered for service. At forty-one, in dubious health and with no military experience, Jack was sent to a makeshift military camp near the racecourse northeast of Richmond. For several sweltering days and nights, he reconnoitered the malarial swamps along the Pamunkey, Mattaponi and Chickahominy Rivers, which the British might use if they were to move on Richmond. When the enemy instead marched north toward Baltimore, Jack was ordered back to camp. There, in early September, he received a letter from Gouverneur Morris that contained the most distressing news yet in a summer of calamities.

The previous April, Jack's nephew Tudor had written to Nancy from Harvard asking his "dear, good Aunt" if he could borrow thirty dollars. Nancy sent him the money and heard from him again several weeks later. He was in Providence, Rhode Island, trying to get home to Virginia, and needed more money. Again Nancy obliged. In July, she received a third letter from Tudor, announcing his intention to visit. On August 4,

Tudor arrived at Morrisania by boat and was so sick that Nancy put him to bed at once. Morris wrote to Jack that the boy was under Nancy's care and was "deeply, perhaps mortally diseased." His family should come immediately. If they could make the trip, Jack, Judith and St. George would be welcome at Morrisania as Nancy's guests.

Jack would have to break the distressing news to Tudor's mother. Tudor had been doing well at Harvard, fulfilling all the expectations the family had for him. Thrilled by the reports of his progress, Judith sometimes feared becoming "an idolator of this dear child." He was "the pride, the sole hope of our family," Jack told Francis Scott Key. "How shall I announce to his wretched mother that the last stay of her widowed life is failing?" Even if Tudor were to recover sufficiently to make it home, Jack wondered how the boy would react to what he would see. "What a scene awaits him there! His birth-place in ashes, his mother worn to a skeleton with disease and grief, his brother cut off from all that distinguishes man to his advantage from the brute beast."

Morris assured the Randolphs that a very different scene awaited them at Morrisania. If Judith felt strong enough to make the journey, she would be treated to "good air, milk, vegetables, and fruit." She will discover upon her arrival "a comfortable House, an affectionate Sister, and a good friend. You will both find a hearty welcome."

Perhaps that was so, but Jack was in no mood to trust anyone's motives. He told Morris that the Randolphs would await further word and would leave if Tudor's condition worsened.

CHAPTER FORTY-TWO

———~~~~~———

*Around September 25, Morris reported, Tudor be-*gan to suffer "violent bleeding from the lungs." Judith borrowed money from St. George Tucker to pay for the trip and left Farmville for New York. Jack was in Richmond and would meet her at Morrisania. When he arrived on Saturday, October 22, he took Nancy in his arms and kissed her on the lips. When she noticed that he was using a cane, he explained that a few days earlier, at an inn at Port Conway, Virginia, he had been roused at three A.M. to catch the stage, mistaken a steep staircase for a hallway and tumbled to the bottom, injuring his ankle and shoulder in the fall. He was in great pain the rest of the journey, but whether he was using opium to ease it, he did not say. If he were relying on the drug in New York, his behavior over the next few weeks might be more easily explained.

Things began uneventfully. Morris's physician, Doctor Hosack, came as expected on Sunday and announced that the boy was improving and might soon regain his strength and be able to travel. After Sunday dinner Jack handed his host a note giving his consent for Tudor and Judith to remain at Morrisania for the fall and winter, if that is what they decided to do. Saying good-bye to Morris, Jack took Nancy in his arms, whispered, "Remember the past," and left.

Later in the day Jack was in New York City when his coach struck a pile of stones on Courtlandt Street and overturned. The spill aggravated Jack's injuries, leaving "the ligaments very much wrenched." When Judith learned of the mishap, the Randolphs and Morrises rushed down to see him.

Judith and Tudor stayed at Bradish's boardinghouse on Greenwich Street, and at some point, Judith left Jack and Tudor alone. During their private moments together, they discussed Tudor's treatment at Morrisania, which Jack apparently found lacking. He also appears to have shared with Tudor his unfavorable opinion of Nancy, which his few hours with her at Morrisania had not altered. Taking his cue from his uncle, Tudor also seems to have been critical of Nancy, which only encouraged Jack's malevolent suspicions. Tudor told him, or so Jack claimed, that when he had lived at Bizarre, the boy had seen his aunt's "love letters" to the slave Billy Ellis.

What motivated Jack to act as he proceeded to do? Perhaps he resented that Nancy was happy, living in a grand house with a rich husband and healthy baby boy, when everyone she had left behind in Virginia was so miserable. Perhaps it was the opium, but Jack shared Tudor's comments and other oddments of gossip, rumor and transmogrified recollection with David Bayard Ogden, one of Morris's nephews, who had been seeking a weapon to use against Nancy for some time. Born at Morrisania in 1775, Ogden was the son of Morris's sister Euphemia. A prominent, if overextended, New York City lawyer and land

DAVID BAYARD OGDEN

speculator, he had on several occasions borrowed large sums of money from his rich uncle and was in debt to Morris when he met with Jack. Resenting both Nancy and her son, Ogden was eager to see the marriage destroyed.

For years, Jack had listened to as much damaging gossip about Nancy as he could, made up some of it and believed it all. What he learned from Gabriela Brockenbrough, from Tudor and from David Ogden came together that week and spurred him to commit an act of breathtaking vengeance against the woman on whom he blamed his brother's death and the family's subsequent miseries.

At some point Jack learned of the correspondence between Gouverneur Morris and John Marshall. Somehow he concluded that Nancy had persuaded Morris that she was of good enough character to be his wife by claiming that Jack had asked her to marry him after the ordeal at Cumberland Court. Jack also concluded that it was Nancy who had suggested that Morris write to Marshall, her defense attorney, and ask him what had happened in Virginia twenty years earlier.

Whether any of these allegations was true or not, Jack seems to have believed them and decided that Nancy had lied about him to convince Morris that she was worthy of him. After talking with Ogden, Jack decided that their marriage was based on fraud. Ogden apparently told Jack that it was a sham and claimed that little "Gouverno" was not Morris's son but "the offspring of an illicit amour" with a servant at Morrisania who had quit as soon as Nancy became pregnant. Ogden also said Nancy was plotting to kill everyone who knew her true character, as he did, to prevent them from revealing it to her husband. He claimed that he feared for his life whenever he stayed at Morrisania. He said that on a recent visit, Nancy had tried to murder him by introducing a "noxious and offensive-smelling vapour" into his bedroom. Ogden said Jack should talk to Martin Wilkins, another nephew of Morris's, to whom the same thing had happened.

"Something very like this happened to me," Jack replied. "I was obliged to sleep with my door open all night."

Jack and Ogden then discussed the likelihood that Richard "came unfairly by his death" and that Morris might face a similar fate. They agreed that the old man should be warned.

CHAPTER FORTY-THREE

———~~~~~~~~———

*Leaving Tudor in the care of the Morrises, Judith de-*parted for Virginia, while Jack stayed in New York City waiting for his injuries to heal. Over the next few days, he met with Martin Wilkins, with Harmanus Bleecker, who had served with Jack in Congress, and with Captain Stephen Decatur and shared with each of them his feelings about Nancy and his opinions of her marriage. Apparently, they offered information that confirmed his suspicions.

Convinced that Nancy had used his good name to trick Morris into marrying her, Jack decided that he was released from any obligation to conceal the truth about her and her activities in Virginia. On the night of November 27, Nancy responded to a note from Jack addressed to Morris requesting a private meeting. Morris was too ill to write, much less to travel, she said, and "too ill to leave the house." While Jack fumed in New York City, Morris began feeling better, and on the last day of October, he, Nancy and little Gouverno took advantage of clear, brisk weather to take a long carriage ride across the Harlem Bridge into New Jersey and back. Jack spent All Hallow's Eve in his boardinghouse writing a letter that would be waiting for them when they returned. The letter was addressed to Nancy, but Jack wanted her husband to read it first.

Madam: When, at my departure from Morrisania, in your sister's presence, I bade you remember the past, I was not aprised of the whole extent of your guilty machinations. I had nevertheless seen and heard enough in the course of my short visit to satisfy me that your own dear experience had availed nothing toward the amendment of your life. My object was to let you know that the eye of man as well as of that God, of whom you seek not, was upon you—to impress upon your mind some of your duty towards your husband, and, if possible, to rouse some dormant spark of virtue, if haply any such should slumber in your bosom. The conscience of the most hardened criminal has, by a sudden stroke, been alarmed into repentance and contrition. Yours, I perceive, is not made of penetrable stuff. Unhappy woman, why will you tempt the forbearance of that Maker who has, perhaps, permitted you to run your course of vice and sin that you might feel it to be a life of wretchedness, alarm and suspicion? You now live in the daily and nightly dread of discovery. Detection itself can hardly be worse. Some of the proofs of your guilt (you know to which of them I allude); those which in despair you sent me through Dr. Meade on your leaving Virginia; those proofs, I say, had not been produced against you had you not falsely used my name in imposing upon the generous man to whose arms you have brought pollution! to whom next to my unfortunate brother you were most indebted, and whom next to him you have most deeply injured. You told Mr. Morris that I had offered you marriage subsequent to your arraignment for the most horrible of crimes, when you were conscious that I never at any time made such proposals. . . .

Your inveterate disregard of truth has been too well known to me for many years to cause any surprise on my part at those or any other falsehood that you may coin to serve a turn. In like manner, you instigated Mr. Morris against the Chief Justice whom you knew to have been misled with respect to the transactions at R. Harrisons, and who knew no more of your general or subsequent life than the Archbishop of Canterbury. Cunning and guilt are no match for wisdom and truth, yet you persevere in your wicked course. Your apprehensions for the life of your child first flashed conviction on my mind that your hands had deprived of life that of which you were delivered in October, 1792, at R. Harrison's. The child, to interest his feelings in its behalf, you told my brother Richard (whom you entrusted to him the secret of your pregnancy and implored him to hide your shame) was begotten by my brother Theodorick, who died at Bizarre of a long decline the preceding February. You knew long before his death (nearly a year) he was reduced to a mere skeleton; that he was unable to walk; and that his bones had worked through his skin. Such was the inviting object whose bed (agreeably to your own account) you sought and with whom, to use your own paraphrase, you played 'Alonzo and Cora,' and to screen the character of such a creature, was the life and fame of this most gallant of men put in jeopardy. He passed his word, and the pledge was redeemed at the hazard of all that men can hold dear. Domestic peace, reputation and life, all suffered but the last. His hands received the burthen, bloody from the womb, and already lifeless. Who stifled its cries, God only knows and you. His hands consigned it to an uncoffined grave. To the prudence of R. Harrison, who [refrained] from a search under the pile of shingles, some of which were marked with blood—to this cautious conduct it was owing that my brother Richard did not perish on the same gibbet by your side, and that the foul stain of incest and murder is not indelibly stamped on his memory and associated with the idea of his offspring. Your alleged reason for not declaring the truth (fear of your brothers) does not hold against a disclosure to his wife, your sister, to whom he was not allowed to impart the secret.

But her own observation supplied all defect of positive information and, had you been first proceeded against at law, your sister being a competent witness, you must have been convicted, and the conviction of her husband would have been followed as a necessary consequence; for whom would have believed your sister to have been sincere in her declaration that she suspected no criminal intercourse between her husband and yourself?

When, some years ago, I imparted to her the facts (she had a right to know them), she expressed no surprise but only said, she was always satisfied in her own mind that it was so. My brother died *suddenly* in June, 1797, only three years after his trial. I was from home. Tudor, because he believes you capable of anything, imparted to me the morning I left Morrisania his misgivings that you had been the perpetrator of that act, and, when I found your mind running upon poisonings and murders, I too had my former suspicions strengthened. If I am wrong, I ask forgiveness of God and even of you. A dose of medicine was the avowed cause of his death. Mrs. Dudley, to whom my brother had offered an asylum in his house, who descended from our mother's sister, you drove away. Your quarrels with your own sister, before fierce and angry, now knew no remission. You tried to force her to turn you out of doors that you might have some plausible reason to assign for quitting Bizarre. But, after what my poor brother had been made to suffer, in mind, body and estate, after her own suffering as wife and widow from your machinations, it was not worth while to try to save anything from the wreck of her happiness, and she endured you as well as she could, and you poured on. But your intimacy with one of the slaves, your '*dear* Billy Ellis,' thus you commenced your epistles to this Othello!, attracted notice. You could stay no longer at Bizarre, you abandoned it under the plea of ill usage, and, after various shiftings of your quarters, you threw yourself on the humanity of Capt. and Mrs. Murray (never appealed to in vain), and here you made a bold stroke for a husband—Dr. Meade. Foiled in this game, your advances became so immodest you had to leave Grovebrook. You, afterwards, took lodgings at Prior's (a public garden), whither I sent by your sister's request, and in her name $100. You returned them by the bearer, Tudor, then a schoolboy, because sent in her name which you covered with obloquy. But to S. G. Tucker, Esq., you represented that I had sent the money, suppressing your sister's name, and he asked me if I was not going to see 'poor Nancy'? You sent this, a direct message, and I went. You were at that time fastidiously neat, and so was the apartment. I *now* see *why* the bank note was returned—but the bait did not take—I left the apartment and never beheld you more until in Washington as the wife of Mr. Morris. Your subsequent association with the players—your decline into a very *drab*—I was informed of by a friend in Richmond. . . . From Rhode Island, you wrote to me, begging for money. I did not answer your letter. Mr. Sturgis, of Connecticut, with whom you had formed an acquaintance, and with whom you corresponded! often brought me messages from you. He knows how coolly they were received. When Mr. Morris brought you to Washington, he knew that I held aloof from you. At his instance, who asked me if I intended to mortify his wife by not visiting her, I went. I repeated my visit to ascertain whether change of circumstances had made any change in your conduct. I was led to hope that you had seen your errors and were smoothing his passage through life. A knowledge that he held the staff in his own hands and a mistaken idea of his character (for I had not done justice to the kindness of his nature) fortified this hope. Let me say that, when I heard of your living with Mr. Morris as his *housekeeper,* I was glad of it as a means of keeping you from worse company and courses. Considering him as a perfect man of the world, who, in courts and cities at home and abroad, had in vain been assailed by female blandishments, the idea of his marrying you never entered my head. Another connection did. My first intimation of the marriage was its announcement in the newspapers. I then thought, Mr. Morris being a travelled man, might have formed his taste on a foreign model. Silence was my only course. Chance has again thrown you under my eye, What do I see? A vampire that, after sucking the best blood of my race, has flitted off to the North, and struck her harpy fangs into an infirm old man. To what condition of being have you reduced him? Have you made him a prisoner in his own house that there may be witness of your lewd amours, or have you driven away his friends and old domestics that there may be no witness of his death? Or do you mean to force him to Europe, where he will be more at your mercy and, dropping the boy on the highway, rid yourself of all encumbrances at once? "Uncle," said Tudor, "if ever Mr. Morris' eyes are opened, it will be through this child whom, with all her grimaces in her husband's presence, 'tis easy to see she cares nothing for except as an instrument of power. How shocking she looks! I have not met her eyes three times since I have been in the house. My first impression of her character, as far back as I can remember, is that she was an unchaste woman. My brother knew her even better than I. She could never do anything with him."

I have done. Before this reaches your eye, it will have been perused by him, to whom, next to my brother, you are most deeply indebted, and whom, next to him, you have most deeply wronged. If he be not both blind and deaf, he must sooner or later unmask you unless *he too die of cramps* in his *stomach*. You understand me. If I were persuaded that his life is safe in your custody, I might forbear from making this communication to him. Repent before it is too late. May I hear of that repentance and never see you more.—John Randolph of Roanoke.

CHAPTER FORTY-FOUR

Jack's letter seems to have done nothing to lessen Morris's love and admiration for Nancy and may have endeared her to him all the more. Nancy, however, was horrified. She felt betrayed by Tudor, who, still sick, was now on his way back to Virginia. And she was appalled that Judith would repay her kindness by helping Jack try to destroy her marriage. After all Nancy had done for Tudor, he had obviously told the most appalling lies to Jack, who claimed that now even Judith believed that Nancy had murdered Richard.

In the days after Jack's charges went out, Nancy's health faltered "under the wounds inflicted by relations, whom she believed to be friends," Morris said. Theirs remained a happy household all the same, and little Gouverno, too young to have any comprehension of the torment the visitors had caused, remained healthy and affectionate. "His Blandishments and mine," Morris said, "are required to soothe his Mother's anguish." Their efforts seemed to work. In time Nancy felt stronger and, on occasion, even defiant.

On such days Nancy was ready to do battle with her accusers, but Morris believed the less said, the better. Some of his friends were urging Morris to sue Jack, but Morris did not "want his money and [could] see no use in keeping up, much less spreading his filthy tales." There was nothing in Nancy's past that Morris had not already known and come to terms with. They had discussed her life in Virginia before she had come to live at Morrisania, and her "candor had blunted [Jack's] arrow."

Even if the Randolphs had misled John Marshall, as Jack claimed, *"She never deceived me,"* and that was all that mattered. The world will never lack for slanderers "while we have among us envious women and flagitious men," and what such people say should not be taken too seriously. "Those who cried aloud against this Houseless child of want that I took to my bosom and hate her because she is happy" would have to answer to a Higher Authority.

Some of them were not willing to wait that long. They wanted justice—or their perverse notion of it—in this life. As soon as Jack's bombshell exploded, they set about getting as much money as they could from Morris while he was still alive, tried to figure out how much they would get when he was dead and pressed him to tell them whether he intended to divorce his wife or not.

Obsequious as ever, David Ogden came to Morrisania on November 2 and asked his uncle to renew a note for one of the loans Morris had made him for $10,000. Morris complied. A few days later, another nephew, Martin Wilkins, wrote to Morris, mentioning Jack's charges against Nancy, and asked flat out where he now stood in the old man's will. Morris professed astonishment that Jack would dare share his malicious slanders with someone as dear to his aunt Nancy as Wilkins and refused to discuss his will. "What my intentions respecting my property were," Morris continued, "it is useless to conjecture. What they are it would answer no honest purpose to communicate. I am not without hopes, however, that some of these may enable me to be useful to you while I yet linger on the stage of mortality."

A third letter arrived, addressed to Morris. Unsigned, it repeated Jack's charges against Nancy. Believing that Ogden was its author, Nancy wrote to him and he then wrote to Morris, demanding an explanation of why Nancy had written to him about the matter. With characteristic forbearance and a rich lather of irony, Morris said she had done so only because she viewed him as a friend who would be "disposed, from the sentiments you entertain for me, to defend the reputation of my wife."

Through these difficult days Nancy was sustained by the support of her gallant husband and her "dear lovely Babe." Sometimes, when she realized how blessed she was, she felt sorry for Jack, who had set out to destroy her, and for Judith, who had done nothing to stop him and might even have helped. If Judith could say, "I was simple in my heart and the Lord helped me," she would be a much happier person, Nancy thought.

There were moments that Nancy said made every hardship and hurt she had suffered seem trivial. One night, when little Gouverno was sleeping in the same bed with his parents, he woke up, and Nancy gave him a cup of milk. When he had finished, he grabbed his mother and father by their nightcaps and drew them together on each side of him. "Come, Papa," he murmured. "Come, Mama." Then, "with one of his dear little hands held by each parent," Nancy said, "he fell into a sweet sleep."

At such times she considered Jack a "poor creature" condemned to live alone because no one would live with him. "Could his heart experience one glow of parental or conjugal affection," Nancy said, "he would afterward behold his own malignity with horror." But while Nancy pitied Jack, she did not intend to let his misdeeds go unpunished.

CHAPTER FORTY-FIVE

On January 15, while Jack was still in Philadelphia,
Nancy responded to his allegations, made twenty copies of her
letter and sent them to his political opponents, so "that your
former constituents should know the creature in whom they
put their trust." These included Senator William Branch Giles,
whom Nancy barely knew but had heard that "amid the fury of
[her] enemies," he had once defended her "in a way which
evinced much benevolence of heart."

"In your letter to my husband," Nancy began, "you say, 'I
wish I could withhold the blow but I must in your case do what
under a change of circumstances I would have you do unto me.'
This, Sir, seems fair and friendly." But it only seemed so—and
Jack only wanted it to appear that he was taking Morris into his
confidence, since he had already made to Ogden and others the
"filthy accusations" he was making against her now. Jack also
claimed he wished to inform Morris alone of facts "important
to his happiness and honor, though fatal to [Nancy's] reputation," so that her husband could "display them to the world as
the means of freeing him from a monster unfit to live." Here,
too, Jack lied. He said he had written to Morris out of gratitude
for the care he had given to Tudor. If Jack felt grateful, "at-

tempting to blacken [his wife's] character and destroy his peace" was a peculiar way to show it.

Jack's letter revealed that he either knew what he said was false or that he had completely lost his reason, for his presentation of his case "would have been hissed [at] even by a sisterhood of old maids." If he did indeed believe the allegations he was making against her,

> why did you permit your nephew to be fed from my bounty and nursed by my care during nearly three months? Could you suppose him safe in the power of a wretch who had murdered his father? Does it consist with the dignified pride of family you affect to have him, whom you announce as your heir, and destined to support your name, dependent on the charity of a negro's concubine?

Jack had not only allowed Nancy to take care of Tudor but also had given Judith and Tudor permission to remain at Morrisania: "Recollect, Sir, when you rose from table to leave Morrisania, you put in my husband's hand a note to my sister expressing your willingness that she and her son should pass the winter in his house." And the warm manner in which Jack had greeted Nancy and taken his leave showed that he did not believe the accusations he had made.

> When you entered this house, and when you left it, you impressed upon my lips a kiss which I received as a token of friendship from a near relation. Did you then be-

lieve that you held in your arms, that you pressed to your bosom, that you kissed the lips of a common prostitute, the murderess of her own child and of your brother?

Decent people require proof before they will believe others guilty of such enormities as those of which Jack accused her. Those "who feel themselves capable of committing the blackest crimes," however, have no difficulty believing the worst of others, with no proof at all. To those of a "malevolent heart," mere hearsay is all the evidence they require, and that is all the "proof" Jack had.

The one thing Jack's letter did prove was that, despite all his boasting, he was not a man of honor, for honorable men do not betray confidences. If he were half the man his brother Richard had been, he, too, would have taken his secrets to the grave—if he had any secrets to guard. He would never have kicked a defenseless young woman out of Bizarre, and he would not have lied about her once she had gone.

Nancy had sought refuge at Bizarre because her father's new wife had made her leave. Richard had been kind enough to take her in, and Theodorick had been good enough to love her, even though her father would never allow them to marry. Jack might recall, too, how he had also attempted to court her, though "your stormy passions, your mean selfishness, your wretched appearance, rendered your attentions disagreeable," and Richard, who knew how Jack's interest "annoyed" her, had had to intervene.

Theodorick was the brother Nancy had loved, but her father, knowing that he would not inherit money, had "preferred for my husband a person of clear and considerable estate" and prevented their marriage.

Under these circumstances, I was left at Bizarre, a girl, not yet seventeen, with the man she loved. I was betrothed to him, and considered him as my husband in the presence of that God whose name you presume to invoke on occasions the most trivial and for purposes the most malevolent. We should have married, if Death had not snatched him away a few days after the scene which began the history of my sorrows.

Yes, they had all lied at Cumberland Court. She had given birth that night at Glentivar, but it had been Theodorick's baby, not Richard's, and it had been stillborn, not murdered.

Your brother, Richard, knew every circumstance, but you are mistaken in supposing I exacted from him a promise of secrecy. He was a man of honor. Neither the foul imputations against us both, circulated by that kind of friendship which you have shown to my husband, nor the awful scene, to which he was afterwards called as an accomplice in the horrible crime, with which you attempt to blacken his memory, could induce him to betray the sister of his wife, the wife of his brother; I repeat, Sir, the crime with which you now attempt to blacken his memory. You say that, to screen the character of such a creature as I am, the life and fame of that most generous and gallant of men was put in jeopardy. His life alas! is beyond the reach of your malice, but his fame, which should be dear to a brother's heart, is stabbed by the hand of his brother. You not only charge me with the heinous crime of infanticide, placing him in the condition of an accomplice, but you proceed to say that "had it not been for the prudence of Mr. Harrison, or the mismanagement of not putting *me* first on my trial, we should both have swung on the same gibbet and the foul stain of incest and murder been stamped on his memory and associated with the idea of his off-spring."

Is this the language of one brother's love for another? "What must be the indignation of a feeling heart to behold a wretch rake up the ashes of his deceased brother to blast his fame?" Nancy asked. "Who is there of nerve so strong as not to shudder at your savage regret that we did not swing on the same gibbet?"

Surely Jack remembered what had taken place at Cumberland Court, where they had been cleared of all charges "to the joy of numerous spectators expressed in shouts of exultation." Jack seemed to have forgotten that part of this long-dead story, which for the most depraved of reasons he was now telling others.

This, Sir, passed in a remote county of Virginia more than twenty years ago. You have revived this scandalous tale in the most populous city in the United States. For what? To repay my kindness to your nephew by tearing me from the arms of my husband and blasting the prospects of my child! Poor innocent babe, now playing at my feet, unconscious of his mother's wrongs . . .

Jack even professed to tell others what had happened once Nancy had left Bizarrre, and he lied about that, as well. Yes, when she had nowhere else to go, she had lived at Prior's in Richmond, "where public balls and entertainments were held," in a room "over Mrs. Prior's, a lady of as good birth as Mr. John Randolph and of far more correct principles." He had come to see her there, and it had seemed a pleasant visit, under the circumstances. "You sat on my bedstead, I cannot say my bed, for I had none, I was too poor," she recalled. "When weary, my limbs rested on a blanket, spread over the sacking." A few days later, Jack had Tudor deliver $100 to her, which she would not accept. Her refusal no doubt shocked Jack, "for it must be very difficult for you to conceive how a person in my condition would refuse money" from anyone. She had been too proud "to receive a boon at the hands of those by whom I had been so grievously wounded."

Months later, when she was ill, she had written asking to borrow money. But Jack would not help her, perhaps because he hoped "the poor forlorn creature" he had expelled from Bizarre would "be driven to a vicious course and enable you to justify your barbarity by charges such as you have now invented." Lacking evidence that she had been reduced to such a course,

Jack now merely asserted it. Having listened to the gossip of Gabriela Brockenbrough, he claimed Nancy had become a prostitute. That charge was malicious nonsense, but "if suffering could have driven me to vice, there was no want of suffering."

What proof did Jack have that Nancy was a woman of bad character? None, it seemed, but Gabriela's word and that of the boy Nancy had tried to nurse back to health, at risk to her husband's own. It was difficult for Nancy to talk about Tudor, but it had been Jack's decision—and Tudor's—to drag his name into it. If Tudor had indeed said Nancy was an "unchaste woman," Jack should have asked him

"Why did you stay in that house? Why did you accept her kindness? Why did you accept her presents? Why did you pocket her money?" If Jack had asked Tudor those questions, his reply might have been: "Uncle, I could not help it. I was penniless, in daily expectation that you and my mother would bring relief." The proper response to this explanation would have been: "Why, the wretch, having from necessity or choice, laid yourself under such a load of obligations, do you become the calumniator of your benefactress? Are you yet to learn what is due to the rites of hospitality, or have you at the early age of nineteen, been taught to combine profound hypocrisy with deadly hate and assume the mask of love that you more surely plant the assassin's dagger? Where did you learn these horrible lessons?" This last, Sir, would have been a dangerous question on your part. He might have replied and may yet reply, "Uncle, I learned this from you."

With the help of the man she had been blessed to marry, Nancy hoped to raise her child with sounder and more benevolent principles. The great Randolph of Roanoke would be wise to be more careful when speaking of her husband. Jack knew little of the circumstances of her life with Gouverneur Morris, whose kindness to those in need "might even touch *your* heart." But Jack understood nothing of kindness or love.

"You speak of him as an infirm old man," Nancy wrote, "into whom I have struck the fangs of a harpy, after having acted in your family the part of a vampire." Jack could not be more mistaken. "I loved my husband before he made me his wife. I love him still more now that he has made me the mother of one of the finest boys I ever saw; now that his kindness soothes the anguish which I cannot but feel from your unmanly attack."

There was one last thing. Judith had told her that one of the few items she had been able to save from the fire at Bizarre was a portrait of Nancy. Now that Nancy had become Mrs. Anne C. Morris, Jack could keep it. Perhaps he could hang it in his "castle at Roanoke," as a "trophy of the family's prowess."

She closed with an echo of Jack's own letter, laced with references to the books he had read:

I observe, Sir, in the course of your letter an allusion to one of Shakespeare's best tragedies. I trust you are by this time convinced that you have clumsily performed the part of "honest Iago." Happily for my life, and for my husband's peace, you did not find him a headlong, rash Othello. For a full and proper description of what you have written and spoken on this occasion, I refer you to the same admirable author. He will tell you it is a tale told by an idiot, full of sound and fury, signifying nothing.

CHAPTER FORTY-SIX

Those who read Nancy's letter or learned of its contents seem to have fallen into two camps. Either they knew Jack's nature and detested him or, knowing his nature, they nevertheless recognized his abilities, supported his politics and did not much care how he treated the women in his family. The people of his old congressional district probably knew him as well as anyone did, and so long as they were not the object of his abuse, they enjoyed his outlandish antics. They appreciated him for the florid eccentric that he was. He could always be counted on to give a first-rate speech, and he had been fearless in defense of their interests. By the spring of 1815, they decided he had been right all along about the war with England, which had ended with little resolved and at great cost, with the ratification of the Treaty of Ghent in February. And Eppes, who had replaced Jack in Congress, was not nearly as entertaining.

So in April, to the dismay of his army of despisers, Jack's constituents returned him to Congress. Their support outraged some people of gentler sensibilities, including Nancy's sister-in-law, the former Patsy Jefferson, who viewed Jack's attacks with intense loathing. "What can we think, my Dear Friend," Patsy wrote to one of her daughters, "of the morality of a district who can choose such a man to represent them?" Since writing his original tirade, Jack was now accusing Nancy "of having seduced one of Judy's little boys & attempted the chastity of the other, neither of them nine years old at the time." Patsy wanted to write to Nancy but feared that Nancy resented her. They had not spoken or written for years. For a long time, Nancy had thought that Patsy was intercepting the letters she had sent to her brother Tom Randolph, which was not true. Tom had simply been too lazy to answer them.

If Patsy were to write to Nancy now, her letter might be misunderstood. She and Tom, like so many of the planters, had fallen on hard times. Tobacco prices continued to decline, the land was wearing out and taxes were coming on, as Patsy's father said, like "an approaching wave in a storm." Tom had begun to sell slaves—once he sold a five-year-old girl—just to raise cash. Since Patsy had become poor while Nancy "is now in prosperity," Nancy might think she was trying to ingratiate herself.

Patsy might well have found Nancy more understanding and less suspicious of her childhood friend's motives than she imagined. Nancy was more forgiving than she had been in years. She had also come to a place in her life where she did not much care what Jack or Patsy or anyone else thought. Upon hearing that Peyton Randolph's wife had accused Nancy of forging other people's names to her own letters, Nancy laughed and said that for Peyton's wife to waste her time spreading such gossip, she must "have very little to do."

The year that had begun with such turbulence had gradually become as untroubled as any Nancy had known. One day in June, when the cherries at Morrisania were ripening, she, her husband and little Gouverno, who was now twenty-eight months old, took advantage of the early summer sun and walked all the way to the orchards and back. Napoleon had been crushed that very week at Waterloo. Captain Decatur had defeated the Algerians in the Mediterranean, bringing an end to hostilities against American shipping. Trade with Great Britain had resumed, and workers in Washington were rebuilding the burned-out city. The world, for once, seemed at peace. When the Morrises got back to the house, Gouverno drank wine and milk, "frolicking until dinner." Randolph Harrison would be sending two of his children to Morrisania for a visit, so Nancy would be able to spend time with a niece and a nephew she had not seen in years. They planned to spend some of the hottest weeks of the summer in the Mohawk Valley, in part to ease Morris's gout.

The only unhappy news that summer concerned Tudor Randolph. Earlier in the year, Judith had written to Morris, clearly distraught by Nancy's claim that Tudor had been a source of the allegations Jack had made against her. Had Tudor been party to the conspiracy against Nancy? "It is too true, my dear Madam," Morris replied, "that your son was a principal agent in those transactions which excite your indignation and abhorrence." It saddened Morris to say so, but Judith deserved the truth—and a vigorous defense. Since she herself had been wholly innocent of any involvement in the campaign against her sister, Morris said he would "omit no proper occasion to vindicate your Honor from the imputation."

Still very sick, Tudor had spent the first months of the year in Richmond, sailed from Norfolk on April 25 and reached London on July 2. If he were strong enough, he would travel on to the Mediterranean, where the Randolphs believed the air would be good for his failing lungs. The family had not heard from him since his departure, and Judith was frantic with worry. In late October, Judith heard from the Reverend John Holt Rice, who had a friend who knew someone in Liverpool. The friend had made inquiries about Tudor and was now on his way to Farmville. He would have news for them when he arrived. "Your suspense and mine," Rice told Judith, "will soon be removed."

As Judith soon learned, Tudor had died on Tuesday, August 18, 1815, in Cheltenham, England, three weeks before his twentieth birthday. In her grief, she accepted a long-standing offer from Rice and his wife to live with them in Richmond, which meant leaving Farmville forever.

Nancy's response to the death is not known. She had come to have a poor opinion of the young man by the time he had sailed for England, though there was a time when she "would have made any possible sacrifice for Saint and Tudor, such was my devotion to them."

Jack learned of Tudor's death from John Brockenbrough, "the first intelligence of an event [he] had long expected, yet dreaded to hear." He sought solace in the Anglican faith of his childhood but found that his contempt for his fellow creatures and for life itself presented an insurmountable obstacle to a sincere profession of Christianity. "To me," he explained, "the world is a vast desert, and there is no merit in renouncing it, since there is no difficulty."

His return to Washington when Congress opened in December did little to revive his spirits. The men he had served with in 1799 had long since departed, and the whole town bore the scars of the senseless war with England. The south wing of the Capitol was an unsightly shell, and Congress had to convene at Blodgett's Hotel. After a great deal of debate about whether to abandon the Capitol and move the government back to Philadelphia, Latrobe was called back to restore the old House chamber.

The principles of state sovereignty and strict construction that had inspired Jack's colleagues in Jefferson's first term were gone as well. The Democratic-Republicans still held a majority in both houses, but the two parties seemed to be wearing each other's masks. The Federalists now took the states' rights position, while Democratic-Republicans like Clay and Calhoun had allowed the public debt to explode to finance the war. The militias had been devoured by a standing army.

These new men, many of them from the states to the west, envisioned not the free and peaceful agricultural republic true Jeffersonians dreamed of but a great military empire stretching from the Atlantic to the Pacific, crisscrossed with government roads and canals that connected sprawling cities filled with factories. Even the younger men from the South espoused a Hamiltonian program, with a strong central government and a national bank and tariffs to protect the manufacturing interests. Now the party leaders were pushing for a system of federally sponsored "internal improvements," meaning new roads and canals linking the new states to the old ones. Virginia planters would have to pay for these internal improvements, but no one seemed to care about old Virginia, including its residents.

Jack fought all these measures and more but took no pleasure—or, at best, a perverted one—in the sport. By now, he was making "moderate use" of opium, drinking heavily and suffering from an assortment of afflictions, including "spasms that threatened to terminate all my earthly cares." His ailments became so severe that Chief Justice Marshall helped him draw up his will. Once that was done and he was alone again, he read *King Lear* and cursed his fate. His worst fears, first expressed when he became head of the household at Bizarre nearly thirty years earlier, had come true. "I am 'the last of my family'—of my family at least," he wrote to his half brother Henry St. George Tucker, "and I am content that in my person it should become extinct. In the rapid progress of time and of events, it will quickly disappear from the eye of observation, and whatever of applause or disgrace it may have acquired in the eyes of man, will weigh but little in the estimation of Him by whose doom the everlasting misery or happiness of our condition is to be irrevocably fixed."

Such a cruel fate need not have befallen the Randolphs but for Nancy, he believed. Had Richard lived, things might have been different. The circumstances of his death twenty years earlier continued to weigh heavily on Jack's increasingly disordered mind, and not long after Tudor died, Jack wrote to a still grieving Judith seeking answers to questions that had troubled him for two decades. He remembered being told that an emetic had precipitated Richard's final crisis, and he wanted to know if Nancy had prepared it.

"Did she mix or hand him the medicine? I ask for my own ease and comfort."

If Judith wrote back in response, her answer has long been lost.

CHAPTER FORTY-SEVEN

On March 20, 1816, a year after Tudor's death, Nancy learned that Judith had died. Her body had been taken from the Reverend Rice's home in Richmond to Tuckahoe for burial in the family graveyard. The night Nancy received the news, she sat in front of the fire long after her husband and child had gone to bed. As snow blanketed the terrace, she wrote to a friend, calling her sister "Judy" for the first time in years. Nancy said she had heard that "Judy" had broken off all relations with her brother William because he had defended Nancy. She hoped her sister was "happy now" and that poor St. George "may be protected in a life of comfort—free from every strong emotion."

Nancy wished her siblings could "unite in brotherly Love and Friendship." Time seemed to be running out for all of them. Judith had been forty-four, and an old forty-four at that. Nancy's husband would be sixty-five in January. He insisted he felt like a young man, but he knew he had little time left. His life had been a long, happy and rich one in every sense of the word, and he faced his inevitable demise with courage and grace. He said he considered himself fortunate to have witnessed one of the most remarkable periods "in the history of mankind" and to have played even a small role in it.

Grateful for all his blessings, he wanted nothing more than to live out his days in the company of a wife and son who had been the greatest joys of his earthly existence. Nancy "has much genius, has been well educated, and possesses, with an affectionate temper, industry and a love of order," he wrote to his friend John Parish in July of 1816. "That I did not marry earlier is not to be attributed to any dislike for that connection. On the contrary, it has long been my fixed creed that as love is the only fountain of fidelity, so it is in wedded love that the waters are most pure. To solve the problem of my fate it was required to discover a woman who, with the qualities needful for my happiness, should have also the sentiments. In a word the postulate was that I also find a woman who could love an old man."

Fast approaching his fourth birthday, little Gouverno was such an endearing tyke that he had charmed even the avaricious aunts and uncles "who would have been more content had he never seen the light." His parents, "who see him almost every minute of every day, are chiefly delighted with the benevolence that warms his little heart."

Morris had much to be thankful for, but by the fall of 1816, when Nancy was planning to visit Virginia for the first time since her exile, he felt sick enough to cancel the trip. He was eaten up by gout—and increasingly by worry. For reasons that are difficult to determine with any precision but in retrospect seem to have been well founded, he had come to distrust his nephew David Ogden and feared for the condition of the once-immense Morris fortune. On October 26, he made a new will that superseded one drawn up in 1809.

Already in debt to his uncle, Ogden had purchased vast tracts of land in the northern counties of New York after persuading Morris to cosign the mortgage and making "solemn assurances" that he would make the payments himself. By late October, Morris was confined to bed but had determined that Ogden was failing to make the mortgage payments as promised and without his knowledge had taken out a second mortgage on the newly acquired property. This plunged Ogden into still deeper debt and made it more likely that he would default on the original loan, leaving Morris—or his heirs—liable for his debts.

There are indications that Ogden had engaged in other risky schemes injurious to Morris that Morris knew little or nothing of. As winter came on, the sick old man struggled mightily to figure out what Ogden was up to and what hardship his nephew's schemes might inflict on Nancy and little Gouverno. Morris was able to make little progress, however, though he does not seemed to have shared his anxieties with Nancy, perhaps in the hope that he could resolve the difficulties before he died and spare his wife needless worry.

Ogden came to Morrisania on November 4. Morris was civil to him, but when Dr. Hosack came, Morris complained of Ogden's "villainy."

Hosack examined Morris but decided that there was little he could do for his patient. The gout was worsening daily, and it would soon spread to his internal organs. Morris tried everything—bleeding, cupping, clysters, laudanum and laxatives, even a concoction of guaiacum. Nothing helped. His urinary passage was blocked, and the pain was excruciating. If he died now, he could do nothing to save Nancy from financial ruin, and he would surely die if he could not urinate. He elected to remove the blockage himself. He decided that the insertion of a whalebone, no doubt taken from one of Nancy's corsets, would accomplish the desired effect.

Gouverneur Morris died at five in the morning on Wednesday, November 6, 1816, at the age of sixty-five. A funeral was held at ten A.M. the next day, after which his body was buried in the cherry orchard at Morrisania.

Morris's attempt at self-surgery had resulted in severe lacerations, which had proved fatal. He "died the death of the most noble," Nancy said. He had been in horrendous pain, but "not a murmur escaped him." He was "the best of husbands and the most charming of companions," and her heart was "agonized" by her loss. For days, she said, her son "cried to see his father."

Morris left the bulk of his estate to his son. Nancy would receive the house and its furnishings plus $2,600 a year, as set forth in their prenuptial agreement. He hoped she would remarry, and to encourage her, he stated that she would receive another $600 a year upon taking another husband. This additional sum would "defray the increased expenditure, which may attend that connexion." One nephew, Gouverneur Wilkins, would receive $25,000 when he turned thirty. Ogden got nothing.

These generous bequests would prove more easily expressed in writing than bestowed, as Nancy discovered as soon as she began to sort through the mess of her family's finances. "Borne down by business and sorrow," she forged ahead, learning that Ogden had "swindled us almost out of everything." Her husband had "discovered his villainy too late" and had been able to do nothing in his last days to set things right.

Nancy began corresponding with others whose wealth, generous natures and good names, she discovered, Ogden had also taken advantage of. She learned of the depth of her financial difficulties, which did not end with Ogden's "villainy." He had swindled the estate out of at least $117,000, but a number of others owed her husband money, too, and she was determined to recover it, if it took years of hardship and endless legal battles to do it.

Little was left of the legendary Morris fortune but the mansion, the grounds, the Morrisania farmlands and a great deal of undeveloped land in northern New York State. Taxes were coming due, and people to whom Ogden owed money were demanding payment from her. Three weeks after her husband's death, she was "threatened with having my person seized for the Ogden debts." To prevent such a calamity, she gave up her $2,600 annuity and mortgaged her house and, to pay taxes, began to sell the land. The only thing she did not mortgage, she said, was the vault in which her husband was buried, and for the next several years, she made payments to three New York banks and to the American Insurance Company.

In May of 1818, six months after Morris was buried, James A. Hamilton, the son of her husband's friend Alexander

Hamilton, sued her for nonpayment of legal bills, a claim she disputed. In the weeks after Morris's death, she had paid him what she considered exorbitant fees for "discharging debts," though this work "could not have fatigued him much." She had given him a bust of his father that Morris had owned, for which he thanked her with "gross flattery," for which she figured he must have been charging her, too. Never "having flattered any person," she wrote, "I am ignorant of the price." (They wrangled for almost a decade, and in April 1828, she paid him $4,000 to close the case.) She kept up a constant correspondence with other lawyers, and every new arrival of legal papers that had to be read and responded to aroused in her "sensations like those apparent in a mad dog at the sight of water."

"After passing a long life in the society of such men as Judges Marshall and Tucker, Gouverneur Morris, Mr. Jefferson, etc., etc.," she was saddened to have to spend so much of her energy dealing with far less admirable examples of that "wretched animal man."

All that kept her going during this difficult time, she said, was concern for her son. If she did not have such a "fine boy to protect," she would have been happy "sewing for an honest and quiet life."

She was poor again and, except for little Gouverneur, was alone once more. For a time, she supported them solely from produce grown on the farmland at Morrisania, 400 acres of which she supervised herself. She raised cattle, sheep and hogs, planted corn and sold apples, pears, potatoes and grapes. One summer, the lease of pastureland alone brought in $200 a month, which was enough to "support us comfortably." But when a tenant farmer allowed his cattle and horses to graze over the entire property, they laid waste to the cornfields, depriving her of needed income. He stole wood for his fireplace, moreover, "while I burn coal to save the forests."

Repairs to the house depleted what little money Nancy had almost as soon as her husband was in his grave. Whenever it rained, water poured down through the roof and floor and into the cellar. She paid hundreds of dollars to painters, carpenters and masons, who she felt charged more than their work was worth.

Once during this period of hardship, she heard from her brother William, who was back in Virginia and still broke. William urged her, in light of her circumstances, "not to live in style."

CHAPTER FORTY-EIGHT

The two statesmen agreed to meet near the Little Falls Bridge on the south bank of the Potomac at four-thirty on the afternoon of April 8, 1826. Ravaged by brandy and opium, Jack insisted that the duel be fought on Virginia soil; if he were to die that day, he wanted his home state "to receive [his] blood."

As an orator, his opponent was as accomplished as Jack, but he was a novice with a pistol. Henry Clay had been born in Virginia, too, but he had thrown in his lot with Kentucky and western expansion. A war hawk and promoter of internal improvements, Clay had run for president in 1824 but had come in fourth after Andrew Jackson, John Quincy Adams and William Crawford. When none of the candidates had received a majority of votes and the election had gone to the House, Clay had thrown his support to Adams. Adams had then made Clay his secretary of state. Jack had denounced the appointment as a "corrupt bargain," causing Clay to issue a challenge, which Jack had promptly accepted.

The South needed someone to speak for its interests, and Jack, who had always worked best in opposition, had become that man. When Adams made Virginia Senator James Barbour his secretary of war, the legislature picked Jack to serve out

Barbour's unexpired term, and Jack began to represent the whole South, with its tangle of doomed, almost mystical notions of aristocracy and gentlemanly valor, whose chief support was the sweat of its slaves. That support was increasingly threatened by the North.

The admission of Maine and Missouri, thanks to Clay's "compromise," had brought the number of states to twenty-four, half of which opposed slavery. As northern commerce prospered and abolitionist sentiment built, southerners had begun to think of themselves as united in some larger cause. A clash of interests and cultures was, Jack had concluded, inevitable. "I look," he told his Charlotte County neighbors, "for civil war." He was for secession now, and he would welcome the bloodletting that would come. He was an old man, but they could strap him on his horse, the one called Radical, and he would fight for Virginia to his dying breath. He spoke for all southern gentlemen, and as such, how Randolph of Roanoke conducted himself took on new, even national consequence.

Jack spent the day before the duel in his boardinghouse, reading *Paradise Lost* and talking calmly with his seconds, who included Thomas Hart Benton, the new senator from Missouri. Benton had gone to Clay's house the night before, where the secretary of state's wife, having no idea of her husband's plans, was serene. Clay sat with one of his children asleep on his lap. When Benton told Jack what he had seen, Jack said: "I shall do nothing to disturb the sleep of the child or the repose of the mother."

Jack had already made up his mind. Virginia law now prohibited dueling, and he would neither "insult" the laws of his native state nor kill an honorable man who had a family depending on him.

Jack and his seconds crossed the Little Falls Bridge the next afternoon, and the adversaries took their positions. While the seconds began to go over the rules and Clay was still unarmed, Jack held his pistol in his gloved hand, with the barrel pointed down. There was a sharp explosion, and for several tense moments no one knew what had happened. Jack's gun had gone off by accident. Fearing people would say he had fired at a defenseless man, Jack was humiliated.

When others in the party raised questions about what had happened, Clay spoke up. He declared that the firing "was clearly an accident," and the duel could proceed.

Clay was handed his pistol; the second appointed to conduct the duel called, "Fire!" As he began to count, Jack squeezed the trigger; his bullet hit a stump. Benton tried to call a halt to the proceedings, but Clay waved him off. "This is child's play," he declared, and the adversaries loaded their weapons and resumed their positions.

Jack felt wretched. He had fired at Clay, or at least people would say he had. They would say he had indeed tried to kill his adversary and that by even participating in the duel, he had shown contempt for Virginia. But with a second shot coming, he could redeem himself. Having begun as a contest of wills, the duel had become a struggle within himself. The second shouted, "Fire!"

Calmly, Jack fired straight up into the sky; as he did, he heard another *crack!* and something whistled past, making Jack's coat flutter. No one was hurt, and the seconds exhaled. "I do not fire at you, Mr. Clay," he called. As he offered his hand, Jack saw that there was a hole in his coat.

"You owe me a coat, Mr. Clay."

"I am glad," Clay replied, "the debt is no greater."

It was storming when the steamboat docked at Philadelphia on the evening of May 5, 1833. Jack's manservant, John, managed to hail a hack, but its windows were broken, and the rain soaked the passengers. The carriage splashed through the streets, stopping at inn after inn before they found a place to stay at the City Hotel on North Third Street. Jack planned to catch the packet *Montezuma* bound for England, so he could visit Tudor's grave. He had arrived too late and was so sick that the innkeeper called for Dr. Joseph Parish, though Jack doubted if any physician could help him now.

In a few more weeks, Jack would turn sixty. Andrew Jackson was president, and in 1830, he had appointed Jack U.S. Minister to Russia. Jack had left St. Petersburg after only a week and sailed home in the summer of 1831. The cold had nearly killed him. Back at Roanoke, he stayed drunk most of the time, and in 1832, he lost his mind completely. John Marshall, who had retired to a plantation in Charlotte County, took Jack in. It was about this time that Jack developed a sudden and in many ways inexplicable enthusiasm for the president, to whom he volunteered his service as "an unpaid, secret, confidential agent" to the Court of St. James's. In a letter that surely baffled

Jackson, he praised the rough-and-tumble Tennessean effu-
sively and compared his admiration of the president to that of
Hephaestus for Alexander, "the nature of [whose connection],"
Jack wrote, was, "if I forget not, Greek love."

As soon as Jack regained his reason, he returned to
Roanoke but continued to drink. He carried his "good friend
opium" with him wherever he went and declared that he would
use it to end his life if he should find that he had done anything
dishonorable. His neighbors said he was increasingly obscene
in his speech and abusive to his slaves. When his cook, Queen
Betty, made pudding with a plum in it, instead of the plum pudding he had requested, he had her whipped. After that, Queen
Betty "always made them right and greatly improved in her
soup."

When the doctor arrived at the inn, Jack told him that he
had attended several courses in anatomy in his college days. He
could describe his symptoms with great specificity, using all the
anatomical knowledge accumulated in a lifetime of hypochon-
dria.

"How long have you been sick, Mr. Randolph?" the doctor
asked.

"Don't ask me that question. I have been sick all my life."

Dr. Parish took his pulse.

"You can form no judgment by my pulse," Jack said. "It is so
peculiar."

"You have been so long an invalid, Mr. Randolph, you must
have acquired an accurate knowledge of the general course of
practice adapted to your case."

"Certainly, sir; at forty, a fool or a physician, you know."

"There are idiosyncrasies in many constitutions. I wish to ascertain what is peculiar about you."

"I have been an idiosyncrasy all my life."

In the morning, Dr. Parish recommended a medicine, which Jack refused. The next night he suggested bringing in other doctors, but Jack would not hear of it. "In a multitude of counsel," he argued, "there is confusion; it leads to weakness and indecision; the patient may die while the doctors are staring at each other."

On Thursday night, Parish stayed at Jack's bedside for two hours, and Jack asked him to relieve his congestion by performing a tracheotomy. When he refused, the dying orator barked orders to bring him a knife so he could cut his own throat but soon calmed down. Jack asked Parish to read the newspaper to him. When the doctor came upon the word "omnipotence," and put the accent on the penultimate syllable, Jack corrected his pronunciation. When Parish pronounced "impetus" with a long *e*, Jack again corrected him. When he protested, Jack cut him off and ordered him to continue reading.

The next day, May 24, Jack's condition had worsened and Parish listened patiently as the dying man confirmed the contents of a will he had drawn up, freeing his slaves. When the doctor promised to return as soon as he had seen another patient, Jack objected.

"You must not go. You cannot, you shall not leave me."

The doctor turned away.

"John," Jack called to his servant, "take care that the doctor does not leave the room."

The slave moved quickly toward the door.

"Master, I have locked the door and got the key in my pocket, the doctor can't go now."

Jack told his servant to bring him the breast button that had belonged to his father, a gold stud Jack kept with him at all times. He instructed John to attach it to his shirtfront, but the servant could not secure it. There was no hole, he told his master, who said: "Get a knife and cut one."

Jack slumped back in the bed. A few moments passed, then he suddenly roused himself. His dark eyes seemed to glow, and, sitting up, he shrieked: "Remorse!"

CHAPTER FORTY-NINE

—~~~~~~~—

By the time of Jack's death, Nancy had cleared her late husband's estate of debt. The effort to put the household on a sound footing had been enormously difficult, but she and her son could now live in comfort, if not on the luxurious scale they had enjoyed while Morris had lived. David Ogden's treachery proved a blessing, one of her husband's biographers would theorize. The need to restore the family fortunes, he wrote, "supplied the 'pressures' and tapped the energies without which, in her grief over Morris's death and the continuing shame of the Randolph letter, [Nancy] might not have had the determination to survive." This seems a stretch, though she did exhibit courage and resourcefulness just as she had in other crises in her life. Although her husband had often told her to "spurn the pittance," her circumstances made such magnanimity impossible. Determined to collect the money owed her, Nancy appealed to the courts and won. In January 1818, she obtained a judgment in the Supreme Court of the County of New York for $25,000 against John Swarthout, Samuel Swarthout and Waters Smith, for debts to her husband that he had never bothered to collect. When she discovered that Moss Kent, the coexecutor of the Morris estate, had sold some of the family's lands without her permission and without making provision for the payment of taxes, she sued to have Kent removed and won that lawsuit, too. This victory gave Nancy sole power over the estate, which she exercised with characteristic pluck.

Throughout the 1820s, she struggled to collect large sums and small, while making whatever sacrifices seemed required. On one occasion she apologized to her guests for the "paltry dinner," embarrassed that she had "not even a half cup of wine" to put before them. In June 1831, in what was no doubt a difficult decision, she tried to sell the "elegant pearl set" her husband had given to her as a wedding present.

Throughout the early 1830s, Nancy worked to make the farms at Morrisania productive again, which required draining stagnant ponds, repairing the barn roof and, when the tenant farmer threatened to move, paying for renovations to a tenant house. "Morrisania will give us an income henceforth," she declared when fences finally went up, "but not whilst cows and hogs eat what we plant." In the summer of 1831, as her fifty-seventh birthday approached, she tried to sell her "splendid" watch, having long since concluded that material things no longer much mattered to her. "My trust is in God," she said, "and I consider patience and perseverance" the only sure means of securing contentment in this life.

All her "constant exertion of fortitude" paid off, and that same year, she was able to pass the estate, unencumbered, to her son. By 1833, when he turned twenty, Gouverneur Morris II stood well over six feet tall and showed an aptitude for commerce that would have made his father proud. Nancy also enjoyed warm and amiable relationships with those members of her husband's family who had not connived to get his money. It was a good, if quiet, life. She worked on a genealogy of her son's family going back three generations and tried to supply relevant portions of her late husband's diary for publication in a history of the Erie Canal. Her husband had amassed a "splendid" library that included not only books but also "voluminous correspondence" of the great men of his day. He owned many of George Washington's letters, and reading them took Nancy back to the stirring events of her youth. She never thought of Jack Randolph unless "his attacks on some other persons" were brought up in conversation. Some people thought he was "crazy," but Nancy decided his case was not so much one of insanity as of demonic possession. His malevolent antics seemed like those of people "whom Satan entered in old times." The same might be said of David Ogden, who in 1826 committed suicide.

Other news from Virginia surely saddened her. Her brother's marriage to Patsy Jefferson came to grief. After Thomas Jefferson's death that same year, Patsy left Tom, who had been beating her, and fled to Boston with their two youngest children. She returned to Monticello only when Tom, who had lost everything, was on his deathbed. He died in June 1828, and Patsy could not afford to maintain Monticello, which would have to be sold. The house there had been stripped of its furnishings just as Tuckahoe had been when Nancy sought refuge there. Tom Randolph's financial problems had jeopardized Tuckahoe, too, and in 1830, the house where Nancy had been born would also be sold, passing out of the Randolphs' hands.

The whole Randolph family seemed to labor under a curse,

and Nancy felt relieved to be delivered from "their merciless fangs." In the summer of 1830, one of her Morris in-laws saw St. George Randolph, who was nearly forty and "looks wretchedly." She considered it "fortunate indeed . . . for mankind that the wisdom and mercy of God determined [that that branch of the Randolphs] should soon be extinct." God's judgment of the family had become obvious enough to her. The "nature of St. George's malady" was no mystery. In that pitiful man's inability to speak, one "beheld what the father attempted visited on his child."

Precisely what Nancy meant by this statement remains a matter of conjecture. It seems to suggest that Richard had imposed on her an oath of silence—a silence imposed by nature on St. George—that she was never entirely happy to uphold. Richard had not wanted anyone to know the truth, and she was the only one who could know what that truth was.

Richard and St. George were the only members of the family she spared from judgment, and Richard—or "Dick," as she called him—was the only one she ever again referred to with fondness. Although Theodorick was the Randolph brother she had supposedly loved and to whom she was engaged to be married, it was Richard whose passing she still lamented and whose marriage to her sister she never ceased to resent.

On his deathbed, Richard had told Nancy that, except for his stepfather, she "was the only sincere friend he ever had." What else he might have said she did not reveal, but the intimacy they shared would last a lifetime. "I do think his Nature made of the best materials," she declared, but he had made one fatal mistake. He had married a "coldhearted, malignant haughty woman" who did not understand him and did not bring out his finer qualities.

Richard was the only man Nancy had known whose destiny "seemed entirely to depend on his choice of a wife." Had he married someone else, and Nancy never admitted whom she wished he had married, everything would have been different. But had Richard done differently, Nancy might never have married the "darling husband" she did, nor had the son who proved to be "the richest treasure God could have bestowed on me."

As Nancy pulled herself and her son up from the poverty that had engulfed them when her husband had died, she seems to have found a peace like the one she had known when Gouverneur Morris was alive. It no longer troubled her to learn that people gossiped about her. She strolled in the gardens, spent long hours in her husband's library and looked forward to visits from a favorite, but unnamed, niece who "delights us with the melody of her Harp and voice."

"Thus do our lives glide on," she wrote, "slander sounds like distant thunder . . ."

EPILOGUE

Gouverneur Morris II grew up to be president of the New York and Harlem Railroad, a founder of the Illinois Central and Union Pacific railroads and an anti-slavery Republican. In 1841, at Morrisania, he built, "for the glory of God and in Memory of His Mother," St. Ann's Church. It still stands in the South Bronx, serving a largely black and Hispanic congregation. In the floor of the east aisle a plaque reads:

AND HERE BY HER OWN REQUEST
REPOSE THE REMAINS
OF
THE WIFE AND MOTHER
IN MEMORY OF WHOM
THIS CHURCH
WAS CREATED
TO THE GOD SHE LOVED
BY FILIAL VENERATION

GOUVERNEUR	ANNE CARY
MORRIS	MORRIS
NOV. 6, 1816	MAY 28, 1837
IN HIS 65TH YEAR	IN HER 63RD YEAR

Epilogue

A year after building St. Ann's Church, Gouverneur Morris II married his cousin Patsey Jefferson Cary of Virginia, a daughter of Nancy's sister Virginia Randolph of Tuckahoe.

NOTES

———〰〰〰———

EPIGRAPH

| 7 | "I regret": | Thomas Jefferson. Letter to John Holmes, April 22, 1820. In *Basic Writings of Thomas Jefferson*, edited by Philip S. Foner (Garden City, N.Y.: Halcyon House, 1950), 767–68. |

PROLOGUE

9	"poisoning a man and trying to seduce his sons":	Anne Cary Morris to St. George Tucker, August 27, 1818, Tucker-Coleman Collection, Swem Library, College of William and Mary.
10	boys "of 12 and 14":	Ibid.
10	"with wonder":	Nancy Randolph, no addressee, June 21, 1805, Bruce-Randolph Collection, Virginia State Archives.
11	"I shall rally again":	Nancy Randolph to Mary Johnson, Nancy Randolph Papers, Swem Library, College of William and Mary.

CHAPTER ONE

| 18 | "Don't you think I could make the trip in the carriage?": | William Wirt, *The Life of Patrick Henry, Correspondence and Speeches*, vol. 2 (New York: Scribner's, 1891), 490–91. |
| 22 | "raving mad": | Ibid., 167. |

Notes

22 "ill state of Health":   George Washington to Patrick Henry, September 13, 1778, Charles Campbell Papers, Swem Library, College of William and Mary.

CHAPTER TWO

24 She was born Anne Cary Randolph: *The Douglas Register, being a Detailed Record of Births, Marriages and Deaths together with Other Interesting Notes, as Kept by the Rev. William Douglas* [rector of St. James–Northam Parish], *Goochland County, Virginia, from 1750 to 1797*, transcribed and edited by William Macfarlane Jones (Richmond: J. W. Fergusson & Sons, 1928), 283.

25 "solely to answer the purposes of hospitality":   Thomas Anburey, *Travels Through the Interior Parts of America*, vol. 2 (Boston: Houghton Mifflin, 1923), 203.

27 "tangle of fish-hooks":   Jonathan Daniels, *The Randolphs of Virginia* (Garden City, N.Y.: Doubleday & Co., 1972), 9.

27 "They trace their pedigree":   Thomas Jefferson, "Autobiography," in *The Writings of Thomas Jefferson*, vol. 1, collected and edited by Paul Leicester Ford (New York, London: G. P. Putnam's Sons, 1892), 2.

29 "No doubt":   Anburey, *Travels*, vol. 2, 370.

30 "rash humour":   William Fitzhugh Gordon. Letter to Mrs. Gordon, December 27, 1823. In William H. Gaines, Jr., *Thomas Mann Randolph: Jefferson's Son-in-Law* (Kingsport, Tenn.: Louisiana University Press, 1966), 7.

CHAPTER THREE

32 "small cheerful world":   Henry Adams, *John Randolph* (Boston, New York: Houghton Mifflin Company, 1910), 4–5.

33 "tawny":   Hugh A. Garland, *The Life of John Randolph of Roanoke*, vol. 1 (New York: D. Appleton & Co., 1859), 4.

33 "never marry a widow": St. George Tucker to Robert Wash, October 2, 1812, Tucker-Coleman Collection, Swem Library, College of William and Mary.

35 "Comfortable in this world": Jan Lewis, *The Pursuit of Happiness: Family and Values in Jefferson's Virginia* (New York: Cambridge University Press, 1983), 46.

35 "a fine officer": John Randolph to St. George Tucker, July 10, 1781, Tucker-Coleman Collection, Swem Library, College of William and Mary.

CHAPTER FOUR

39 "smokey Cabbin": Frances Tucker to St. George Tucker, March 2, 1781, Tucker-Coleman Collection, Swem Library, College of William and Mary.

39 "make the militia fight": John Randolph to St. George Tucker, July 10, 1781, Tucker-Coleman Collection, Swem Library, College of William and Mary.

39 "into an old Pumpkin faced, Dropsical, Mope": Frances Tucker to St. George Tucker, March 25, 1779, Tucker-Coleman Collection, Swem Library, College of William and Mary.

39 "without a skin": Benjamin Watkins Leigh, Nathan Loughborough MSS., quoted in William Cabell Bruce, *John Randolph of Roanoke, 1773–1833*, vol. 1 (New York, London: G. P. Putnam's Sons, 1922), 36.

39 "more eagerly than gingerbread": John Randolph. Letter to Theodore Dudley, February 16, 1817. In *Letters of John Randolph, to a Young Relative, from Early Youth, to Mature Manhood* (Philadelphia: Carey, Lea & Blanchard, 1834), 190–91.

40 "have my syntax": Richard Randolph to St. George Tucker, July 9, 1781, Tucker-Coleman Collection, Swem Library, College of William & Mary.

40 "in the best manner": Quoted in Robert Dawidoff, *The Education of John Randolph* (New York: W. W. Norton, 1979), 78.

40 "our little monkeys":   St. George Tucker to Frances Tucker, July 15, 1781, quoted in Mary Haldane Begg Coleman, *Virginia Silhouettes* (Richmond: Press of the Dietz Printing Co., 1934), 66.

41 "quite spoilt":   St. George Tucker to Theodorick and John Randolph, June 12, 1787, Tucker-Coleman Collection, Swem Library, College of William and Mary.

CHAPTER FIVE

42 Richard almost immediately ran out of money: Richard Randolph to St. George Tucker, March 11, 1786, Tucker-Coleman Collection, Swem Library, College of William and Mary.

42 "perfectly futile":   St. George Tucker to Frances Tucker, April 1786, Tucker-Coleman Collection, Swem Library, College of William and Mary.

43 "sublime":   Nancy Randolph to St. George Tucker, February 21, 1805, Bruce-Randolph Papers, Virginia State Archives.

43 Having developed strong opinions: Thomas Mann Randolph, Jr., to Anne Cary Randolph, May 7, 1788, Nicholas P. Trist Papers, part 4, Southern Historical Collection, University of North Carolina at Chapel Hill.

44 "in its meridian splendor":   Peter S. Randolph. Letter to Carr, July 28, 1787. *Virginia Magazine of History and Biography*, Virginia Historical Society, year ending December 31, 1940, 238–39.

45 "I must be sought":   Nancy Randolph to St. George Tucker, February 21, 1805, Bruce-Randolph Papers, Virginia State Archives.

CHAPTER SIX

46 "regular, studious":   John Randolph to Tudor Randolph, December 13, 1813. In William Cabell Bruce, *John Randolph of Roanoke, 1773–1833*, vol. 1 (New York, London: G. P. Putnam's Sons, 1922), 73.

46 "poor crippled, distrest": Richard Randolph to St. George Tucker, July 15, 1787, Tucker-Coleman Collection, Swem Library, College of William and Mary.

47 "master of ceremonies": Howard Swiggett, *The Extraordinary Mr. Morris* (New York: Doubleday & Co., 1952), 81.

47 "elegance of dress": *Chateaubriand's Travels in America*, translated by Richard Switzer (Lexington: University of Kentucky Press, 1969), 15.

47 "profusion of luxury": Quoted in Thomas Fleming, *The Man from Monticello: An Intimate Life of Thomas Jefferson* (New York: William Morrow and Company, 1969), 188.

47 "too affected to be pleasing": Jacques Pierre Brissot de Warville, *New Travels in the United States of America*, edited by Durand Echeverria (Cambridge: Harvard University Press, 1964), 256.

47 "a few European fops": Ibid.

48 "Mansion wits": Peter Markoe, "The Times, a Poem," quoted in Robert C. Alberts, *The Golden Voyage: The Life and Times of William Bingham, 1752–1804* (Boston: Houghton Mifflin, 1969), 218.

48 "repeated cruelty": Frances Tucker. Letter to St. George Tucker. In *Virginia Silhouettes*, edited by Mrs. George P. Coleman (Richmond: Press of Dietz Printing Co., 1934), 304.

48 "much disordered": Frances Tucker to St. George Tucker, December 2, 1787, Tucker-Coleman Collection, Swem Library, College of William and Mary.

49 "vice-regal carriage": Henry Adams, *John Randolph* (Boston, New York: Houghton Mifflin, 1910), 19.

49 "the most manly youth": John Randolph to Tudor Randolph, December 13, 1813. In Bruce, *John Randolph of Roanoke*, vol. 1, 73.

49 "not a single negro":   Hugh Garland, *The Life of John Randolph of Roanoke*, vol. 1 (New York: D. Appleton & Co., 1859), 63.

51 "neither debauched nor dissipated":   Ibid.

51 managed to seduce Betsy Talliafero . . . Kitty Ludlow: Anne Cary Morris to St. George Tucker, February 9, 1815, Tucker-Coleman Collection, Swem Library, College of William and Mary.

52 "govern or resist":   Richard Randolph to Frances Tucker, October 28, 1787, Tucker-Coleman Collection, Swem Library, College of William and Mary.

CHAPTER SEVEN

53 "not in much good health":   Gouverneur Morris. Letter to Alexander Hamilton, June 13, 1788. In *The Papers of Alexander Hamilton*, vol. 5, edited by Harold C. Syrett (New York: Columbia University Press, 1961), 7–8.

53 "little upturned nose":   Dr. Thomas Robinson to unspecified Murray cousin, July 9, 1813. In William Cabell Bruce, *John Randolph of Roanoke, 1773–1833*, vol. 2 (New York, London: G. P. Putnam's Sons, 1922), 639.

54 "eclaircissement":   Nancy Randolph to St. George Tucker, February 21, 1805, Bruce-Randolph Papers, Virginia State Archives.

54 Nancy "offends only the unamiable":   Ibid.

54 "a burning affection tinctured with tender melancholy":   John Leslie to Thomas Mann Randolph, Jr., June 6, 1789, Carr-Cary Papers, Alderman Library, University of Virginia.

55 "personal abilities and exertions":   St. George Tucker to John Randolph and Richard Randolph, quoted in T. H. Breen,

*Tobacco Culture: The Mentality of the Great
Tidewater Planters on the Eve of Revolution*
(Princeton, N.J.: Princeton University Press,
1985), 208.

55 "for deferring a union":   St. George Tucker to Thomas Mann Randolph, Jr., November 15, 1789, Tucker-
Coleman Collection, Swem Library, College
of William and Mary.

55 "will never repent":   Anne Cary Randolph. Letter to St. George
Tucker, September 23, 1780. *Virginia Maga-
zine of History and Biography*, December 31,
1934, 49–50.

56 Judith Randolph,   Author's visit.
Nancy Randolph:

57 "unadvisedly, lightly,   1669 Book of Common Prayer.
or wantonly":

57 "man and wife":   Ibid.

58 "mortified":   Richard Randolph to Neill Buchanan, May
1790, Tucker-Coleman Collection, Swem
Library, College of William and Mary.

58 "a dollar or two":   Richard Randolph to Duncan Rose, June 6,
1790, Tucker-Coleman Collection, Swem
Library, College of William and Mary.

58 "charge as before":   Richard Randolph to Duncan Rose, May 11,
1790, Tucker-Coleman Collection, Swem
Library, College of William and Mary.

58 "to shew her power":   Anne Cary Morris to St. George Tucker,
February 9, 1815, Tucker-Coleman Collec-
tion, Swem Library, College of William and
Mary.

Notes

CHAPTER EIGHT

60 "the link of love":   Thomas Jefferson. Letter to Martha Jeffer-
                          son, June 17, 1790. In Sarah N. Randolph,
                          The Domestic Life of Thomas Jefferson (Char-
                          lottesville: University of Virginia Press,
                          1871), 187.

60 "tear [Nancy]   Anne Cary Morris to St. George Tucker,
    from Dick's arms":   February 9, 1815, Tucker-Coleman Collec-
                          tion, Swem Library, College of William and
                          Mary.

61 "were as sweet and   John Randolph. Letter to John Marshall,
    clean as the tea cups": December 17, 1831. In William Cabell Bruce,
                          John Randolph of Roanoke, 1773–1833, vol. 2
                          (New York, London: G. P. Putnam's Sons,
                          1922), 417.

61 "much happier here   Judith Randolph to Mary Harrison, Novem-
    than where we saw   ber 11, 1790, Harrison Family Papers, Vir-
    more company":   ginia Historical Society.

61 "that dear, sequestered Nancy Randolph to Mary Johnson, n.d.,
    spot":   Nancy Randolph Papers, Swem Library, Col-
                          lege of William and Mary.

62 "What inducement   Hugh Garland, *The Life of John Randolph of
    have I":   Roanoke*, vol. 1 (New York: D. Appleton & Co.,
                          1853), 63.

62 He had . . . a library: "Inventory of the Estate of Richard Ran-
                          dolph, Junr., Esq., of Bizarre," Cumberland
                          County, July 18, 1797.

62 "pestered":   Anne Cary Morris to John Randolph, Janu-
                          ary 1, 1815, Virginia Historical Society.

63 Theodorick was   Ibid.
    "unworthy" of her:

63 "I wish my mother   Anne Cary Morris to St. George Tucker, Feb-
    had lived":   ruary 9, 1815, Tucker-Coleman Collection,
                          Swem Library, College of William and Mary.

Notes

CHAPTER NINE

64 "endeavored to shake": Anne Cary Morris to St. George Tucker, February 9, 1815, Tucker-Coleman Collection, Swem Library, College of William and Mary.

64 "I am engaged": Ibid.

64 "was no more than a jog": Quoted in Sarah N. Randolph, *The Domestic Life of Thomas Jefferson* (Charlottesville: University of Virginia Press, 1871), 294–95, 297.

64 "excess fear": William Buchan, *Domestic Medicine: or, A treatise on the prevention and cure of diseases by regimen and simple medicine. With an appendix, containing a dispensatory for the use of private practitioners* (London: A. Strahan, 1798), 116–17.

65 "she is in danger": Ibid.

65 "who quit the bed too soon": Ibid., 544.

65 "fine son": Martha Jefferson Randolph. Letter to Thomas Jefferson, May 7, 1792. In *The Family Letters of Thomas Jefferson,* edited by Edwin Morris Betts and James Adams Bear, Jr. (Charlottesville: University Press of Virginia © 1966; reprinted by arrangement with the University of Missouri Press, 1986), 98–99.

66 "to draw off the milk": Buchan, *Domestic Medicine,* 547.

67 "too lame to travel": Anne Cary Morris to St. George Tucker, February 9, 1815, Tucker-Coleman Collection, Swem Library, College of William and Mary.

67 "constant wrath": Anne Cary Morris to John Randolph, January 1, 1815, Virginia Historical Society.

68 "bones had worked through his skin": John Randolph. Letter to Anne Cary Morris, October 13, 1814. In ibid., Cabell Bruce, *John Randolph of Roanoke, 1773–1833,* vol. 2

Notes

(New York, London: G. P. Putnam's Sons, 1922), 275.

68 "a mere skeleton":   John Randolph. Letter to Tudor Randolph, December 13, 1813. In ibid., 74.

68 "I have never seen the end":   Martha Jefferson Randolph. Letter to Thomas Jefferson, February 20, 1792. In *The Family Letters of Thomas Jefferson*, edited by Betts and Bear, 94.

CHAPTER TEN

69 "hysterics" from "cholic":   "Notes on Evidence," deposition of Mrs. Randolph Harrison. John Marshall, *Correspondence and Papers, July 1788–December 1795*, vol. 2 of *The Papers of John Marshall*, edited by Charles T. Cullen and Herbert A. Johnson (Chapel Hill: University of North Carolina, 1977), 172.

69 "great sinking of the spirits":   William Buchan, *Domestic Medicine, or, A treatise on the prevention and cure of diseases by regimen and simple medicine. With an appendix, containing a dispensatory for the use of private practitioners* (London: A. Strahan, 1798), 299.

70 "produce an abortion":   "Notes on Evidence," Deposition of Mrs. Martha Jefferson Randolph, in John Marshall, *The Papers of John Marshall, Correspondence and Papers*, vol. 2, *July 1788–December 1795*, 169.

CHAPTER ELEVEN

74 Nancy, who wrote a statement for him to use: Anne Cary Morris to St. George Tucker, February 8, 1815, Tucker-Coleman Collection, Swem Library, College of William and Mary.

75 "had prevailed over the dark":   Richard Randolph to St. George Tucker, March 14, 1793, Virginia Historical Society.

76 "worse than mine":   Ibid.

76 "fatal":   Ibid.

CHAPTER TWELVE

77 "My character":   *The Virginia Gazette, and General Advertiser,* April 17, 1793.

80 "I defy you":   Anne Cary Morris to St. George Tucker, February 9, 1815, Tucker-Coleman Collection, Swem Library, College of William and Mary.

81 Judith lost the baby: Judith Randolph to Mary Harrison, December 21, 1793, Harrison Family Papers, Virginia Historical Society.

81 "too rational" . . . "think or say":   Thomas Jefferson. Letter to Martha Randolph, April 28, 1793. In *The Family Letters of Thomas Jefferson,* edited by Edwin Morris Betts and James Adam Bear, Jr. (Charlottesville: University of Virginia Press, 1966), 115–16.

82 "from her vile seducer":   Martha Jefferson Randolph. Letter to Thomas Jefferson, May 16, 1793. In ibid., 117–18.

82 "feloniously murdering a child":   "*Commonwealth v. Richard Randolph,* Called Court Extra Term, April 29, 1793, Cumberland County Order Book, 29th Day of April 1793, Quarter Session," 89.

CHAPTER THIRTEEN

84 "We were waked":   "Notes on Evidence," in *The Papers of John Marshall, Correspondence and Papers,* vol. 2, *July 1788–December 1795,* edited by Charles T. Cullen and Herbert A. Johnson (Chapel Hill: University of North Carolina Press, 1977), 170.

85 "by loud screams":   Ibid.

85	"proceeded from Miss Nancy":	Ibid.
85	"Mrs. [Mary] Harrison soon went up":	Ibid.
85	"heard some person":	Ibid., 171.
85	"from the weight of the step":	Ibid.
85	"frequently passed up & down":	Ibid.
85	"had probably had an hysteric fit":	Ibid.
85	"two or three days before":	Ibid.
85	"Mr. Randolph and I went into her room":	Ibid.
86	"remarkable, except considerable paleness":	Ibid.
86	"to a cause totally different":	Ibid.
86	"Mrs. Harrison, Mrs. Randolph & Mr. Randolph":	Ibid.
86	"behaviour of the Ladies":	Ibid.
86	"except that Mr. Randolph":	Ibid.
86	"she had miscarried":	Ibid.
87	"a negro-woman":	Ibid.
87	"heard a Report":	Ibid.
87	"on a pile of shingles":	Ibid.
87	"six or seven weeks afterward":	Ibid.

87 "observed . . .   Ibid.
   familiarities":

87 "too high an opinion": Ibid., 170.

88 "had the hysterics":   Ibid., 172.

88 "some blood":   Ibid.

88 "an attempt had been   Ibid.
   made":

88 "entertained no   Ibid.
   suspicion":

88 "miscarried":   Ibid.

88 "might be expected":   Ibid.

88 "only appeared un-   Ibid.
   easy":

89 "entire harmony   Ibid.
   existed between Mr.
   Randolph & his lady":

89 "were too fond of   Ibid., 173.
   each other":

89 "extremely weak":   Ibid., 174.

89 "a disagreeable smell": Ibid.

90 "a child or miscar-   Ibid.
   ried":

90 "fondness for each   Ibid.
   other":

90 "miscarried":   Ibid.

90 by "friendship":   Ibid.

90 "kissing":   Ibid., 168.

90 "an apparent alteration Ibid., 173.
   in her size":

90 "very attentive to   Ibid.
   Miss Nancy":

90 "without any loose covering":   Ibid.

90 "encreased":   Ibid.

90 "removal of her ill Health":   Ibid.

90 "discovered no mark":   Ibid.

90 "with a more chearful [*sic*] countenance":   Ibid.

90 "dangerous":   Ibid., 169.

90 "Miss Nancy was pregnant":   Ibid.

CHAPTER FOURTEEN

91 "Mr. Randolph and Miss Nancy were only company for themselves":   "Notes on Evidence," in *The Papers of John Marshall, Correspondence and Papers*, vol. 2, *July 1788–December 1795*, edited by Charles T. Cullen and Herbert A. Johnson (Chapel Hill: University of North Carolina Press, 1977), 169.

91 "fondness":   Ibid.

91 "a criminal inter-course":   Ibid.

91 "Miss Nancy's shape to alter":   Ibid.

91 "unwilling to undress":   Ibid.

92 "give no further satisfaction":   Ibid., 170.

92 "she thought she was any smaller":   Ibid.

92 "look down at her waist":   Ibid.

92 "suspicious of her situation":   Ibid.

92	"Great God, deliver us from eavesdroppers!":	Robert Douthat Meade, *Patrick Henry: Practical Revolutionary* (Philadelphia: Lippincott, 1969), 420.
93	"the most impudent youth":	E. S. Thomas, *Reminiscence of the Last Sixty-Five Years*, vol. 1 (Hartford, Conn.: Garland, 1840), 65.
94	"burst into tears":	"Notes on Evidence," in *The Papers of John Marshall*, Correspondence and Papers, vol. 2, *July 1788–December 1795*, 174.
94	"the most perfect harmony":	Ibid.
94	"often observed how much fonder":	Ibid.
94	"fondness had increased":	Ibid.
94	"frequently lounged on the bed":	Ibid.
96	"Let us examine":	Ibid., 175.
96	"Is it wonderful":	Ibid., 176.
96	"would have suppressed":	Ibid.
96	"was under the eye":	Ibid.
96	"she must have been advanced":	Ibid.
96	"the size of a woman":	Ibid.
97	"she would have taken it at home":	Ibid., 177.
97	"no person on earth":	Ibid.
97	"The most innocent person on earth":	Ibid., 178.
97	"heart conscious of it's [*sic*] own purity":	Ibid.

97 "the pride of conscious   Ibid.
     innocence":

97 "cannot deny, that   Ibid.
     there is some
     foundation":

97 "In this Situation":   Ibid.

97 Thomas Jefferson   John Eppes to Thomas Jefferson, May 1,
     learned of the decision: 1793, Alderman Library, Bryan Family Pa-
                                 pers, University of Virginia.

98 Jefferson told Judge   Thomas Jefferson to St. George Tucker,
     Tucker: April 26, 1793, Tucker-Coleman Collection,
                                 College of William and Mary.

98 "The Trial. Return.   William Cabell Bruce, *John Randolph of*
     Quarrels of the   *Roanoke*, vol. 2 (New York, London: G. P.
     women":   Putnam's Sons, 1922), 118.

CHAPTER FIFTEEN

99 Richard Randolph ap-   "Cumberland County Court Order Book,"
     peared a second time: 18, 1792–1797, Cumberland County, Va., 217.

99 "could not possibly   "To the Public," St. George Tucker circular,
     have taken place":   May 5, 1793, Tucker-Coleman Collection,
                                 Swem Library, College of William and Mary.

99 "perfect state of   Judith Randolph. Letter to Mary Harrison,
     misery":   May 12, 1793. In Howard Swiggett, *The*
                                 Extraordinary Mr. Morris (New York:
                                 Doubleday & Co., 1952), 273.

100 "those corroding   Judith Randolph to Mary Harrison, Febru-
     reflections":   ary 15, 1796, Harrison Family Papers, Vir-
                                 ginia Historical Society.

100 "you alone":   Judith Randolph. Letter to Mary Harrison,
                                 May 12, 1793. In Swiggett, *The Extraordi-*
                                 nary Mr. Morris, 273.

Notes

CHAPTER SIXTEEN

104 "the bones of Men, women, and Children": Benjamin Henry Latrobe, *The Virginia Journals of Benjamin Henry Latrobe*, vol. 1, *1795–1797*, edited by Edward C. Carter, II (New Haven: Yale University Press, 1977), 8.

104 "went mad": Ibid., 89.

104 "his reason by degrees": Ibid.

104 "young puppies waiting to be pilfered": Benjamin Henry Labrobe. Letter to Thomas Blackburn, April 21, 1796. In ibid., 99.

105 "great a fool as myself": Lee W. Formwalt, "Benjamin Henry Latrobe and Jeffersonian Virginia," *Virginia Cavalcade*, Summer 1979, 12.

105 "often Captain, sometimes Major": Benjamin Henry Latrobe. Letter to Thomas Blackburn, April 23, 1796. In ibid., 99.

105 "fancied myself in a society": Benjamin Henry Latrobe. Letter to Thomas Blackburn, May 17, 1796. In ibid., 99.

105 "An unlucky boy": Latrobe, *Virginia Journals*, vol. 1, 8.

106 "too distressing": Benjamin Latrobe diary entry, June 10, 1796. In ibid., 137.

106 "there is hospitality": Ibid.

107 "indeed seems to have implanted": Benjamin Latrobe diary entry, May 17, 1796. In ibid., 127.

107 "ought to be like a coat of Mail": Ibid., 128.

CHAPTER SEVENTEEN

108 "inflammatory fever": Benjamin Latrobe diary entry, June 12, 1796. In *The Virginia Journals of Benjamin Henry Latrobe*, vol. 1, *1795–1797*, edited by Edward C. Carter II (New Haven: Yale University Press, 1977), 143.

109 "a long string of hopes and technical phrases": Benjamin Latrobe diary entry, June 17, 1796. In ibid., 144.

109 "much worse": Benjamin Latrobe diary entry, June 12, 1796. In ibid., 143.

109 "every attention and kindness in their power": Ibid.

109 "a promise which I held sacred": Anne Cary Morris to St. George Tucker, February 9, 1815, Tucker-Coleman Collection, Swem Library, College of William and Mary.

110 "and will be rewarded": Nancy Randolph to St. George Tucker, June 1796, Tucker-Coleman Collection, Swem Library, College of William and Mary.

110 "perfect madness": Ibid.

CHAPTER EIGHTEEN

112 "the deranged state": Judith Randolph to John Randolph, September 25, 1796, Bryan Family Papers, Alderman Library, University of Virginia.

112 "her helpless and destitute little ones": Judith Randolph to St. George Tucker, July 24, 1796, Tucker-Coleman Collection, Swem Library, College of William and Mary.

113 "utmost ingratitude": Nancy Randolph to St. George Tucker, July 14, 1796, Tucker-Coleman Collection, Swem Library, College of William and Mary.

114 "keenest sufferings": Nancy Randolph to St. George Tucker, May 29, 1798, Tucker-Coleman Collection, Swem Library, College of William and Mary.

114 "the time of retribution": Ibid.

114 "mere lounger": John Randolph. Letter to Tudor Randolph. In Gerald W. Johnson, *Randolph of Roanoke* (New York: Minton, Balch & Co., 1929), 91.

114 "fleshy portion":   Lemuel Sawyer, *A Biography of John Randolph, with a Selection from His Speeches* (New York: William Robinson, 1844), 9.

115 "Johnny, all the land":   Hugh Garland, *The Life of John Randolph of Roanoke*, vol. 1 (New York: D. Appleton & Co., 1859), 18.

115 Richard's will: "Will of Richard Randolph of Bizarre, Prince Edward County," District Will Book, vol. 1, 4.

116 "Macbeth hath murdered sleep":   Quoted in Garland, *The Life of John Randolph of Roanoke*, vol. 1, 70.

116 "verging toward extinction":   John Randolph. Letter to Elizabeth T. Coalter, March 22, 1824. In William Cabell Bruce, *John Randolph of Roanoke, 1773–1833*, vol. 1 (New York, London: G. P. Putnam's Sons, 1922), 101.

116 "more tender":   John Randolph, January 31, 1826. In Garland, *The Life of John Randolph of Roanoke*, vol. 1, 11.

CHAPTER NINETEEN

118 Virginians had been building an informal opposition: Norman K. Risjord, *The Old Republicans: Southern Conservatism in the Age of Jefferson* (New York: Columbia University Press, 1965).

121 as great a speaker as Edmund Randolph: Hugh Garland, *The Life of John Randolph of Roanoke*, vol. 1 (New York: D. Appleton & Co., 1859), 23.

CHAPTER TWENTY

123 "I see":   Gouverneur Morris, *The Diary and Letters of Gouverneur Morris*, vol. 2, edited by Anne Cary Morris (New York: Charles Scribner's Sons, 1888), vol. 1, 4.

123 "An *aristocrat?*":   Ibid., vol. 1, 14.

124 "You argue the matter so handsomely":   Ibid., 13.

124 "almost tempted to wish he had lost *something else*": John Jay. Letter to Robert Morris. In Howard Swiggett, *The Extraordinary Mr. Morris* (New York: Doubleday & Co., 1952), 80.

124 "milk is mixed": Gouverneur Morris diary entry, November 13, 1789, *The Diary and Letters*, vol. 1, 226.

124 "in his own way— as a bachelor": Gouverneur Morris diary entry, May 2, 1799, *The Diary and Letters*, vol. 2, 379.

125 "Hamilton tells me": Ibid.

125 "to lead a private life": Gouverneur Morris diary entry, December 26, 1798, *The Diary and Letters*, vol. 2, 377.

126 Dickinson had a daughter: Swiggett, *The Extraordinary Mr. Morris*, 340.

126 Roger Sherman: Ibid., 225.

126 Washington stuck by Morris: Ibid., 225–26.

127 "leaky and ruinous": Ibid., 338.

127 "bath room $50": Ibid.

127 "the most salubrious air in the world": Gouverneur Morris. Letter to James Parish, February 16, 1802. In *The Diary and Letters*, vol. 2, 419.

128 Jonathan Mason on Morris: Swiggett, *The Extraordinary Mr. Morris*, 378.

CHAPTER TWENTY-ONE

129 "only a *very little* to one side": Judith Randolph to Mary Harrison, February 16, 1798, Harrison Family Papers, Virginia Historical Society.

130 "hearts [were] light as air": Ibid.

130 "the keen dart of misfortune": Ibid.

Notes

130	"having transgressed the bounds of decorum":	Nancy Randolph to St. George Tucker, May 29, 1798, Tucker-Coleman Collection, Swem Library, College of William and Mary.
130	"endangered by [Jack's] uncommon attention to his own":	Ibid.
131	"So, you have begun to blab":	Nancy Randolph to St. George Tucker, May 29, 1798, Tucker-Coleman Collection, Swem Library, College of William and Mary.
131	"simple piety":	Quoted in William Maxwell, *Memoir of the Rev. John H. Rice, D.D.* (Philadelphia: J. Whethem, 1835), 60.
132	her "aversion to me":	Nancy Randolph to St. George Tucker, February 8, 1799, Tucker-Coleman Collection, Swem Library, College of William and Mary.
133	"the blaster of my happiness":	Ibid.
133	"my being obliged to leave Bizarre":	Ibid.

CHAPTER TWENTY-TWO

135	Henry began in a voice:	Hugh Garland, *The Life of John Randolph of Roanoke*, vol. 1 (New York: D. Appleton & Co., 1859), 129–33.
136	As Jack got up to speak:	Ibid., 180.
136	"Young man":	Ibid., 141.
137	"I haven't seen":	Ibid.
137	"the slightest expectation":	William Cabell Bruce, *John Randolph of Roanoke*, vol. 1 (New York, London: G. P. Putnam's Sons, 1922), 154.

Notes

CHAPTER TWENTY-THREE

138 "unwholesome chill-
ing mists":
Nancy Randolph, no addressee, n.d., Bruce
Randolph Collection, Virginia State Archives.

139 "terrible state of dilapidation":
Nancy Randolph to St. George Tucker, August 15, 1799, Tucker-Coleman Collection,
Swem Library, College of William and Mary.

139 "constant succession
of company":
Ibid.

140 "cause of republi-
canism":
Thomas Jefferson. Letter to Archibald Stu-
art, May 14, 1799. In *The Writings of Thomas
Jefferson*, vol. 7, collected and edited by Paul
Leicester Ford (New York, London: G. P.
Putnam's Sons, 1896), 378.

140 "foolish things":
Gouverneur Morris diary entry, November
13, 1801. In *The Diary and Letters of Gouverneur Morris*, vol. 2, edited by Anne Cary
Morris (New York: Charles Scribner's Sons,
1888), 415.

140 "Mr. Jefferson's
presence":
Nancy Randolph to St. George Tucker, August 15, 1799, Tucker-Coleman Collection,
Swem Library, College of William and Mary.

CHAPTER TWENTY-FOUR

141 "Go ask my con-
stituents":
William Cabell Bruce, *John Randolph of
Roanoke*, vol. 1 (New York, London: G. P.
Putnam's Sons, 1922), 155.

142 "put no confidence":
Ibid., 159.

142 Before the orchestra:
Randolph's account appears in Hugh Garland,
The Life of John Randolph of Roanoke, vol. 1
(New York: D. Appleton & Co., 1859), 157–61;
see also William Ewart Stokes, "Randolph of
Roanoke: A Virginia Patriot: The Early Career of John Randolph of Roanoke, 1773–
1803" (Ph.D. diss., University of Virginia,
1955), 176–89.

144 *"youth* will find":	Quoted in Page Smith, *John Adams*, vol. 2, *1784–1826* (New York: Doubleday, 1962), 1023.
144 "with great splendor":	Thomas Jefferson. Letter to Maria J. Eppes, January 17, 1800. Quoted in Willard Sterne Randall, *Thomas Jefferson: A Life*, vol. 2 (New York: Henry Holt, 1993), 534.

CHAPTER TWENTY-FIVE

145 "more dear":	William Thompson. Letter to John Randolph, n.d. In Hugh Garland, *The Life of John Randolph of Roanoke*, vol. 1 (New York: D. Appleton & Co., 1859), 163.
145 "is cheerful":	Ibid., 174.
145 "gloomy disposition":	Judith Randolph to St. George Tucker, October 18, 1801, Tucker-Coleman Collection, Swem Library, College of William and Mary.
146 "bad health and worse spirits":	Judith Randolph to St. George Tucker, March 16, 1800, Tucker-Coleman Collection, Swem Library, College of William and Mary.
146 "one of the most promising":	John Randolph, no addressee, August 12, 1800. Bruce-Randolph Collection, Virginia State Archives.
146 "a scene of horror":	Virginius Dabney, *Richmond: The Story of a City* (Charlottesville: University Press of Virginia, 1990), 56.
146 "deluge the Southern country in blood":	Ibid., 57.
147 "soothe and conciliate":	Judith Randolph to St. George Tucker, October 18, 1801, Tucker-Coleman Collection, Swem Library, College of William and Mary.
147 "groundless and absurd":	Ibid.

147 "conviction of impending ruin":

Nancy Randolph to St. George Tucker,
March 8, 1800, Tucker-Coleman Collection,
Swem Library, College of William and Mary.

147 "an incomparable
servant":

Nancy Randolph to St. George Tucker, February 21, 1805, Bruce-Randolph Papers, Virginia State Archives.

148 "some species of
drudgery":

Ibid.

148 "the long last hope
of negotiating
ascendancy":

Nancy Randolph to St. George Tucker,
March 8, 1800, Tucker-Coleman Collection,
Swem Library, College of William and Mary.

CHAPTER TWENTY-SIX

149 "We want nothing
here":

Gouverneur Morris, *The Diary and Letters of
Gouverneur Morris*, vol. 2, edited by Anne
Cary Morris (New York: Charles Scribner's
Sons, 1888), 394.

150 "I busy myself here at
the trade of a senator":

Gouverneur Morris. Letter to the Princesse
de la Tour et Taxis, December 14, 1800. In
ibid., 395.

150 "You who are tem-
perate in drinking":

Gouverneur Morris. Letter to Alexander
Hamilton, January 5, 1801. In ibid., 398–99.

151 "I believe it my duty":

Frank Van Der Linden, *The Turning Point:
Jefferson's Battle for the Presidency* (Washington, D.C.: Luce, 1962), 306.

152 "on political grounds
only":

Ibid., 308.

152 "vehement reproaches":

Dumas Malone, *Jefferson and the Ordeal of
Liberty* (Boston: Little, Brown, 1962), 504.

153 "On the thirty-six
ballot":

John Randolph to St. George Tucker, Febru-
ary 17, 1801. In Hugh Garland, *The Life of
John Randolph of Roanoke*, vol. 1 (New York:
D. Appleton & Co., 1859), 187.

Notes

CHAPTER TWENTY-SEVEN

154 "paltry expense . . . decayed politicians": William Cabell Bruce, *John Randolph of Roanoke, 1773–1833*, vol. 1 (New York, London: G. P. Putnam's Sons, 1922), 174.

155 "adulation and toad-eating": *Richmond Examiner*, January 28, 1800.

155 "I don't get": Bruce, *John Randolph of Roanoke*, vol. 2, 766.

156 "hated of men and scorned of women": Ibid., 322.

156 "strong suspicions of a physical disability": Samuel Taggart to the Rev. John Taylor, January 13, 1804, *Proceedings of the American Antiquarian Society* 33 (1924): 125.

156 "You pride yourself": Bruce, *John Randolph of Roanoke*, vol. 2, 321.

156 "We have indeed a set of madmen": Gouverneur Morris. Letter to James Parish, February 16, 1802. In *The Diary and Letters of Gouverneur Morris*, vol. 2, edited by Anne Cary Morris (New York: Charles Scribner's Sons, 1888), 418.

157 "cold as a frog": Gouverneur Morris diary entry, May 4, 1802. In ibid., 424.

157 "forget, as fast as I can": Ibid.

157 "that enchanting Yankee": Gouverneur Morris diary entry, May 24, 1803. In ibid., 438.

157 "especially at my time of life": Ibid.

158 "*monsieur* was cordial": Howard Swiggett, *The Extraordinary Mr. Morris* (New York: Doubleday & Co., 1952), 363.

158 "My political enemies": Gouverneur Morris. Letter to John Dickenson, April 13, 1803. In *The Diary and Letters of Gouverneur Morris*, vol. 2, 436.

158 "No good domestics": Gouverneur Morris diary entry, March 14, 1801. In ibid., 406.

CHAPTER TWENTY-EIGHT

160 "[W]hen I consider": Judith Randolph to John Randolph, April 12, 1803, Bryan Family Papers, Alderman Library, University of Virginia.

160 "Soon, my boy": Anne Cary Morris to John Randolph, January 1, 1815, Virginia Historical Society.

161 "in the full tide of successful experiment": Hugh Garland, *The Life of John Randolph of Roanoke*, vol. 1 (New York: D. Appleton & Co., 1859), 198.

162 "faithfully report to you": John Randolph to James Monroe, November 7, 1803, Monroe Papers, Library of Congress.

162 "Can I venture": Ibid.

163 "becoming each day more calamitous": Judith Randolph to John Randolph, April, 1803, Bryan Family Papers, Alderman Library, University of Virginia.

163 "only in the hopes": Judith Randolph to St. George Tucker, June 30, 1803, Tucker-Coleman Collection, Swem Library, College of William and Mary.

163 "Heaven cannot sanction such oppression": Nancy Randolph to St. George Tucker, January 30, 1803, Tucker-Coleman Collection, Swem Library, College of William and Mary.

163 "at a distance": Judith Randolph to St. George Tucker, April 12, 1803, Tucker-Coleman Collection, Swem Library, College of William and Mary.

CHAPTER TWENTY-NINE

164 *"without any consideration of the quarter from which a motion comes"*: Dumas Malone, *Jefferson the President, First Term, 1801–1805*, vol. 4 of *Jefferson and His Time* (Boston: Little, Brown and Company, 1970), 409.

165 "historically": Thomas Jefferson. Letter to John Randolph, December 1, 1803. In *The Writings of Thomas Jefferson*, vol. 8, collected and edited by Paul Leicester Ford (New York, London: G. P. Putnam's Sons, 1892), 281.

Notes

165 "very assuming":   William Plumer, January 26, 1804. In *William Plumer's Memorandum of Proceedings in the United States Senate, 1803–1807*, edited by Everett S. Brown (New York: Da Capo Press, 1969), 122–23.

166 "with as little relation":   William Cabell Bruce, *John Randolph of Roanoke*, vol. 1 (New York, London: G. P. Putnam's Sons, 1922), 207.

166 "weak, feeble, and deranged":   Ibid., 208.

166 "cried like a baby":   Ibid., 210.

166 "have performed our duty":   Ibid., 213.

166 "as disgusting as his harangue":   Plumer, *William Plumer's Memorandum*, 302.

167 "father of a nobleman":   Quoted in G. S. Rowe, *Thomas McKean: The Shaping of an American Republicanism* (Boulder: Colorado Associated University Press, 1978), 302–3.

167 "vast affability":   Nancy Randolph to St. George Tucker, February 21, 1805, Bruce-Randolph Papers, Virginia State Archives.

167 "the most ridiculous thing":   Ibid.

168 "retained her veracity unimpaired":   Ibid.

168 "of saying what I did not think":   Ibid.

168 "I am indeed metamorphosed":   Ibid.

169 "Nancy, when do you leave this house?":   Anne Cary Morris to John Randolph, January 1, 1815, Virginia Historical Society.

169 "in a tavern":   Ibid.

CHAPTER THIRTY

173 "condition of total despair": Anne Cary Morris to St. George Tucker, December 26, 1814, Tucker-Coleman Collection, Swem Library, College of William and Mary.

175 "advances became so immodest": John Randolph to Anne Cary Morris, October 31, 1814, Virginia Historical Society.

175 "folly": Anne Cary Morris to St. George Tucker, February 9, 1815, Tucker-Coleman Collection, Swem Library, College of William and Mary.

175 Jack began telling people: Anne Cary Morris to St. George Tucker, December 16, 1814, Tucker-Coleman Collection, Swem Library, College of William and Mary.

176 "dangerous to virtue": Virginius Dabney, *Richmond: The Story of a City* (Charlottesville: University Press of Virginia, 1990), 85.

CHAPTER THIRTY-ONE

178 "beware that his proboscis": Henry Adams, *John Randolph* (Boston: Houghton Mifflin, 1920), 173.

179 *"tertium quid"*: Ibid., 181.

179 "The Constitution was in its chrysalis state": Hugh Garland, *The Life of John Randolph of Roanoke*, vol. 1 (New York: D. Appleton & Co., 1859), 28.

179 "contumely and hostility": William H. Gaines, Jr., *Thomas Mann Randolph: Jefferson's Son-in-Law* (Kingsport, Tenn.: Louisiana State University Press, 1966), 61.

180 "lead and even steel": Ibid., 1104–06.

180 "cut each other's throats": John Taylor to Wilson Cary Nicholas, June 26, 1806, Jefferson Papers, Massachusetts Historical Society.

181 "Seven children": Thomas Jefferson to Thomas Mann Randolph, June 23, 1806, Edgehill-Randolph

Notes

Papers, Alderman Library, University of Virginia.

CHAPTER THIRTY-TWO

182 "a very severe one": Judith Randolph to John Randolph, November 21, 1807, Tucker-Coleman Collection, Swem Library, College of William and Mary.

182 "blasted [her] youth": Judith Randolph to Mary Harrison, November 21, 1805, Harrison Family Papers, Virginia Historical Society.

182 "as if he were [their] own son": John Randolph to James Monroe, July 29, 1804, Monroe Papers, Library of Congress.

183 "is at once the most odious": John Randolph to St. George Randolph, September 6, 1806, John Randolph Letters, Virginia State Archives.

183 "in good health": James Monroe to John Randolph, June 16, 1806, Monroe Papers, Library of Congress.

183 "holds the relation": Ibid.

183 "conduct continues to merit": James Monroe to John Randolph, November 12, 1806, Monroe Papers, Library of Congress.

183 "They are really in a miserable plight": Judith Randolph to John Randolph, November 21, 1807, John Randolph Papers, Library of Congress.

184 "In quitting Virginia": Nancy Randolph to St. George Tucker, December 19, 1808, Tucker-Coleman Collection, Swem Library, College of William and Mary.

185 "Sturges loves wine and women": William Plumer, March 4, 1806. In *William Plumer's Memorandum of Proceedings in the United States Senate, 1803–1807*, edited by Everett S. Brown (New York: Da Capo Press, 1969), 443.

Notes

CHAPTER THIRTY-THREE

188 "manners a queen might envy": Jonathan Daniels, *The Randolphs of Virginia* (Garden City, N.Y.: Doubleday & Co., 1972), 131.

189 Jack believed that Jefferson: Leonard Levy, *Jefferson and Civil Liberties*, (Chicago: Ivan R. Dee, 1989), 162.

CHAPTER THIRTY-FOUR

191 "provoked the servants": Gouverneur Morris to Anne Cary Randolph, March 9, 1809, Gouverneur Morris Letters, Library of Congress.

191 "Talk not of gratitude": Gouverneur Morris to Anne Cary Randolph, March 3, 1809, Gouverneur Morris Letters, Library of Congress.

192 "The Incidents of Pleasure": Ibid.

192 "Since Fortune's Favor": Ibid.

193 "If we ever": Ibid.

194 "Pride may proclaim": Ibid.

194 "for future storms": Ibid.

194 "The numerous Ladies": Ibid.

195 "I can only answer": Ibid.

195 "brought home Miss Randolph of Virginia": Howard Swiggett, *The Extraordinary Mr. Morris* (New York: Doubleday & Co., 1952), 399.

CHAPTER THIRTY-FIVE

196 "not only the Morals, but the Decencies, of Life": Gouverneur Morris to John Marshall, December 2, 1809, Gouverneur Morris Letters, Library of Congress.

197 "plunge the country": Gouverneur Morris. Letter to Simeon DeWitt, December 18, 1808. In *The Diary and Letters of Gouverneur Morris*, vol. 2, edited by Anne Cary Morris (New York: Charles Scribner's Sons, 1888), 508.

197 "The object": Ibid.

197 "rumor": John Marshall to Gouverneur Morris, December 12, 1809, Gouverneur Morris Letters, Library of Congress.

197 "who had the fairest means": Ibid.

198 "I marry this day": Gouverneur Morris. In *The Diary and Letters of Gouverneur Morris*, vol. 2, 516.

198 "I glory": Anne Cary Morris to Joseph C. Cabell, May 30, 1828, Bruce-Randolph Collection, Virginia State Archives.

CHAPTER THIRTY-SIX

199 "has her Share": Gouverneur Morris to John Marshall, December 28, 1809, Gouverneur Morris Letters, Library of Congress.

200 "fifteen years": Ibid.

200 "already tarnished": Ibid.

201 "we have the pleasure": Gouverneur Morris to Gertrude Meredith, January 10, 1810, Gouverneur Morris Letters, Library of Congress.

201 "with the best of husbands": Nancy Randolph to St. George Tucker, June 14, 1810, Tucker-Coleman Collection, Swem Library, College of William and Mary.

201 "are the best": Ibid.

201 "agreeable conversation": Katherine McCook Knox, *The Sharples: Their Portraits of George Washington, and His Contemporaries. A Diary and an Account of the Life*

and Work of James Sharples and His Family in
England and America (New York: Da Capo
Press, 1972), 38.

202 "on a magnificent ser-   Ibid.
vice of silver":

202 "demure":   Howard Swiggett, *The Extraordinary Mr. Mor-*
ris (New York: Doubleday & Co., 1952), 407.

204 "Nothing would give   Ibid., 406.
me more pleasure":

204 "thundering in [their]   Gouverneur Morris, *The Diary and Letters of*
ears":   *Gouverneur Morris*, vol. 2, edited by Anne
Cary Morris (New York: Charles Scribner's
Sons, 1888), 520.

204 "unnatural and impious   Swiggett, *The Extraordinary Mr. Morris,*
doctrine":   408.

CHAPTER THIRTY-SEVEN

206 "for a thousand dollars":   John Randolph. Letter to John Marshall,
December 17, 1831. In William Cabell Bruce,
John Randolph of Roanoke, 1773–1833, vol. 2
(New York, London: G. P. Putnam's Sons,
1922), 417–18.

206 "stay at home":   Judith Randolph to Mary Harrison, n.d.,
Harrison Family Papers, Virginia Historical
Society.

206 "never contemplated   Judith Randolph to John Randolph, August
for poor St. George":   22, 1809, Bryan Family Papers, Alderman
Library, University of Virginia.

207 "fortunes are narrow":   Judith Randolph to John Randolph, August
27, 1809, Bryan Family Papers, Alderman
Library, University of Virginia.

207 "was there a nobler   Ibid.
child":

208 "some large, bare, rect- Bruce, *John Randolph of Roanoke*, vol. 2, 138.
angular frame":

208 "savage solitude": John Randolph to Theodore Dudley, Febru-
ary 5, 1813. In *Letters of John Randolph, to a Young Relative, from Early Youth, to Mature Manhood* (Philadelphia: Carey, Lea & Blanchard, 1834), 133.

209 "almost to a jelly": John Randolph to Theodore Dudley, October 29, 1810. In ibid., 71.

209 "large dose of opium": John Randolph to Theodore Dudley, November 16, 1810. In ibid., 74.

CHAPTER THIRTY-EIGHT

210 "Tantrums of Mrs. R.": John Randolph's diary, October 15, 1810. In William Cabell Bruce, *John Randolph of Roanoke, 1773–1883*, vol. 2 (New York, London: G. P. Putnam's Sons, 1922), 394.

210 "I have a mind to cane Lemuel Sawyer, *A Biography of John Ran-
him": dolph, with a Selection from His Speeches* (New York: William Robinson, 1844), 42.

211 "appraisement of Ibid.
Alston's head":

211 "All the bastard wit": Robert Dawidoff, *The Education of John Randolph* (New York: W. W. Norton, 1979), 63.

211 "Asking one of the Gerald W. Johnson, *Randolph of Roanoke*
states": (New York: Minton, Balch & Co., 1929), 236.

211 "like the chameleon on Bruce, *John Randolph of Roanoke*, vol. 2, 202.
the aspen":

211 "a man of splendid Quoted in Powhatan Bouldin, *Home Reminis-
abilities": cences of John Randolph of Roanoke* (Richmond: Clemmit & Jones, Printers, 1876),139.

211 "carving knife whetted Armistead C. Gordon, *William Fitzhugh Gor-
on a brickbat": don* (New York: Neale Publishing Company, 1909), 278.

211 "rowed to his object with muffled oars":   Bruce, *John Randolph of Roanoke*, vol. 2, 203.

211 "too weak for the plow":   Ibid., 202.

212 "in saying":   Bruce, *John Randolph of Roanoke*, 366–67.

212 "anything short of that bloody scourge":   Gouverneur Morris. Letter to James Parish, April 8, 1812. In *The Diary and Letters of Gouverneur Morris*, vol. 2, edited by Anne Cary Morris (New York: Scribner, 1888), 538.

213 "much-admired":   Gouverneur Morris diary entry, December 16, 1811. In ibid., 538.

213 "intended to mortify":   John Randolph to Anne Cary Morris, October 31, 1814, Virginia Historical Society.

214 "renewed spring of life":   Gouverneur Morris. Letter to James Parish, April 8, 1812. In *The Diary and Letters of Gouverneur Morris*, vol. 2, 537.

214 "As to other folks":   Gouverneur Morris. Letter to Anne Cary Morris, June 5, 1812. In Howard Swiggett, *The Extraordinary Mr. Morris* (New York: Doubleday & Co., 1952), 414.

214 "quiet, happy home":   Ibid., 415.

CHAPTER THIRTY-NINE

215 "How do you do?":   Powhatan Bouldin, *Home Reminiscences of John Randolph of Roanoke* (Richmond: Clemmit & Jones, Printers, 1876), p. 41. Under the Virginia Constitution of 1776, suffrage in Virginia was limited to free white males who owned either 1200 acres of uncultivated land, 25 acres of improved land, or a house and lot in a town. Only about one-quarter to one-third of free white men met the property requirements, leaving even most white men disenfranchised. See D. Bruce Dickson, Jr., *The Virginia Convention of 1829–30 and the Conservative Tradition in the*

South (San Marino, Calif.: Huntington Library, 1982). Also, J. A. C. Chandler, "History of Suffrage in Virginia," *Johns Hopkins University Studies in Historical and Political Science*, series 19, no. 6–7 (1901), 8–94.

216 "A new broom sweeps clean, but": William Cabell Bruce, *John Randolph of Roanoke, 1773–1833*, vol. 1 (New York, London: G. P. Putnam's Sons, 1822), 591.

217 "cabins and hovels of the lowest": Randolph to Josiah Quincy, April 19, 1813, quoted in ibid., 593.

218 "My once comfortable & peaceful dwelling": Judith Randolph to St. George Tucker, April 4, 1813, Tucker-Coleman Collection, Swem Library, College of William and Mary.

218 "and all my hoard": Judith Randolph to St. George Tucker, March 21, 1813, Tucker-Coleman Collection, Swem Library, College of William and Mary.

219 "or he would have been beaten to a jelly": John Randolph. Letter to Josiah Quincy, April 19, 1813. In Bruce, *John Randolph of Roanoke*, vol. 1, 593.

219 "The days of my boyhood": John Randolph. Letter to Francis Scott Key, March 20, 1814. In Hugh Garland, *The Life of John Randolph of Roanoke*, vol. 2 (New York: D. Appleton & Co., 1859), 2.

219 "What a spectacle": Ibid.

220 "to pay for every mouthful": Anne Cary Morris to St. George Tucker, December 16, 1814, Tucker-Coleman Collection, Swem Library, College of William and Mary.

CHAPTER FORTY

221 They might have called him Kutuzoff: Howard Swiggett quotes letter from Anne Cary Morris to Joseph C. Cabell attributing nickname of "Cutusoff" to invention of Martin Wilkins and Isabella Morris. See *The Extraordinary Mr. Morris* (New York: Doubleday & Co., 1952), 417.

221 "with cordial wishes
     for Mrs. Morris's
     speedy and perfect
     recovery":

John Randolph to Gouverneur Morris. In
Ibid., 407.

222 "odious thraldom":

Hugh Garland, *The Life of John Randolph of
Roanoke*, vol. 1 (New York: D. Appleton &
Co., 1859), 9.

222 "sheer hypocrisy":

John Randolph. Letter to Francis Scott Key,
May 7, 1814. In Hugh Garland, *The Life of
John Randolph of Roanoke*, vol. 2 (New York:
D. Appleton & Co., 1859), 36.

222 "Peace or war . . .
     manufactures on a
     grand scale":

John Randolph to Francis Scott Key, December 15, 1814. In ibid., 29.

222 "commerce and do-
     mestic slavery":

Gouverneur Morris. Letter to Harrison
Gray Otis, April 29, 1813. In *The Diary and
Letters of Gouverneur Morris*, vol. 2, edited by
Anne Cary Morris (New York: Scribner,
1888), 552.

222 "union of the North-
     ern states":

Swiggett, *The Extraordinary Mr. Morris*, 545.

223 "hellishly frightened":

Ibid.

223 "Kiss for me":

Ibid.

CHAPTER FORTY-ONE

224 "intolerably hot'"

John Randolph. Letter to Dr. John Brocken-
brough, July 15, 1814. In Hugh Garland, *The
Life of John Randolph of Roanoke*, vol. 2
(New York: D. Appleton & Co., 1859), 42.

224 "shut [his] heart":

Ibid.

225 "must be the Yahoo's
     paradise":

John Randolph. Letter to Dr. John Brockenbrough, June 2, 1813. In ibid., 15.

225 "very amiable, exemp-
     lary girl":

Judith Randolph to John Randolph, July 24,
1813. In William Cabell Bruce, *John Randolph of Roanoke, 1773–1833*, vol. 2 (New

York, London: G. P. Putnam's Sons, 1922), 496.

225 "no hopes for his restoration":

John Randolph. Letter to Francis Scott Key, June 3, 1814. In Garland, *The Life of John Randolph of Roanoke*, vol. 2, 39.

225 "terrors of future punishments":

John Randolph. Letter to Francis Scott Key, July 14, 1814. In ibid.

225 "incurably alienated":

Ibid.

226 "dear, good Aunt":

Anne Cary Morris to John Randolph, January 1, 1815, Virginia Historical Society.

227 "deeply, perhaps mortally diseased":

Gouverneur Morris to John Randolph, July 29, 1814, Gouverneur Morris Letters, Library of Congress.

227 "an idolator of this dear child":

Judith Randolph to John Randolph, October 16, 1813, Bryan Family Papers, Alderman Library, University of Virginia.

227 "the pride, the sole hope":

John Randolph. Letter to Francis Scott Key, July 31, 1814. In Garland, *The Life of John Randolph of Roanoke*, vol. 2, 43.

227 "What a scene awaits him there":

Ibid.

227 "good air, milk, vegetables":

Gouverneur Morris to John Randolph, July 29, 1814, Gouverneur Morris Letters, Library of Congress.

CHAPTER FORTY-TWO

228 "violent bleeding from the lungs":

Anne Cary Morris to Joseph Cabell, October 14, 1831, Bruce-Randolph Papers, Virginia States Archives.

229 "Remember the past":

John Randolph to Anne Cary Morris, October 31, 1814, Virginia Historical Society.

229 "the ligaments very much wrenched":

John Randolph. Letter to Theodore Dudley, October 13, 1814. In *Letters of John Randolph, to a Young Relative, from Early Youth, to*

		Mature Manhood (Philadelphia: Carey, Lea & Blanchard, 1834), 21.
229	"love letters":	Anne Cary Morris to John Randolph, January 1, 1815, Virginia Historical Society.
231	"the offspring of an illicit amour":	Memo of John Randolph, November 23, 1814, John Randolph Collection, Library of Congress, witnessed by David B. Ogden.
231	"noxious and offensive-smelling vapour":	Ibid.
232	"Something very like this happened":	Ibid.
232	"came unfairly by his death":	Ibid.

CHAPTER FORTY-THREE

233	"too ill to leave the house":	Memo of John Randolph, November 23, 1814, John Randolph Collection, Library of Congress, witnessed by David B. Ogden.
233	Jack spent All Hallow's Eve:	John Randolph. Letter to Anne Cary Morris, October 31, 1814. In William Cabell Bruce, *John Randolph of Roanoke, 1773–1833*, vol. 2 (New York, London: G. P. Putnam's Sons, 1922), 273–78.

CHAPTER FORTY-FOUR

241	"under the wounds":	Gouverneur Morris to Randolph Harrison, January 22, 1815, Morris Papers, Butler Library, Columbia University.
242	"candor":	Gouverneur Morris to Randolph Harrison, May 25, 1815, Morris Papers, Butler Library, Columbia University.
242	*"She never deceived me":*	Gouverneur Morris to Randolph Harrison, January 22, 1815, Morris Papers, Butler Library, Columbia University.

242 "Those who cried aloud":   Gouverneur Morris to Randolph Harrison, May 25, 1815, Morris Papers, Butler Library, Columbia University.

243 "What my intentions respecting my property were":   Howard Swiggett, *The Extraordinary Mr. Morris* (New York: Doubleday & Co., 1952), 428.

243 "disposed":   Ibid.

243 "dear lovely Babe":   Anne Cary Morris to St. George Tucker, November 24, 1814, Tucker-Coleman Collection, Swem Library, College of William and Mary.

243 "I was simple in my heart":   Anne Cary Morris to St. George Tucker, November 28, 1814, Tucker-Coleman Collection, Swem Library, College of William and Mary.

244 "Come, Papa . . . Come, Mama":   Anne Cary Morris to St. George Tucker, November 24, 1814, Tucker-Coleman Collection, Swem Library, College of William and Mary.

244 "Could his heart experience":   Anne Cary Morris to William B. Giles, February 17, 1815, Giles Papers, Virginia Historical Society.

CHAPTER FORTY-FIVE

245 "in a way which evinced much benevolence of heart":   Anne Cary Morris, no addressee, March 14, 1815, Giles Papers, Virginia Historical Society.

245 "In your letter":   Anne Cary Morris to John Randolph, January 1, 1815, Virginia Historical Society.

CHAPTER FORTY-SIX

254 "What can we think":   Martha Randolph to Mrs. Nicholas Trist, May 31, 1815, Elizabeth Trist (House) Papers, Virginia Historical Society.

255 "of having seduced":   Ibid.

255 "an approaching wave in a storm":   Thomas Jefferson. Letter to Mrs. Elizabeth Trist, December 26, 1814. In Sarah N. Randolph, *The Domestic Life of Thomas Jefferson* (Charlottesville: University of Virginia Press, 1871), 360.

255 "is now in prosperity":   Martha Randolph to Mrs. Nicholas Trist, May 31, 1815, Elizabeth Trist (House) Papers, Virginia Historical Society.

255 "have very little to do":   Anne C. Morris to William B. Giles, March 22, 1815, Giles Papers, Virginia Historical Society.

256 "frolicking until dinner":   Howard Swiggett, *The Extraordinary Mr. Morris* (New York: Doubleday & Co., 1952), 437.

256 "omit no proper occasion":   Gouverneur Morris to Mrs. Judith Randolph, March 13, 1815, Morris Papers, Butler Library, Columbia University.

257 "Your suspense and mine":   The Reverend John Holt Rice. Letter to Mrs. Judith Randolph, October 20, 1815. In William Maxwell, ed., *Memoir of the Reverend John H. Rice* (Philadelphia: J. Whetham, 1835), 118.

257 "would have made any possible sacrifice":   Anne Cary Morris to St. George Tucker, March 20, 1816, Tucker-Coleman Collection, Swem Library, College of William and Mary.

257 "To me":   John Randolph. Letter to Francis Scott Key, June 16, 1816. In William Cabell Bruce, *John Randolph of Roanoke, 1773–1833*, vol. 2 (New York, London: G. P. Putnam's Sons, 1922), 88.

259 "moderate use":   John Randolph diary entry, February 23, 1817. Quoted in Hugh Garland, *The Life of John Randolph of Roanoke*, vol. 2 (New York: D. Appleton & Co., 1859), 91.

259 "spasms": John Randolph diary entry, February 18, 1817. In ibid., 91.

259 "and I am content": Ibid.

259 "Did she mix": John Randolph to Judith Randolph, January 20, 1816, Tucker-Grinnan Papers, Virginia State Archives.

CHAPTER FORTY-SEVEN

260 "may be protected": Anne Cary Morris to St. George Tucker, March 20, 1816, Tucker-Coleman Collection, Swem Library, College of William and Mary.

260 "unite in brotherly Love and Friendship": Ibid.

261 "in the history of man- kind": Gouverneur Morris. Letter to John Parish, July 6, 1816. In *The Diary and Letters of Gouverneur Morris*, vol. 2, edited by Anne Cary Morris (New York: Charles Scribner's Sons, 1888), 6200–01.

261 "That I did not marry earlier": Ibid.

261 "who see him almost every minute": Ibid.

262 "solemn assurances": Anne Cary Morris to William Short, No- vember 25, 1816, William Short Papers, Library of Congress.

262 "villainy": Anne Cary Morris to St. George Tucker, December 2, 1816, Tucker-Coleman Collec- tion, Swem Library, College of William and Mary.

263 His urinary passage was blocked . . . inser- tion of a whalebone: Rufus King to Christopher Gore, November 5, 1816. In *The Life and Correspondence of Rufus King*, vol. 6, edited by Charles R. King (New York: G. P. Putnam's Sons, 1900), 35.

263 "died the death of the most noble": Anne Cary Morris to St. George Tucker, December 2, 1816, Tucker-Coleman Collection, Swem Library, College of William and Mary.

263 "cried to see his father": Ibid.

263 Morris left the bulk of his estate: Morris's will is quoted in full in Jared Sparks, *The Life of Gouverneur Morris with Selections from His Correspondence and Miscellaneous Papers*, vol. 1 (Boston: Gray and Bowen, 1832), 504–05.

264 "Borne down by business and sorrow": Anne Cary Morris to St. George Tucker, December 2, 1816, Tucker-Coleman Collection, Swem Library, College of William and Mary.

264 "threatened with having my person seized": Ibid.

265 "discharging debts": Anne Cary Morris to Henry Munro, April 10, 1828, Gouverneur Morris Papers, Museum of the City of New York.

265 "I am ignorant of the price": Ibid.

265 "sensations like those apparent in a mad dog": Ibid.

265 "After passing a long life": Anne Cary Morris to Henry Munro, n.d. [1828], Gouverneur Morris Papers, Museum of the City of New York.

265 "fine boy to protect": Anne Cary Morris to Peter Jay Munro, May 10, 1822, Gouverneur Morris Papers, Museum of the City of New York.

266 "support us comfortably": Anne Cary Morris to Henry Munro, n.d. [1828], Gouverneur Morris Papers, Museum of the City of New York.

266 "while I burn coal": Anne Cary Morris to Henry Munro, n.d. [1828], Gouverneur Morris Papers, Museum of the City of New York.

266 "not to live in style" William Randolph to Anne Cary Morris. Quoted in Howard Swiggett, *The Extraordi-*

Notes

nary Mr. Morris (New York: Doubleday & Co., 1952), 447.

CHAPTER FORTY-EIGHT

267 "to receive [his] blood":
Thomas Hart Benton, *Thirty Years' View,* vol. 1 (New York: Greenwood Press, 1968), 71, 73.

267 "corrupt bargain":
Kenneth S. Greenberg, *Honor & Slavery* (Princeton, N.J.: Princeton University Press, 1996), 62.

268 "I look . . . for civil war":
John Randolph to William Wallace, March 17, 1832, Randolph MSS., Duke University.

268 "I shall do nothing":
Benton, *Thirty Years' View,* vol. 1, 71–74.

269 "was clearly an accident":
Benton, quoted in Powhatan Bouldin, *Home Reminiscences of John Randolph of Roanoke* (Richmond: Clemmit & Jones, Printers, 1876), 151.

269 "This is child's play":
William Cabell Bruce, *John Randolph of Roanoke, 1773–1833,* vol. 1 (New York, London: G. P. Putnam's Sons, 1922), 522.

270 "I am glad":
Ibid., 523.

270 "an unpaid, secret, confidential agent":
Bruce, *John Randolph of Roanoke, 1773–1833,* vol. 2 (New York, London: G. P. Putnam's Sons, 1922), 14.

271 "the nature of [whose connection]":
John Randolph to Andrew Jackson, March 1, 1832, Jackson Papers, vol. 80, Library of Congress.

271 "good friend opium":
John Randolph. Letter to Nathaniel Macon, n.d. In Bruce, *John Randolph of Roanoke,* vol. 2, 443.

271 "always made them right":
Bouldin, *Home Reminiscences,* 103.

271 "Don't ask me":
Ibid., 258.

271 "You can form":
Ibid.

272	"Certainly, sir":	Ibid.
272	"There are idiosyn-crasies":	Ibid.
272	"In a multitude":	Ibid., 258–59.
272	"omnipotence":	Ibid., 259.
272	"impetus":	Ibid.
272	"You must not go":	Ibid., 260.
273	"Master":	Ibid.
273	"Get a knife and cut one":	Ibid.
273	"Remorse!":	Ibid.

CHAPTER FORTY-NINE

274	"supplied the 'pressures'":	Howard Swiggett, *The Extraordinary Mr. Morris* (New York: Doubleday & Co., 1952), 443.
274	"spurn the pittance":	Anne Cary Morris to Isaac Bronson, May 29, 1829, Bronson Papers, Jefferson County, New York, Historical Society.
275	"paltry dinner":	Ibid.
275	"not even a half cup of wine":	Ibid.
275	"elegant pearl set":	Anne Cary Morris to Isaac Bronson, June 1, 1831, Bronson Papers, Jefferson County, New York, Historical Society.
275	"Morrisania will give":	Ibid.
275	her "splendid" watch:	Anne Cary Morris to Isaac Bronson, August 18, 1831, Bronson Papers, Jefferson County, New York, Historical Society.
275	"My trust . . . patience and perseverance":	Anne Cary Morris to Isaac Bronson, July 23, 1831, Bronson Papers, Jefferson County, New York, Historical Society.

276 "voluminous corre-
spondence":

Anne Cary Morris to Joseph C. Cabell, May
30, 1828, Bruce-Randolph Collection, Virginia State Archives.

276 "whom Satan entered
in old times":

Anne Cary Randolph, no addressee, June 7,
1830, Bruce-Randolph Collection, Virginia
State Archives.

277 "their merciless fangs":

Anne Cary Randolph to Joseph C. Cabell,
May 30, 1828, Bruce-Randolph Papers, Virginia State Archives.

277 "looks wretchedly":

Anne Cary Morris, no addressee, June 7,
1830, Bruce-Randolph Collection, Virginia
State Archives.

277 "fortunate indeed":

Anne Cary Morris to Joseph C. Cabell, May
30, 1828, Bruce-Randolph Papers, Virginia
State Archives.

277 "beheld what the
father attempted":

Anne Cary Morris to John Randolph, December 17, 1822, Tucker-Coleman Collection, Swem Library, College of William and
Mary.

277 "Dick":

Anne Cary Randolph to St. George Tucker,
December 16, 1814, Tucker-Coleman Collec-
tion, Swem Library, College of William and
Mary.

277 "was the only sincere
friend":

Anne Cary Randolph to St. George Tucker,
February 9, 1815, Tucker-Coleman Collec-
tion, Swem Library, College of William and
Mary.

277 "coldhearted, malig-
nant haughty woman":

Ibid.

278 "seemed entirely to
depend":

Ibid.

278 "darling husband":

Anne Cary Morris to St. George Tucker,
December 2, 1816, Tucker-Coleman Collec-
tion, Swem Library, College of William and
Mary.

278 "the richest treasure": Anne Cary Morris to Joseph C. Cabell, May 30, 1828, Bruce-Randolph Collection, Virginia State Archives.

278 "delights us with the melody": Ibid.

278 "Thus do our lives glide on": Ibid.

EPILOGUE

279 St. Ann's Church: Author's visit. See also Barbaralee Diamonstein, *The Landmarks of New York* (New York: Harry N. Abrams, 1988), 87.

Photo Credits

The Virginia Historical Society: Patrick Henry, Tuckahoe Interior, Col. Thomas Mann Randolph, Frances Bland Randolph Tucker, Martha (Patsy) Jefferson Randolph, Thomas Mann Randolph, Jr., Randolph Harrison, Mary Harrison, John Randolph by Stuart, John Marshall, Gouverneur Morris, Tuckahoe Exterior, Roanoke Plantation, John Randolph

Maryland Historical Society: Nancy Randolph

Library of Virginia: *The Virginia Gazette*

White House Historical Association: Benjamin Latrobe

National Portrait Gallery: Gouverneur Morris by Sharples

John Randolph Bruce: Anne Cary Morris by Sharples

Yale University Art Gallery: David Bayard Ogden

ACKNOWLEDGMENTS

Any errors in this book are, of course, my own. The credit for whatever I managed to get right is to be shared by many, especially my editor, Michael Korda of Simon & Schuster, and my agent, Clyde Taylor of Curtis Brown, Ltd. I would also like to acknowledge the contributions of Mrs. Margaret Cook of Swem Library's Special Collections at the College of William and Mary in Williamsburg; Joseph R. Slay, Wirt Shapard Confroy and Kenneth M. Shores in Richmond; and the late Marie Delaney of Farmville. Dan Bartges of Richmond and Dyanne Petersen of Dublin, California, offered valuable editorial suggestions. Ned and Tim Crawford made contributions that, while not strictly editorial, I nonetheless cherish. Finally, I want to thank Kent Owen of Bloomington, Indiana, my debt of gratitude to whom is such that I will forever be paying the interest, never the principal.

ABOUT THE AUTHOR

Alan Pell Crawford is a former U.S. Senate speechwriter and congressional press secretary. A contributor to *Vogue, The Wall Street Journal* and *The Nation,* Crawford is also the author of *Thunder on the Right.* A vice-president of Emergence Brand Labs, he lives in Richmond, Virginia, with his wife, Sally Curran, and their two sons, Ned and Tim.